THE GREAT DECEPTION

10 Shocking Dangers and the Blueprint for Rescuing The American Dream

CRAIG A. HUEY

MEDIA SPECIALISTS

The Great Deception: 10 Shocking Dangers and the Blueprint for Rescuing The American Dream

Media Specialists, 1313 4th Ave N., Nashville, TN 37208, USA

Acknowledgments

I want to thank my beautiful bride, Shelly, for her support and encouragement — not only throughout the writing of this book but through every adventure we've shared over a long, beautiful life together.

My children, Asher, Julia, Caleb, Kelly, and Cory, and my grandchildren, Cassandra and Paul, were the inspiration for me to spend the time to research and write this book in the prayerful expectation that their lives can be as good as mine has been.

I started off in business with nothing and was able to achieve success beyond my wildest dreams. I want this for my kids and grandkids.

I also want to thank Allen Harris for his help in creating clarity in this book, as well as my staff at Creative Direct Marketing Group that helped make this book possible.

Craig A. Huey

Craig A. Huey, Author

Table of Contents

Preface

The Epic Battle: Statism and Collectivism vs. Freedom and Prosperity

In the 16th century, Niccolo Machiavelli first popularized the word *state* in his book *The Prince,* published in 1532, giving us the modern concept of a government of complete political power and control. Today, we call it the *Deep State.*

Machiavelli described the state as a governing body made up of a ruling elite class that controlled all aspects of our lives through a centralized power.

He believed, like many aristocrats and royalty at the time, that only *they* were smart enough to run things, that the "average" citizen was too stupid to know what was good for them. The logical conclusion, then, was that the general population should trust thc state and its governing elite to take care of them, to provide for the people what they needed but were too ignorant and helpless to provide for themselves.

All the state asked for in return was power — absolute power and authority over every aspect of the citizenry's lives. And, of course, that means that citizens put the needs of their own condition over the needs and the financial well-being of their families.

Seems fair enough, right?

This type of coercive power of government (the state) has been the status quo throughout human history.

Governmental recognition of the God-given rights of individuals, such as freedom of speech, freedom of religion, and freedom of the press, was almost entirely nonexistent.

An average person had nearly zero chance of becoming successful and starting a business — unless they were well-connected to the ruling elite. In fact, the opportunity to start with nothing and go on to achieve incredible levels of success is unique in human history. It is, in fact, an American invention, thanks to the U.S. Constitution's protection of private and intellectual property.

Allowing people to act freely, without repressive government regulations and oversight, has been key to The American Dream. Our Founding Fathers proved to the world that the revolutionary absence of government control and micromanagement creates a better, freer society. We call it *free enterprise* or *capitalism.*

The ability of the individuals to do what they wish, as long as it doesn't hurt anyone else or infringe on *their* rights, is a freedom that people could only dream about before 1776. Yet within a generation, everything changed — not just in the United States, but throughout the world. America became a "shining city on a hill," a beacon of hope, and an example of freedom in action worldwide.

Two and a half centuries ago, our freedoms literally changed the world for the better. But today, our individual freedom is in danger.

Indeed, the danger is so intense that those who study history wonder why America would ever turn its back on freedom.

Many wonder if America can ever recover.

Are we near the end? Is this the coming death of the Republic?

That's up to us, the American people. It depends on what we do next, on the decisions we make in the very near future about who and what we want to be as a nation.

This book is about reclaiming The American Dream.

It's about hope — our great hope — for a better America.

The freedom to think, act, believe, and speak without worrying about suppression, censorship or some form of coercion by a government entity is critical. It's an American gift, another unique blessing enshrined in our Constitution.

I experienced what I believe is America's greatest gift — our freedom of worship — in college. It was there that I accepted Jesus Christ as my personal Savior and discovered the freedom that only Christ can bring for salvation, joy, love, peace, and hope ... despite any circumstances.

America has been so, so good to me.

It has been good to you.

And it has been good to every single anti-American, anti-capitalism, anti-God, pro-socialism protester who hates the U.S. Constitution — the same document that *gave* them the right to hold and fight for those very beliefs.

America is in danger. Our way of life, our founding documents, our legislative bodies, our culture ... *our freedoms* ... are less than one generation away from potentially being lost forever.

It's time to open our eyes to the dangers we're facing.

It's time to fight back.

My hope is that this book will be an inspiration to you to work and fight hard as we strive to rescue The American Dream ... together.

Chapter 1

A Dangerous Plunge: Why You, Your Family, and Your Future Are in Danger

America is at a tipping point.

What happens in the next election and policy decisions that are made in the very near future will alter America forever.

It's a tipping point between:

- A country where you are free to live your life as you want ... or a country where you are coerced to do what the government dictates.
- A better standard of living and opportunity ... or going backwards to fewer or no opportunities.
- A country evolving with a wide selection of products and services ... or one of no or very limited choices.
- A country governed by three distinct branches of government ... or a country governed by unelected bureaucrats who operate in secret with no accountability.
- A country with free, fair, and honest elections ... or a One-Party-State.
- A country with rights and freedoms enshrined in the U.S. Constitution and laws passed by Congress ... or a country run by activist judges who circumvent the Constitution and laws passed by Congress and legislate from the bench.

- A country run by artificial intelligence ... or a country run by living, breathing Americans with a brain and a conscience.
- A country where parents are free to provide input and accountability for what their children are learning in school ... or a country where parents fully surrender their children to political brainwashing and the radical Marxist, anti-God propaganda of government.
- A country where you can worship and live according to the dictates of your conscience ... or a country where you are forbidden to worship.
- A country where words have meaning and that recognizes basic right and wrong ... or a country where "truth" is constantly redefined according to the latest radical pro-socialist ideological craze or attack on our Judeo-Christian beliefs.

In short, we are facing dangers to our economy, individual freedoms, and even our national sovereignty that we have never faced before.

When I was in high school, I heard Ronald Reagan give a powerful speech we've come to know as his "A Time for Choosing" speech. That was in 1964, two years before he became Governor of California and long before he was elected the 40th President of the United States. He summarized the dangers to individual freedom and economic prosperity at that time. He didn't use the words *tipping point;* he called it America's "Rendezvous with Destiny."

Reagan warned of the dangers facing America at home and abroad, saying our future depended on the choices we would make between socialism (communism) and individual liberty.

I was struck by a powerful point: If America failed then, the voters would sentence our children to take "the last step into a thousand years of darkness." [1]

It was the start of a tipping point in American history as our nation faced aggressive external enemies, and an even bigger and more dangerous socialist enemy from within.

I believe we have reached as big or bigger tipping point today.

We face dangers we've never experienced before. And the battle is just ...

AN ELECTION AWAY FROM DESTRUCTION

America is on the verge of destruction ... but it could get much worse.

Can you imagine four more years of:

- Crippling inflation and stagflation.
- Burdensome and job-killing regulations.
- The potential collapse of our economy.
- Foreign policy blunders, appeasement, and failures leading to war in Ukraine, Israel, and Taiwan.
- Not taking China's threats and aggression seriously.
- Unbridled lawlessness.
- Unfettered illegal immigration, including terrorists sneaking into our country.
- Radical transgender ideology and other depravities taught to our children.
- The ideological weaponization of the government bureaucracy attacking Conservatives, Republicans, Libertarians, and Christians.
- The double standard of justice, where if you support the "right" politics, the law favors you, and if you support the "wrong" politics, they throw the book at you.

- Reinstating radical late — and even post — abortion policies, including the actual murder of abortion survivors.

And what about the unseen dangers of Artificial Intelligence or "AI": government and media technologically enabled deception and messaging, the Deep State's weaponization of government to crush its political opposition, the war on Christianity and other issues that are either seldom discussed or tragically misunderstood?

You and I must do all we can to stop the insanity and the evil.

You and I must cut through the confusion, disinformation, and misinformation being forced on us by the radical pro-socialist "Mainstream" media and the government — Big Tech censorship of social media.

There's too much at stake for our country to simply sit back and let events play out.

Unfortunately, the radical pro-socialists are not sitting it out. And they are winning.

They are doubling down with advanced Get-Out-the-Vote tactics and strategies to win an election.

They are brainwashing and persuading family, friends, and neighbors, all too often, and they are succeeding.

And tragically, we keep losing elections — winnable races — in 2018, 2020, 2022, and 2023.

You, your family, and America cannot afford to keep losing! We can't afford to lose our freedoms, our standard of living, and our way of life.

You and I must step up now and say, *"Enough losing. Let's start winning again!"*

The starting point is understanding the very real dangers we face ... and having intelligent and powerful answers to them.

This book will reveal information you'll likely find nowhere else.

It will reveal how not to be deceived.

It will reveal how you can talk to your friends, family, and neighbors.

It will show you how we can turn America around and restore The American Dream.

Chapter 2

Danger #1: The Road to Socialism: America's Epic Battle Between Collectivism vs. The Individual

A civil war is brewing in America.

It's an *ideological* battle between free-market capitalists, who understand that individual freedom, entrepreneurialism, and innovation are the bedrock of America's success — and Big-Government, central-planning, Democratic socialists, who believe the system is rigged, that workers are exploited by the wealthy, and that only Big Government and its bureaucracy can bring about "equity."

Pockets of Americans have fallen for socialism in recent American history, but the ideological war has gotten very serious and threatening with stunning speed.

Celebrities, politicians, educators, and influencers from all walks of life are promoting socialist ideas under the alluring banner of *fairness* and *equity*. As you'll see below, a shocking number of Americans across several generations is turning their backs on free enterprise and individual freedom, and embracing a new form of socialism that makes the same old empty promises of a new utopia ... but is destined to deliver the same old devastating results of failure, and loss of freedom, and tyranny.

Socialism is a political theory that calls for governmental ownership and administration of the means of production and the distribution of goods. That means the government, not individuals in a free market, decides what products will be available and how much they will cost.

It's an epic battle between collectivism verses the individual.

In theory, the goal of socialism is to guarantee equal outcomes for all. No person should have an economic advantage over any other person. And, in a *pure* socialist society, there is no private property. Everything is owned by everyone, "collectively."

That is, the state owns it all.

Despite the false promise of equity and fairness, the heart of socialism is *coercion* — forcing people to behave a certain way and to obey the commands of the elite government leaders.

It's about control.

It's about domination.

It's about a ruling elite demanding submission to the government's total power.

And it's spreading throughout America.

SOCIALISM IS A SERIOUS DANGER TO THE UNITED STATES

Winston Churchill famously said, *"Socialism is the philosophy of failure, the creed of ignorance, and the gospel of envy."* Specifically:

- *The philosophy of failure,* because government is never as efficient nor as quality-conscious as private enterprise in the production of goods and services.
- *The creed of ignorance,* because socialism ignores basic human nature, and assumes that individuals will work just as hard when the results of their labor are turned over to the government as they will when they get to keep the fruits of their labor.

- *The gospel of envy,* because socialism creates a society in which most people want what others have even if they have to take it by force. As long as the object of the envy — those with more than they have — have it, it's an "injustice." And, if they can't have it, they want to destroy it so *no one* can have it.

Modern socialism in America, however, is different in strategy than what was envisioned by Karl Marx, the "Father" of socialism, and the socialists of the late-19th and early/mid-20th centuries. Today's socialists want to use the power of the state to regulate and control all business and consumer choice. The elites accomplish this using taxes, regulations, and "executive orders" by pro-socialist, ideologically driven bureaucrats who control and manage the countless agencies in Washington, D.C.

Socialists today achieve their goals by overseeing those federal government bureaucracies that are imposing new and radical regulations without legislation or debate. They use harmful economic policies to force business owners, property owners, and everyday citizens to change how they live, work, and run their businesses or what they can buy.

It's still built on central planning like the old socialist model, but it's done without legislation or dictatorship. Instead, unelected bureaucrats and judges simply change a rule here and a regulation there, slowly turning the entire economy away from the free-market engine that built America and toward a new "socialist utopia" that history has proven is impossible to achieve and destined to fail.

New strategy or not, this rebranded socialism has the same devastating consequences of economic strangulation, destruction of individual choices, and elimination of individual freedom that results in political favoritism and a powerful controlling elite.

Sadly, the shift toward socialism doesn't stop with nameless, faceless bureaucrats.

If you had told the average American even 25 years ago that a Marxist/socialist would not only become a U.S. Senator but would also run for president (with a huge base of support), that person probably would have laughed in your face.

Not anymore.

Sen. Bernie Sanders is a self-proclaimed socialist. He's been one all of his adult life, even honeymooning in the former Soviet Union at the height of its communist power. Sanders has been an apologist for every socialist dictator, from Cuba's Fidel Castro to Venezuela's Hugo Chavez. We can't imagine the type of horrific changes a "President Bernie" would unleash upon our great nation.

How has socialism become so acceptable so quickly? It partly comes down to what you might call a *rebranding effort* by socialists that have taken control over the Democratic party.

Politicians like Sanders, and radical, antisemitic Alexandria Ocasio-Cortez (AOC), and groups like Democratic Socialists of America (DSA) often try to redefine socialism or communism as *Democratic socialism* — doing so to make it more acceptable to ordinary people. They argue that socialism itself isn't flawed; it just hasn't been implemented correctly. But America, they say, can do it right ... this time.

They try to "put lipstick on a pig" by sticking the word *Democratic* in front of *socialism.* Bernie, AOC, and the DSA want you to believe that their brand of socialism is a beneficial form of democracy because we will still have free elections under their system.

However, they still want a government-controlled economy. And government-controlled social institutions. And government-controlled bureaucracies. And government-controlled wealth redistribution. And government-controlled healthcare.

They want everything every other socialist snake-oil salesman throughout history has wanted — more government control and less individual freedom. And they want your permission to do it.

But as Marion Smith, former Director of the Victims of Communism Foundation, has said, "Socialists cannot redefine the term *socialism.* It's a term for an ideology, an imperfectly practiced system that affected the lives of millions of people ... They don't get to redefine it." [1]

Why would Bernie and AOC have to even admit that socialism hasn't been implemented correctly yet? Because it has been tried so many times over the past 200 years. And it has failed. Every time. Without exception.

The only things socialism has achieved are bringing economic collapse, the loss of individual liberty and a free press, and creating a totalitarian police state in every country where it's been implemented. And this is while those brave enough to oppose the state are labeled *class enemies* and are imprisoned or executed — more than 100 million in the 20th Century — all with the lie of saving and improving "society" or "democracy."

And if you're a person of faith in a socialist country? Prepare for even greater hardships.

Religion is one of the first things to go in a socialist society. That's because citizens must effectively worship the state, not God. God isn't needed, they say, because the state is here to provide everything you could ever need.

Karl Marx himself wrote that *"religion is the opium of the people"* and a hindrance to socialist progress.

There is no greater enemy to socialism than the Christian faith. That is why the socialists must ban, censor, ridicule, and marginalize religion. That's also why the socialists here in the United States and throughout the world hate it.

Economic collapse, a police state, complete bureaucratic control of our lives, cracking down on religious thought and practices ...

Sadly, it is becoming too easy to imagine such a dark, state-driven totalitarian future for our country.

SOCIALISM IS GROWING IN POPULARITY

How did we get to a point where a socialist future is even a remote possibility in America? How did the term "socialist" go from being a curse of failure and genocide to something considered good by a new generation of Americans?

I believe that one of the primary culprits — if not the *main* culprit — is a shift to socialist ideology in the education "industry" over the past two decades.

There are more than 68 million Generation Zers (born between 1997 and 2012) in the United States today. That's more than 20 percent.

Millennials comprise more than 72 million (born between 1981 and 1996), or 21 percent of Americans.

Today's generation of high school, college, and post-graduate students includes Gen Z, those born between 1997 and 2012. This generation leans toward more Left, and outright socialist policies. In fact, a recent survey of "Gen Zers" found that one in four favored gradually abolishing capitalism in the United States. Even more troubling, 12 percent of Gen Zers (along with 10 percent of Millennials) believe that *"society would be better off if all private property was abolished and controlled by the government."* [2]

As if that weren't disturbing enough, nearly half of Gen Z (49 percent) and 47 percent of Millennials have favorable opinions of socialism, calling it *fair.* [3]

They wouldn't be so enthusiastic about socialism if they were being taught true history, (or lived in a socialist country) instead of the Marxist propaganda that's filling our schools and colleges.

The truth is, communist regimes massacred more than 100 million people since the Bolshevik Party seized power during the Russian Revolution in 1917. In 1922, the Union of Soviet

Socialist Republics (USSR) was born, becoming the world's first "self-declared" socialist state.

Government "programs" in the Soviet Union, China, North Korea, Cambodia, Cuba, Venezuela, and all other socialist regimes promised radical social transformation, prosperity, and equity for all — but that false hope never materialized. Instead, those dictatorships wound up delivering mass starvation, poverty, misery, and death to the people who had once believed the governments' false promises. And those who opposed those governments faced arrest, torture, and execution for daring to question the authority of the state.

People of faith were persecuted, jailed, and murdered. Churches were closed, home church gatherings were outlawed, and the Bible was banned.

Schools from kindergartens to Ph.D. programs are teaching Gen Z students that socialism is fair and equalizes the society, so everyone shares in the wealth and prosperity. And how does socialism allegedly ensure these goals? Because, unlike greedy corporations and "the rich," the "benevolent" government is "altruistic" and doesn't operate on "greed."

This couldn't be further from the truth.

In every socialist or communist society, government leaders and their handpicked cronies are incredibly wealthy and live in the lap of luxury. Those who balk at Donald Trump's affluence would be shocked to see the opulence in which communist leaders like Nicolas Maduro (Venezuela), Miguel Diaz-Canel (Cuba), and Xi Jinping (China) live.

But what about the average citizen in these socialist and communist nations? Are they living in *equity* with their leaders?

No. Of course not.

Instead, the people must labor long hours for little pay and struggle for scarce resources. Because the government controls the means of production, the output can't support the needs of the populace, and the economy constantly teeters on collapse.

Citizens who are disillusioned by the socialist dream rarely have any options for escape. *Escape* is indeed the right word, too. For example, the Berlin Wall separated the Soviet side of Germany from the free side from 1961 to 1989. The Soviet side had armed soldiers, barbed wire, sandbags, and massive concrete and barbed-wire blockades to stop people from trying to escape from the horrors of communism. Anyone caught trying to cross over was shot.

If communism were so great, why would they need a wall and armed soldiers to keep the people from escaping?

Schools have long ignored the legacy of socialism, portraying it instead as a pathway to equity and fairness for all. So, students learn little about the actual, historical hardships and the crimes of socialists leaders and are instead taught the idealistic promises of a failed and anti-human ideology.

Another reason for the rise in socialism in America is the increased legitimacy and support many of our elected leaders give this ideology.

The Democratic Socialists of America's (DSA) stated goal is to participate in *"fights for reforms today that will weaken the power of corporations and increase the power of working people,"* with a long-term aim of social ownership of production as public enterprises, worker cooperatives, or decentralized planning. [4]

DSA's membership has ballooned from 6,000 members in 2015, to more than 90,000 today, making them a significant political machine. [5]

That statistic is frightening enough, but what's even more ominous is that members of the U.S. Senate and Congress are proud members of the DSA, including Alexandrea Ocasio-Cortez, Rashida Tlaib, Cori Bush, Jamaal Bowman, Greg Casar,

Seattle Councilwoman Kshama Sawant, and, of course, senator and former presidential candidate Bernie Sanders.

The socialist education initiatives, combined with the "cool" factor many modern Democrats give it on social media, plus the false promise of *fairness* and *democracy* that organizations like the DSA claim, have not only made socialism a legitimate option for today's younger generations; it's made it an *attractive* choice.

Sadly, the younger generations are placing unjustified trust in socialist promises and the government's ability to live up to them. They also lose sight of where the government would get all the money it would need to provide such extravagant benefits — from hard-working taxpayers through ever-increasing taxes.

As 19th century French economist Frederic Bastiat put it, "The State is the great fictitious entity by which everyone seeks to live at the expense of everyone else."

WHY SOCIALISM FAILS ... EVERY TIME

The only people who like Democratic socialism are the elected and approved professional politicians and government bureaucrats who force the rest of us to:

- Buy products and services we don't want ... or outlaw or restrict what we do want.
- Pay taxes to support causes we oppose.
- Pay higher prices for everything.
- Suffer shortages and long wait times for things we need.

When the government takes over an industry and sets prices for a product or commodity, shortages result. This creates economic upheaval and personal misery.

We see this in the severe shortages of basic utility services — water, gas, and electricity — in Venezuela. Thousands of

Venezuelans have been protesting in the streets. They know that the only real *equality* socialism offers is an equal share of misery for everyone.

Well, *almost* everyone.

You can be sure the government elites in Venezuela have more than enough electricity to power their luxury homes and plenty of food, water, energy and other items to meet all their needs.

The bottom line is that socialism in all its forms has failed everywhere it has been implemented:

- Cuba.
- North Korea.
- Venezuela.
- The USSR.
- Nazi Germany.

Nazi, by the way, is short for the National *Socialist* German Workers' Party. So, every time a radical socialist attacks a conservative by calling him a *Nazi,* they're actually testifying to the horrors of socialism themselves!

Hitler was elected as a socialist. He became a dictator as a socialist.

He divided people between the oppressed and the oppressors.

He instituted central planning of the economy ... crushed freedom of speech and the press ... demanded submission and obedience from Christians by threat of imprisonment or death.

And, of course, he set out to eliminate Jews, murdering more than 6 million Jewish men, women, and children and at least five million prisoners of war.

But what about here in America? Surely we can figure out the *correct* way to implement socialism, right?

That is one of the biggest lies about socialism — that, while it has totally failed wherever it has been tried, the problem wasn't the concept of socialism itself; the problem was that those who implemented it *did it all wrong.*

"But not us!" said every elite ruling class who's ever attempted it. *"We'll succeed where all others have failed!"*

For example, in the 1970s, Cambodia was one of the poorest, most poverty-stricken countries in the world. Their leader, Pol Pot — a mass-murdering communist — claimed to have the solution for the failing country's problems: a socialist reorganization! Inspired by Communist Chinese leader Mao Zedong's "Great Leap Forward," Pol Pot instituted a socialist campaign he called a "*Super* Great Leap Forward."

The reference to Mao was ... problematic, to say the least. The program Pol Pot based his brand of socialism on was responsible for one of the most destructive events in world history, measured in the loss of individual freedoms, the creation of crushing poverty, and the deaths of nearly 100 million innocent Chinese people.

Mao's "Five-Year Plan" began in 1958, but it led to widespread starvation and was abandoned early in 1961. The goal of modernizing China's agricultural sector using communist central planning had the exact opposite result: it created 40 years of famine, causing roughly 30 million Chinese to starve to death.

Did Mao's failure stop Pol Pot from implementing his version of a government-controlled farming system? Of course not. Every socialist leader begins with the unwavering assumption that *he* or *she* is the one person in human history who can make socialism work, who can finally create the socialist utopia that's long been *lauded in theory* by academics but *disproven in practice* over and over again — with ordinary people paying the price, often with their lives.

In Cambodia, the result was not only grinding poverty and the loss of freedom, but the mass murder of more than 2 million people. Of course, religious minorities, including Christians, were a primary target.

You may have seen the movie *The Killing Fields,* which depicted the horrific events that occurred in Cambodia during Pol Pot's communist dictatorship. The movie gave an accurate portrayal of the terror and evils of socialism.

There is a powerful and compelling reason why no country or world leader will *ever* "succeed" with socialism. By its very nature, socialism creates poverty, hopelessness, terror, and oppression. In my previous book, *The Deep State: 15 Surprising Dangers You Should Know,* I outlined 10 ways that socialism can and will harm the typical American family. I think a quick flyover of those dangers will help illustrate why socialism has failed every nation that has tried it — and why it will destroy America, too:

1. **Socialism creates a powerful, expanding, and unresponsive federal government.** This is contrary to the preservation of liberty and free enterprise, which focus on the private sector and local control.

2. **Socialism creates an inefficient, and ineffective, and self-serving bureaucracy.** Bureaucracies are unaccountable entities that constantly want to grow and expand, but are always inefficient, ineffective, and hostile to change. When I was in college, I had a chance to hear an amazing economist, Ludwig von Mises. His book outlined the intrinsic evil and ineffectiveness of socialism. Dr. Mark Skousen, in his book, *The Making of Moder Economics,* points out that Mises was the first to expose the failure of central planning.

3. **Socialism crushes economic growth.** Economic growth means new jobs are created, incomes rise, and new economic and entrepreneurial opportunities boom. But socialism destroys economic growth. Socialist leaders and their elite allies maintain their power by redistributing

wealth and pitting people against one another, rather than creating more wealth, innovation, prosperity, and jobs.

4. **Socialism kills innovation and progress.** New products and services would never make it to market if not for free enterprise and the profit motive. A new cancer drug, for example, could make the company and its investors billions of dollars — while also saving countless lives. Innovations in technology, drugs, and inventions require a free people and individuals who are not shackled by bureaucracy.

5. **Socialism discourages entrepreneurship.** While capitalism gives people greater opportunities to thrive and prosper, socialism crushes individual and national prosperity by its burdensome and excessive regulations, and anti-competitive and power-focused bureaucracies. And simply ensures equal results — no matter how dismal or impoverishing. That means people are robbed of their motivation to start new businesses.

6. **Socialism wastes resources and money.** In a capitalist society, there are harsher penalties for a business that fails. It will run out of resources. But in a socialist society, the government may allocate an incredible amount of resources to a government program that is performing poorly, meaning money, time, and resources are wasted.

7. **Socialism relies on a top-down, command-and-control approach that can't match the free market.** A free economy is self-correcting because it operates out of self-interest, not a top-down approach.

8. **Socialism means everyone is equally poor — except for an elite few.** Socialism eventually descends into political corruption, causing the ruling elite to become extremely wealthy while the rest of the country suffers. People may be struggling to put dinner on the table in a socialist economy, but the government freely hands out benefits and resources to the politically connected.

9. **Socialism is obsessed with expanding centralized power.** As Lord Acton said, *"Power corrupts, and absolute power corrupts absolutely."* The genius of the U.S. Constitution includes its overarching restraint on government, as it also prevents the creation of a centralized power that will lead to coercion and dictatorship.

10. **Socialism works against human nature.** People will always work harder to support themselves and their families than they will to make money for the government. Likewise, they will always take care of their own resources and property more carefully than they will take care of someone else's. Put simply, that's human nature!

Former British Prime Minister Margaret Thatcher, a close friend and ally of Ronald Reagan, perfectly summed up why socialism is doomed to failure: *"The problem with socialism is that you eventually run out of other peoples' money."*

A SURPRISING HISTORY LESSON ON SOCIALISM

Reviewing the entire history of socialism is beyond the scope of this book, and I could not come close to detailing its horrors and failings throughout history in so short a space here. However, I thought it might be interesting to give you one example of a (failed) socialist society that will probably surprise you. This one is closer to home for us because it was an early *American* brand of socialism.

When the Pilgrims came to America to escape religious persecution from the English government, they adopted an economic system of shared property and imposed *communal service* on the small population of settlers. Every person was given an equal share of food, property, and compensation for their labor, regardless of how hard they worked — and even if they did not work at all.

In other words, they set up a socialist system. [6]

The results were predictable from a historical standpoint:

- An anemic economy.
- Poverty.
- Famine.
- Discontent.
- Resentment.
- Envy.

The colony grew sick, weak, and hungry, as the able-bodied men and women weren't given an incentive to work hard.

The Pilgrim settlement was a community of people who had come to America together with a shared vision. They formed enduring bonds on the harsh overseas voyage to the New World, they built a community together, and they cared deeply for one other.

Despite that, the colonists were fed up with the *inequity* of the *equitable* system they had put in place upon their arrival. They knew in their hearts that rewards should be proportional to the amount of work each individual contributed to the job at hand.

After three years of economic failure and hardship, the colony abandoned socialism and adopted a new system: every family unit would plant and grow *their own* crops ... and they would get to keep *for themselves* the produce of their labor.

In other words, they switched from a socialist system to a capitalist system. And they thrived. They were happier, more industrious, and exponentially more productive.

Think about the economic lesson of the Pilgrims the next time you sit down for Thanksgiving dinner. As we give thanks, we should certainly celebrate God's protection for the Pilgrims and the grace and kindness with which the Native Americans received them and helped them survive. But we should also celebrate their industrious ingenuity in implementing an economic system that enabled them to thrive — just as it has enabled us to do for the past four centuries.

AN ATTACK ON CAPITALISM AND LIBERTY

Socialists hate capitalism because they are enemies of individual freedom. Therefore, socialism is nothing short of an attack on both capitalism and liberty. Socialism and liberty simply cannot coexist.

Socialism vs. capitalism (or free enterprise) is not merely a *conflict* between competing ideas about which economic system is most-efficient, effective, or even more equal. Instead, it's more of a *life-and-death struggle* because it deals with the core issue of freedom vs. coercion, and individual liberty vs. a modern form of serfdom, where individual rights are subject to the overlords or the bureaucratic state.

Capitalism is a unique economic system. It's a moral system that operates without coercion and respects individual choice.

All others require the government to impose its will on individuals. There is no voluntary compliance. It's required by the state and imposed by force with the threat of fines, jail, and even death.

In communist Cuba, economic destruction, loss of freedom, jails, torture chambers, and mass executions have kept its leaders in power from the beginning.

That is the history of socialism, whether it's wrapped in communism or some other type of Marxism in which central planning rules and the individual is crushed. In a central-planning economy, individual freedom and choice are replaced by command and control from the top ... from the bureaucrats. In capitalism, economic activity is something that people voluntarily pursue if they want to (and don't pursue if they don't want to).

It's the most natural system of all, as it respects and protects freedom of choice, press, religion, and more.

In a capitalist system, individuals are free to act as they choose according to the dictates of their conscience and their personal desires. This is a moral view of *God-given* and *unalienable* rights — rights the government should not violate.

Through my ad agency, I have spent years helping everyday men and women become millionaires. All these individuals have had dreams — and almost always no starting capital. I've been in a great position to help them succeed in achieving their dreams.

These innovators and entrepreneurs needed capital to fund their ventures, and they would seek ways to generate that capital from investors. The investors provided the capital because they wanted to create profits — knowing that this, like any investment, involved the risk of losing their money. They were willing to take that risk in exchange for the promise of greater reward.

That kind of risk/reward exchange is only possible under capitalism.

Those who provide products or services that people want can succeed.

Those with products or services people don't want will fail.

Taxpayers don't lose; investors do.

That's why America became the greatest economic engine in human history.

And that's why more people have been lifted out of grinding poverty and into wealth in America than in any other country in the world.

Whenever countries adopt a free-market economy, they grow. When they impose socialism, they stagnate and collapse.

The socialists call it exploitation when investors "get rich off the backs of workers." It's just the opposite. Investors and entrepreneurs increase job opportunities, increase wages, and increase mobility within society to move up and beyond anyone's expectations.

Social capitalism is not exploitation. It's opportunity. As Ludwig von Mises, one of the great economists of the Austrian School of Economics, wrote in his essay, *Planning for Freedom:*

> *"[Central] Planning and capitalism are utterly incompatible. Within a system of planning production is conducted according to the government's orders, not according to the plans of capitalists and entrepreneurs eager to profit by best filling the wants of the consumers.* [7]
>
> *Our products and services were not the brainchild of a government bureaucrat. They were the dreams of businessmen, entrepreneurs, and innovators who identified a need in the marketplace, determined how best to meet it, and took the risks required to make it to flourish. And hopefully, they're rewarded for it."*

Von Mises concluded, *"The idea that political freedom can be preserved in the absence of economic freedom, and vice versa, is an illusion."* [8]

And that's the central problem with socialism. You cannot have socialism *and* political freedom. They are wholly incompatible. The only way for socialism to work is by coercion. They must crush economic freedom. Socialists must also crush political freedom. There cannot be any dissent. There cannot be criticism. There cannot be any obstacle to their planned economy.

The radical pro-socialists want to expand the power of government at the expense of individual freedom. That's why this growing curse of socialism in America is such grave danger. No matter how attractive and compelling politicians like Elizabeth Warren, AOC, Gavin Newsom and Bernie Sanders make it sound, socialism is dangerous, immoral, and a threat to the very foundation of what made America the greatest nation on earth.

HOW CREEPING SOCIALISM IMPACTS YOU TODAY

Of all the moral wrongs and economic damage socialism and socialist policies inflict on society, the two issues I see increasingly causing serious problems for hard-working Americans can be summed up in two words: *dependency* and *regulations.*

The State of Dependency

First, let's address dependency — specifically *government dependency.*

In recent years, a growing number of people is relying on the government to care for them ... like a parent taking care of their children. They rely on the government to take care of them from cradle to grave — essentially for free, without the recipient having to contribute anything.

In fact, most well-meaning welfare-state policies actually *discourage* people from seeking meaningful work. Someone can make about the same amount of money doing *nothing* than they can by working 40 hours a week. A growing number of dead-beats are saying, *"Why not?"*

These people live off the hard work and hard-earned success of others, and the government is only too happy to oblige because it wins them votes and increases their power and control. And again, why not? From the government's perspective, it doesn't cost them anything — because they use other people's money to provide these benefits — and it further cements the dependency many in government want to create in the minds of most Americans.

To paraphrase the great Irish playwright George Bernard Shaw, *"A government that robs Peter to pay Paul can always depend on Paul's support."*

Put another way, if a government is your main source of income, you're much more likely to vote for the people or political party that will provide and even increase your benefits. It is one way that socialist governments are actively "buying votes," and they're doing it right out in the open.

The federal government spends roughly $1.19 trillion of your hard-earned taxes on more than 80 different welfare programs, representing almost 20 percent of total federal spending, including $890 billion for Medicaid for 11.1 million individuals.

Welfare spending accounts for 6.3 percent of GDP, and it's growing.

And although the amount of welfare received varies from state to state, most states pay more than $8 per hour for a 40-hour-a-week job. Some states pay even more than that — even up to a $29 an hour.

If that seems unbelievable to you, take a moment to review the "How does your state rank?" chart to the right. This comes from the Cato Institute's eye-opening report, "The Work Versus Welfare Trade-Off: 2013."[9] See how much welfare recipients in your state can earn on the government dole. And, as your jaw drops at the dollar amounts you see, keep in mind that these figures are from more than 10 years ago. I'm horrified to think of what the Cato Institute's *next* report will find.

This welfare state, dependency mentality is killing incentive. It's also unsustainable — eventually, as Margaret Thatcher said, you eventually run out of other people's money.

Of all the challenges facing America today, and in the days ahead, one of the most serious is the government's insistence on creating a state of dependency, through which the bureaucratic or technocratic elite can manipulate and control the economy, society's values, and the people.

RANK	JURISDICTION	PRE-TAX EQUIV ($)	HRLY EQUIV ($)*
1	Hawaii	60,590	29.13
2	District of Columbia	50,820	24.43
3	Massachusetts	50,540	24.30
4	Connecticut	44,370	21.33
5	New York	43,700	21.01
6	New Jersey	43,450	20.89
7	Rhode Island	43,330	20.83
8	Vermont	42,350	20.36
9	New Hampshire	39,750	19.11
10	Maryland	38,160	18.35
11	California	37,160	17.87
12	Oregon	34,300	16.49
13	Wyoming	32,620	15.68
14	Nevada	29,820	14.34
15	Minnesota	29,350	14.11
16	Delaware	29,220	14.05
17	Washington	28,840	13.87
18	North Dakota	28,830	13.86
19	Pennsylvania	28,670	13.78
20	New Mexico	27,900	13.41
21	Montana	26,930	12.95
22	South Dakota	26,610	12.79
23	Kansas	26,490	12.74
24	Michigan	26,430	12.71
25	Alaska	26,400	12.69
26	Ohio	26,200	12.60
27	North Carolina	25,760	12.38
28	West Virginia	24,900	11.97
29	Alabama	23,310	11.21
30	Indiana	22,900	11.01
31	Missouri	22,800	10.96
32	Oklahoma	22,480	10.81
33	Louisiana	22,250	10.70
34	South Carolina	21,910	10.53
35	Arizona	15,320	7.37
36	Wisconsin	14,890	7.16
37	Virginia	14,870	7.15
38	Colorado	14,750	7.09
39	Nebraska	14,420	6.93
40	Iowa	14,200	6.83
41	Georgia	14,060	6.76
42	Utah	13,950	6.71
43	Maine	13,920	6.69
44	Illinois	13,580	6.53
45	Kentucky	13,350	6.42
46	Florida	12,600	6.06
47	Texas	12,550	6.03
48	Arkansas	12,230	5.88
49	Tennessee	12,120	5.83
50	Mississippi	11,830	5.69
51	Idaho	11,150	5.36

**Based on 2,080-hour work year*

As investor and economist George Gilder said, *"Nothing is more deadly to achievement than the belief that effort will not be rewarded, that the world is a bleak and discriminatory place in which only the predatory and the specially preferred can get ahead."* [10]

Americans from all walks of life have so much to contribute to our country and to the world. This country was built by everyday Americans who put their God-given skills, talents, minds, and hands to work — work that provided for their families and served their communities. Those hard-working men and women changed the world.

I pray the dependency state doesn't rob us of the value of an honest day's work.

The Regulatory State

The second way these socialist policies are affecting everyday Americans is in the form of regulations and Presidential Executive Orders — all bypassing congressional debates and voters — creating miles and miles of red tape and an endless amount of "fees" that the government forces companies to pay.

I'll discuss regulations in general in Chapter 3. For now, let's simply see how government regulations are affecting your life every day: the price of gasoline.

We keep hearing all about how the "greedy" oil companies are hurting hard-working people in the middle class by their price-gouging and Marxist manipulation. But there's a dirty little secret about our historically high gas prices that the radical Socialists don't want you to know. It's mostly *their* fault, not the oil companies.

California is often the testing ground for socialist policies that later spread like a cancer across the rest of the country. And it may surprise you to know that California is at war with the oil industry.

This isn't because the oil industry has done anything bad. That might shock you, because the Democrats are so persuasive and persistent in spreading the myth that oil companies are making excessive profits at the expense of the average person and need to be punished and stopped.

There's no evidence of this, of course, because it's not true. But by saying it over and over, they're making the general public *think* it's true.

The federal government and the California state government aren't telling you why gas prices are so much higher in California and some other states than they are in others. And nobody is telling you how much of the money you pay at the pump is going to the federal and state governments themselves, rather than the oil companies.

So, I'll tell you.

The federal government's gas tax is 18.4 cents per gallon for gasoline and 24.4 cents per gallon for diesel fuel. But that's just the beginning.

Each state, plus the District of Columbia, adds its own taxes — ranging from 14.4 cents per gallon in Alaska to 58.7 cents per gallon in Pennsylvania. Some counties and cities pile even more taxes on top of the federal and state taxes. Every level of government bureaucracy gets a cut of your money.

And then, of course, we can't forget the additional fees on top of all those taxes.

California's combined gasoline taxes and fees — totaling $1.03 for every gallon of gas you buy — are by far the highest in the nation. But this outrageous amount doesn't even include the 18.4 cents per gallon federal gasoline tax or the state *sales* tax on the price of gasoline — which includes sales tax on the federal, state and local taxes!

That's right: they're taxing you on what you spent on other taxes!

Accounting for that, the state sales tax is about 14.4 cents per gallon for gasoline purchased in California. On top of all that, California's switch to summer gasoline blends adds 10–15 cents per gallon due to the higher cost of refining and production.

All that may have been hard to keep up with, and I haven't even mentioned the fees yet, so let's break down all the taxes and fees per gallon in California:

- 18.4 cents – Federal excise tax.
- 54.1 cents – State gas tax.
- 25 cents – Cap and Trade fee (estimate).
- 22 cents – Low-Carbon Fuel Standard fee (estimate).
- 2 cents – Underground-storage fee.
- 14.4 cents – State sales tax (varies with price of gas at the pump).
- 10 to 15 cents – Summer-blend price add-on between April 1 and October 1.

All that comes to around $1.50 per gallon in taxes and fees. So, if you're in California and choke at paying $5.25 per gallon, keep in mind that almost 30 percent of that is going to all the bureaucracies standing between you and the oil company.

As if the state taxes on gasoline weren't bad enough, California is also gouging its residents with a ton of extra fees that are included when Californians register their vehicles with the state and county. State fees include:

- Registration Fee.
- California Highway Patrol (CHP) Fees.
- Transportation Improvement Fee (TIF).
- Vehicle License Fee (VLF) – 0.65% of car's value.

- Miscellaneous Registration and Service Fees.

And we can't forget the additional county and district fees based on where in the state you live:

- Service Authority for Freeway Emergencies Fee (SAFE).
- Air Quality Fee.
- Auto Theft Deterrence/DUI Fee.
- Abandoned Vehicle Abatement Fee.
- Fingerprint ID Fee.
- County Transportation Project Fee (CTPF).

These are all hidden fees collected by the California DMV that don't show up on a registration renewal notice. No wonder California's total vehicle registration costs are the highest in the nation!

If the radical pro-socialists have their way, every state in the country will face this same oppressive opposition to car owners. High gasoline prices and car registration fees hurt us all, and the poor and middle class suffer the most. And this is just *one tiny area* where a bloated out-of-control bureaucracy and socialist regulatory policies are crushing the California economy, destroying people's lives and forcing more than one million residents to flee the state. But high costs for gasoline-powered cars is the socialist dream: to discourage cars that are powered by fossil fuels and to promote the adoption of electric vehicles (in most cases, also powered by electricity generated by fossil fuels at other locations).

FREE ENTERPRISE: THE ROAD TO PROSPERITY AND FREEDOM

As I've said, socialism seeks to crush innovation — but it can't stop it.

Why?

Because innovation is inherent in our design by God, we are creative beings, and creative beings *create.* We have a drive to do more, to go further, to push the limits, to solve problems. That drive leads to miraculous inventions and innovations that literally change the world.

However, socialists seek to stamp out that creative spark of innovation by squashing free enterprise, demonizing the very basic human drive that has led to all the wonders in our modern society.

Today's students have learned the lesson, as younger generations have grown increasingly critical of capitalism. That's ironic, though, because these same young people (along with the rest of us) are doing a fantastic job of advancing and *driving* capitalism, stirred by our collective need for more, newer, and better *stuff.*

As Ludwig von Mises put it, *"All people, however fanatical they may be in their zeal to disparage and to fight capitalism, implicitly pay homage to it by passionately clamoring for the products it turns out."*

The computer on your desk, the iPhone in your pocket, the car in your garage, the carefully selected wardrobe in your closet ... all are made possible thanks to capitalism and freedom.

With this clear view of a free market economy in mind, let's pick apart two of the most common socialist arguments against capitalism and see why, despite how loudly people shout them, they fall completely flat.

Spread the Wealth

Socialist Democrats like to claim that we need the government to "spread the wealth around."

This is a myth — a barely believable one at that. In truth,

free-market capitalism produces far more wealth to far more people than any socialist government ever can or will.

You don't spread wealth around by taking it from the rich and giving it to the poor. You spread wealth around by freeing the rich and the entrepreneurs to create more of it — by investing in new businesses and by expanding *existing* businesses. This creates new jobs for more people while raising the wages of existing employees.

The jobs that create real wealth are the jobs that produce energy, commodities, manufactured goods, and services that people need or want to buy ... not government jobs that produce nothing.

More manufacturing and goods-producing jobs were created — and more people were raised above the poverty level — during President Trump's first two-and-a-half years in office than during the entire eight-year Obama administration that preceded him.

Trump brought a revitalized free-market mindset to the American economy, proving that the expansion of wealth is market-driven, not government-mandated and controlled.

Government Can't Solve Your Problems

Another popular lie the radical pro-socialists like to spread is that only the government can solve our nation's social and economic problems. But again, free-market approaches provide far superior, far more workable and achievable solutions.

Why?

Because the free market rewards one thing that socialism destroys: *incentive.*

A socialist government has three goals:

1. To perpetuate itself.

2. To expand its reach.

3. To increase its power and control.

None of these goals is compatible with solving problems.

If government actually solved problems, it would put itself out of business. Federal departments created to solve housing problems, health problems, economic problems, energy shortages, and so on would be shut down because they would no longer be needed. Government employees would be furloughed permanently.

That never happens.

Instead, government agencies grow even larger — along with the problems they're *supposed* to be solving. More government employees are hired. Bureaucracies expand. Rules and regulations, along with their forms and paperwork, snowball.

As Ronald Reagan once said, *"No government ever voluntarily reduces itself in size. Government programs, once launched, never disappear. Actually, a government bureau is the nearest thing to eternal life we'll ever see on this earth!"*

A federal government-based, top-down approach to solving social problems can never match the efficiency and effectiveness of an entrepreneurial, free-market approach.

Bureaucrats sitting behind desks in large office buildings aren't going to care as much about people suffering in crime-ridden inner cities or in poor rural communities as the entrepreneurs and companies that actually live there and conduct business among the people.

There is no real, personal incentive for government bureaucrats to solve problems. All they care about is collecting their fat paychecks and receiving their taxpayer-funded healthcare.

Just imagine being dependent on a healthcare system being operated with all the care, passion, and dedication you encounter at your local DMV!

TALKING ABOUT SOCIALISM IS A LUXURY

Former World Chess Champion and human-rights leader Garry Kasparov grew up in the former Soviet Union and is now a vocal critic of socialist and communist regimes around the world.

Writing on behalf of all those who have suffered under such governments, Kasparov shared in a 2016 Facebook post:

> *"I'm enjoying the irony of American [Bernie] Sanders supporters lecturing me, a former Soviet citizen, on the glories of Socialism and what it really means! Socialism sounds great in speech soundbites and on Facebook, but please keep it there. In practice, it corrodes not only the economy but the human spirit itself, and the ambition and achievement that made modern capitalism possible and brought billions of people out of poverty. Talking about Socialism is a huge luxury, a luxury that was paid for by the successes of capitalism."* [11]

That last line bears repeating: *"Talking about Socialism is a huge luxury, a luxury that was paid for by the successes of capitalism."*

If America, the greatest and largest free-market economy in the world, falls into the folly and tyranny of socialism, like so many other now-failed nations, I genuinely fear the horrific effect it will have, not only on Americans, but on every other man, woman, and child throughout the world.

As Ronald Reagan put it, *"If we lose freedom in America, there is no place to escape to. This is the last stand on Earth."*

President Reagan was right.

A strong and free America makes the world a better, safer, more moral place. And socialism is *not* the path to a strong, good, and prosperous America.

Chapter 3

Danger #2: The Growing Economic Crisis: 7 Misunderstood Problems That Are Crippling Our Economy

I have bad news — bad news that represents a growing danger to you, your family, and our nation as a whole. It's a danger that affects your job and salary. It's a danger to your investments and retirement accounts. It's a danger to entrepreneurs and to your ability to start your own business. It's a danger to innovation. And, on a much more practical level, it's a danger to how much you'll pay for the things in your grocery cart each week.

The danger is economic mismanagement by politicians and ideologically driven bureaucrats.

And the bad news is that these decision-makers don't understand what they're doing with your money.

Even more disturbing is that economic crisis is causing millions to fear, worry, and stress, resulting in an increase in needless worry, hopelessness, drug and alcohol abuse, and even suicide.

The state of our personal finances affects every part of our lives, and it often seems like the government and bureaucracy are doing everything they can to cause damage to the U.S. economy. So, in this chapter, we'll dig into the danger of crippling economic mismanagement by examining seven specific problem areas you need to be aware of and understand ... things the politicians and media hope you don't know.

PROBLEM #1: THE DANGER AND IMMORALITY OF INFLATION

If you lived through the late 1970s, you saw prices going up practically every month. America experienced a high inflation rate during that period because of wasteful and out-of-control spending by Congress and the disastrous Carter Administration.

According to the Bureau of Labor Statistics Consumer-Price Index, the U.S. dollar had an average inflation rate of 9.0 percent per year between 1975 and 1980 — a cumulative increase of more than 53 percent!

But that overspending was just a fraction of what it is today.

Back then, every time you went to the store for groceries, put gas in your car or paid a bill, you saw that the cost of the things you purchased had gone up.

The value of the dollar goes down when the money supply is increased above and beyond the proper production cost of goods and services. This happens when the government overspends and when the Federal Reserve — "The Fed" — increases the money supply through the banking system.

Basically, when government spending exceeds the amount of money it takes in from all sources, the more inflation — *and prices* — increase.

This was bad in the '70s, but government overspending and excessive regulations have been on overdrive in the past few years as Congress spent more than $21.17 trillion from 2020 to 2023.

Just as bad, the Fed simultaneously increased the money supply, only slowing it down in March of 2022 with the start of its money supply contraction and raising of interest rates. Since then, they have raised interest rates from 0 percent to more than 5.5 percent. According to the National Debt Clock, the U.S. national debt is at a historic and unsustainable $33.5 trillion.

Of course, they won't admit that inflation is their fault.

Everybody from Deep State bureaucrats to Big Tech to the biased media to the President of the United States is trying to fool you, saying it's not due to the massive overspending. They are all saying, *"Don't worry! Inflation is going down! The economy is getting better! Don't worry about the recession!"*

Do not believe it.

You see higher prices every time you go to the store.

And they are not going down.

The amount of massive and historic money in circulation caused by government overspending is threatening the health and security of our economy for generations to come.

By raising interest rates to slow down the economy, the Fed is having a devastating effect on all of us — individuals, businesses, homebuyers, car purchasers, and wage-earners. The theory is that raising interest rates will cause prices to go down, lowering inflation. There were a total of 10 rate hikes between March 2022 and May 2023. Interest rates increased more in those 14 months than in the previous 15 *years* combined!

There is no logic nor wisdom in this *raise-rates-to-lower-prices* theory.

It's an insufficient Band-Aid on an open wound. It slows economic growth and distorts economic activity, but it still doesn't stop the source of the increase: Government overspending and the Federal Reserve's money-printing policies.

History shows that as the government keeps overspending and the Federal Reserve keeps increasing the money supply, their actions devalue the dollar. This monetary devaluation causes inflation, and inflation raises prices.

And the massive overspending by President Biden and Congress is still spiked with historic new money in circulation (with more to come), meaning the current inflation rates will continue — or get even worse.

To be clear, whatever inflation rate is "officially" announced by the government and media is never the *actual* rate of inflation that you experience in real life. The Biden Administration can't stop touting their economic success at "lowering" inflation and helping the middle class keep more money from their paychecks.

They are either delusional or lying. Or both.

The "official" rate of inflation — the dressed-up number they use to make themselves look better — goes down some months and goes up other months. From Biden's first day in office until the writing of this book, annual average rate of inflation is really up 18 percent. In fact, the price of many goods and services is going up well beyond 18 percent.

The *actual* inflation rate since Biden took office is much different than figures like the 3 or 4 percent we sometimes hear reported for very limited time periods.

You don't have to be an economist to understand that prices that are consistently rising and never going down hurts everyone — especially those on fixed incomes or retirees and, of course, lower-income Americans, the middle class, and business owners.

And it is not just the price of goods and services you buy; inflation also affects income. People's incomes in real terms fell between February 2021 and October 2023. You have lost roughly $7,500–$8,500 per year as prices have risen. How? Because you now have to earn almost 18 percent *more* than you did the last few years just to pay for the same products and services.

If you haven't gotten an 18 percent raise in the last couple of years, you've lost money.

Of course, most people have not received an 18 percent raise recently. In fact, real wages have fallen by –3.2 percent. By late fall 2023, real wages were down for 27 straight months, with everyone becoming a little poorer and falling behind each and every month.

In fact, inflation has risen so high and so fast that prices will never come down to where they once were. But according to President Biden and Treasury Secretary Janet Yellen, everything is great.

I personally don't know any American families who would agree with their claim.

That's the problem with central government planning, and that's the problem with the Federal Reserve utilizing outdated, ideologically driven Modern Monetary Theory: It doesn't work.

As the great economist Dr. Milton Freidman said, *"Inflation is made in Washington because only Washington can create money. And any other attribution to other groups for inflation is wrong. Consumers don't produce it. Producers don't produce it. Foreign sheiks don't produce it. Oil imports don't produce it. What produces it is too much government spending and too much government creation of money and nothing else."*

A clean sweep in the House, Senate, and The White House — and a dramatic change in the Federal Reserve — will be the only remedies that can turn this economy around, and start things moving in the right direction and getting better.

That means your vote and every other voter matters in every single national election.

PROBLEM #2: DEFICIT SPENDING AND NATIONAL DEBT

The media have focused on President Biden and the socialist Democrats' massive trillion-dollar spending programs with the promise of creating jobs and turning the economy around post-pandemic.

But that's not the reality.

In fact, it's just the opposite. And the media are silent about it.

The trillions in government overspending are leading to job losses, increasing prices, and economic crisis. This should not come as a surprise to anyone. Massive deficit spending *always* leads to disaster.

In fact, Biden's Big Government, massive overspending policies have failed in every country that has tried it.

It's failed in Red China.

It's failed in Europe.

It's failed in Cuba and Venezuela.

It's failed in Putin's Russia and the former Communist Union of Soviet Socialist Republics.

It's failed in Nazi Germany (National Socialist German Workers' Party).

Why? Because a central government and its bureaucrats can't make the best decisions that only a free market can make. Having government take money from the successful and productive members of society for redistribution always produces less, not more, for everyone.

The bureaucrats controlling how government money is spent always produce waste and inefficiency. Bureaucrats don't allocate the money to the most-efficient use. In fact, they do just the opposite. They destroy jobs, economic growth … and freedom.

As I write this, the U.S. national debt is nearly $33 trillion and rising. It will be much higher by the time this book is published and even higher by the time you read these words.

Year over year, the debt has not decreased even once since 1957.

Think about what happens if you spend money on your credit card and you can't pay it back.

Bankruptcy.

Now, think about what that would look like on a national scale. Put simply, we are headed for national bankruptcy. The bankruptcy will be so big and the consequences so horrific that every American should be concerned about the future and especially the future of their children and grandchildren.

If you follow the news, you might read that and think, *well, we'll just raise the debt limit. Problem solved!* That absolutely will happen, but that is not an effective long-term strategy, and it certainly will not solve the problem.

You've probably heard politicians and talking heads in the media discuss the need to "raise the debt limit" (or "debt ceiling") several times over the years, but what does that actually mean?

The debt limit/ceiling is simply the legally established maximum on how much the government can borrow to pay its bills — everything from social welfare programs to salaries for the military.

To be blunt, *raising the debt ceiling* is another way of saying *kick the can down the road.* It's sticking future generations with our crippling debt. But that hasn't stopped us from doing it over and over.

In fact, the debt ceiling has been raised 78 times since 1960 under both Democrat and Republican presidents. *Seventy-eight times!* And yet, the problem keeps getting worse. You'd think our leaders would have learned the lesson by now.

Every time the government borrows money, it has to pay it back with interest, and since we, The People, *elect* the government — our taxes fund the government (not including what they borrowed) — we all are on the hook to pay back the money.

That means you, your children, your grandchildren, and generations to come will be saddled with paying back the debt.

It also means higher inflation and higher taxes for us all.

Here's how it works:

Imagine you "max" out on all your credit cards, and you borrow money from your family and friends to pay it back. However, you only raise enough money to pay the interest on the credit cards without touching the balance.

So, you call the credit card company and ask them to raise your credit limit from its current limit of $5,000 to an increased limit of $15,000.

Then, you immediately max out that $15,000 and ask your family and friends to give you even more money to pay the interest on that new, bigger balance.

Then, you call the credit card company and ask them to raise your credit limit again, this time to $30,000. You max *that* out, borrow more money to pay the interest payment on the new balance, call the credit card company to ask for *another* increase, and the cycle continues.

You keep borrowing money and spending, each time maxing out your credit limit. But everything you borrow from your family and friends only goes to pay the interest on your debt, so the amount you owe just keeps growing and growing.

Does this sound like a winning financial strategy? Would you do this in your personal life and expect things to get better?

Of course not.

But that's exactly what the federal government does.

It spends more than it takes in through taxes and then borrows money from the Federal Reserve (and other countries like China), while it continues to spend money it doesn't have.

Then, when it can't afford to pay the interest payments on the money it borrowed, Congress again holds a vote to raise the debt limit, which allows the federal government to borrow more money just to cover its obligations.

It's a vicious cycle that never ends.

Of course, Congress wouldn't have to raise the debt ceiling if they just cut their out-of-control spending, ended borrowing, balanced their yearly budgets, and only spent the money they took in through taxes.

If only ...

But they won't cut their wild and wasteful spending. And they won't heed the basic lesson every family in America has to learn at some point: endless debt with no plan to repay it is a fast track to bankruptcy.

And yet, like death and taxes, it's a sure bet Congress will raise the debt ceiling again.

PROBLEM #3: THE FEDERAL RESERVE

I've mentioned the Fed several times already, but let's take a moment to dig in here and explore why I think the Federal Reserve itself is a contributing factor to America's crippling economic mismanagement.

As I discussed above, the inflation we are seeing today is caused by massive government overspending and the historic money-creation spike by the Federal Reserve, which has flooded the economy with money — what they sometimes call *quantitative easing.*

They've been printing money and thereby devaluing the dollar ever since the Federal Reserve's inception, in 1913. During that time, under the destructive actions of the Fed, the U.S. dollar has lost more than 95 percent of its value. So, $1 in 1913 is equal to about $30 dollars today.

Here's the problem: Excess money sparks misallocations of resources and spikes inflation. The Fed's quantitative-easing policy of propping up the economy and the market with an endless supply of cash has a *security blanket* effect on investors.

This investor security blanket creates demand for investment opportunities, which creates bigger profits for investors, which makes the stock market go up. It also creates a need for more jobs and better wages — growth based on a seemingly "stimulated" economy.

The Fed, in recent attempted to stimulate the economy by keeping interest rates *artificially low,* or below market rates. By keeping interest rates artificially low, the Fed has caused a bogus and delusive economic boom, overvaluing the stock market and creating more inflation.

This overvaluation fools many investors, entrepreneurs, and companies into believing that the economy is growing *naturally* and that it is strong, when, in fact, it was *artificially stimulated.*

This false sense of investor security usually ends badly, as inflation continues to grow and a massive correction in the market occurs, leading to an inevitable crash.

Even if the Fed's and our politicians' intentions were good (and I'm not convinced they are most of the time), we all end up in worse shape after a stock market crash and an economic downturn.

Today, we have an economy that is artificially stimulated. It's built on a house of cards — one gentle breeze away from total collapse.

Money manipulation almost always leads to a recession or depression. Virtually every financial crisis since 1913, including the stagflation of the Carter presidency in the 1970s or the economic meltdown in 2008, can be linked to the Federal Reserve's disastrous monetary policies, endless printing of cash, their expansion of credit, and their artificial stimuli and their eventual tightening and their interest-rate manipulations.

For example, President Franklin Roosevelt and the Federal Reserve had no confidence in the free market to sort itself out. They instead relied on their own human judgment and limitations to steer the economy back on track.

Unfortunately, their counterproductive and coercive policies intended to fix the complexities of our economy made the Great Depression more damaging and much worse, dragging it on and on for almost a decade longer than it should have lasted.

Things are not all that different today. As inflation continues to rise, the Fed continues to tinker with the economy, making presumptuous guesses about what will help. So, they slow down the printing presses, raise interest rates, and restrict the flow of money to banks. Less money to banks means less money to lend, which means less money is available for investors to borrow. With fewer lending options, businesses and individuals slow or stop their investments in new projects, expansions, and new businesses.

With less investment capital, companies that produce products and services shrink. Investors pull back, and stock prices drop. This causes the economy to spiral downward into a recession, as the country's total output of goods and services (or GDP) slows to a point of little or no growth.

This can result in *stagflation,* when the economy is stalling and prices are rising. This is where we are today.

With low GDP and continued spending by the government (helped by the Fed's overheated printing press), the dollar's value shrinks even further, along with the economy, leading to *shrinkflation.*

And this leads to companies charging the same prices (or more) for less of the product or service.

As things get worse, companies start to lay off workers and the unemployment rate rises. Companies file for bankruptcy — and we're in a full-blown recession again.

However, as inflation rises along with interest rates, what was a bad *recession* can quickly turn into a *depression,* unless the government stops its wild spending and returns to policies that are favorable for economic growth.

The results of the Fed's unending attempts at money manipulation have been disastrous throughout its history.

Today's Federal Reserve does not deserve our trust. It's failed. They have proven over and over again that they don't know what they're doing and can't predict the future. And yet they keep trying to solve our growing economic crises … but just end up making things worse.

In a PragerU video titled, "No Free Lunch," Johan Norberg recalls Nobel Laureate economist Milton Friedman's observation that: "Excessive government control, regulation, and taxation distorted incentives and put money in the hands of politicians and bureaucrats who had not earned it and suffered no consequences if their policies failed." [1]

All this nightmarish economic chaos confirms what I've been saying for more than 40 years:

It's time to abolish the Fed.

It's the problem, not the solution to achieving economic prosperity.

PROBLEM #4: GOVERNMENT WASTE

The government always wastes money. The amount of spending and debt that bureaucrats and elected leaders are comfortable with is mind-boggling.

But it's worse than just the wasteful use of taxpayers' money that helps fuel inflation; it's also money used for ideological or partisan purposes.

For example, on January 3, 2023, Congress passed a $1.7 trillion spending bill giving millions to blatantly partisan, pro-Democrat, socialist groups. The full text of the bill was more than *4,000* pages, and no Senator nor House Member read it before casting a vote.

To paraphrase Nancy Pelosi's legendary 2010 nonsensical outburst, they had to *pass* the bill before they could find out what was *in* the bill.

And what *was* in the bill? Unsurprisingly, it was filled with all kinds of pork, wasteful spending, pet projects, and political favors. Billions went to socialist political groups to register and mobilize new voters and brainwash Americans. More went to *pork,* or contrived, unnecessary, and unproductive projects that benefit no one except the friends and political cronies of the Senators and House Members who voted for them.

Here are some examples of what your tax money was spent on:

- $1.2 million was earmarked for LGBTQI+ and "Pride Centers."
- $500,000 for "anti-racism" training for Rhode Island teachers.
- $3 million for the American LGBTQI+ Museum in New York City.
- $1.5 million to help illegal immigrants get legal status.
- $410 million to secure the borders of countries like Jordan, Lebanon, Egypt, Tunisia, and Oman — but nothing to protect our own borders.
- $65 million for Pacific Coastal Salmon "recovery."
- $3 million for bee-friendly highways.
- $3.6 million for the Michelle Obama Trail in Georgia.

- $5 billion (that's *billion* with a "B") for low-income Home Energy Assistance.
- $200 million for "gender and equity" funding.
- $575 million for "family planning" in areas where population growth threatens endangered species.
- $1 million for Zora's House, a coworking and community space for women and "gender-expansive people of color" in Ohio.
- $750,000 for LGBTQI+ and gender non-conforming housing.
- $2 million for a wax museum dedicated to African Americans.

And remember, this is just a handful of the items that are in that outrageous 2023 spending bill.

Every Democrat in both houses of Congress voted for this monstrosity, as did 18 Republican senators and nine Republican House Members.

When you look at these numbers and what this money went toward, don't forget where the money came from:

It came from you, the taxpayer, through taxes and higher inflation.

The only money government has to spend on these things is the money it takes from us.

How many of these items, then, would you have personally chosen to spend your money on? Frankly, if these were options for my own charitable giving, *none* of them would have passed the sniff test. In fact, I'd consider giving money to *stop* many of them from happening!

My guess is you might feel the same way — at least about *some* of these ridiculous expenses. Why, then, is it even remotely acceptable for our elected politicians and bureaucrats to spend our money on this junk?

Answer: It's not.

But they do it anyway.

If you agree most of these things represent wasteful use of your tax dollars, *it's time to vote on a President who will pledge to cut spending ... and a Congress that agrees.*

PROBLEM #5:
REGULATIONS: AN IMPOSSIBLE WEB OF RED TAPE

Business journalist Neil Cavuto once asked me during an interview segment on his Fox TV show, "What is the worst thing that can happen to business owners and to Americans?"

Neil expected me to say taxes. I surprised him.

"Regulations," I said. "Regulations are the worst thing to happen to everyone."

I said that because regulations kill more jobs, opportunities, and businesses than anything else. It's the hidden evil that spikes prices higher, destroys jobs, limits your choices, and crushes opportunities.

This is not just a federal government issue; it's a state issue as well.

A perfect example is what's happening in California, where I lived for most of my life. Californians are feeling the consequences of out-of-control state insurance regulators. Their tight regulatory policies and requirements have driven up the costs for insurance companies and made it impossible for them to operate in California, with the government's price controls and long delays in making decisions, despite constantly rising rates.

Compound that with the state's failure to clear brush, which led to massive wildfires in California, and you have a perfect storm for insurance companies to stop offering homeowner's insurance.

That's right, homeowners' insurance, a necessity for any homeowner, is disappearing. And Californians have no one to blame but the elected Department of Insurance commissioner and the bureaucratic regulatory agencies.

Here's a flyover of the damage that's already been done:

- Geico has closed all 38 of its offices in California.
- The largest property and casualty insurance company in California, State Farm, is no longer accepting new applications for any kind of insurance other than personal vehicle insurance — and they're having to raise those rates, too.
- Allstate is no longer issuing new policies in California.

This will be a terrible nightmare for any homeowner in California.

State Farm was California's largest home-insurance company, and Allstate was the fourth largest. With these companies gone, there will be fewer choices and less competition for all Californians, which will lead to increased rates … because of regulatory overreach.

People may actually have to take out personal loans just to get insurance!

The politicians' solution is to punish the insurance companies, hold hearings on how the insurance companies are "price gouging," demand more price controls, increase more regulations, and impose greater government control.

In other words, they want to solve the problem by doing even more of what created the problem in the first place. Some politicians in California are even suggesting that the state completely take over the insurance industry.

It's a march to complete socialism in the insurance industry —

a form of totalitarianism, the absolute control and regulation over public (and private) life.

Government control of business is never effective and never works efficiently. This is yet another reason for Californians to leave the state. It's also another reason for other states to make sure they don't follow in the disastrous footsteps of "trendsetting" California.

This is an issue more people are starting to speak out against. Millionaire businessman and investment expert Kevin O'Leary is best known as "Mr. Wonderful" on the hit TV series *Shark Tank.* His success in business and marketing is legendary. But he is also not scared to ruffle feathers and speak the truth.

On political commentator Tucker Carlson's show, O'Leary warned that politicians like Elizabeth Warren are at war with entrepreneurship and will punish business owners for their success in the form of high taxes.

He stated, "The regulatory environment there [Warren's home state of Massachusetts] is prohibitive for business. New York? Even worse. New Jersey? Forget about it ... California? You can't do business there, and they're leaving in droves out of there." [2]

I personally had to move my marketing and advertising company from California, where I started it in college. I directly and individually created hundreds of jobs in the state but could not continue because of the regulations. I moved my company to Tennessee, with no regrets.

O'Leary called these states "no longer investable."

For example, say you want to open a small business, that will provide a dozen or so jobs to your local community. Great! But you better be prepared to pay the government for the opportunity to give these people jobs.

One study found that the annual regulatory cost of a small business with fewer than 20 employees, was $10,585 *per employee.* So, as you budget your hires, you have to add an additional $10,585 to your overhead on top of the person's salary! This was 36 percent higher than the annual regulatory cost per employee of a company with more than 500 employees.

The result?

The disadvantages facing an entrepreneur attempting to start a small business to compete with large companies is often so overwhelming that the entrepreneur gives up.

Not only do excessive regulations hurt entrepreneurs and investors, but the cost of those regulations is passed down to us, the American consumers. The regulatory cost passed down to us is around $2 trillion per year, which amounts to nearly 20 cents out of every dollar we spend! All this red tape isn't just annoying; it's expensive!

Worse, excessive regulations slowly but surely remove control from the people and centralize it in the hands of "Washington elites." The genius of the U.S. Constitution is that it is designed to prevent the creation of a centralized power that leads to coercion and dictatorship. But career politicians have found a workaround for what is prohibited in the Constitution: they have created regulatory agencies to consolidate and expand their control over you and me. This includes the FEC, SEC, Department of Labor, Department of Commerce, and hundreds of other departments and agencies that 99 percent of Americans have never even heard of.

And we can't overlook the devastating effect regulations have on innovation and progress in this country.

Take the Food and Drug Administration (FDA), for example. Many effective drugs and new therapies never get to market because the innovating company can't afford the exorbitant cost of government approval.

In other cases, the drug *works* and is approved, but the costs of the FDA approval process are so high that the drug is priced beyond what the market will bear. Can you imagine if a pharmaceutical startup literally cured cancer — but the regulatory costs made the treatment effectively unavailable to suffering cancer patients?

How on earth did we get here?

Because government regulators are virtually free from oversight.

Up until 1983, Congress could exercise a legislative veto over unnecessary or burdensome regulations. But not anymore.

Since 2011, Congress has introduced more than 200 laws to reform federal government regulatory agencies, but so far none of them has been signed into law.

None.

Zero out of *two hundred.*

Meanwhile, 430 federal departments, agencies, and sub-agencies continue working year-round, producing an average of 10 new regulations every single day with virtually no oversight from any of the three branches of government.

So, between 2008 and 2016, approximately 2,500–4,500 new government regulations were unleashed upon the American people — *every year.*

That represents 70,000 to 80,000 additional legal-size pages being added to the Federal Register every single year! The number of pages of regulations for the Affordable Care Act alone is eight times greater than the length of the Bible!

PROBLEM #6:
NEVER-ENDING TAX HIKES

Higher taxes hurt people — and they don't just hurt the "rich people" or "corporations" that the Democrats like to blame for every problem facing America today. Higher taxes hurt everyday, middle-America, blue-collar workers and their families. They hurt small businesses and small business owners. They hurt retired people and everyone living on fixed incomes.

Higher taxes mean less opportunity, fewer jobs, and less freedom.

But that's not what you hear on mainstream news and from socialist politicians.

Instead, you hear how everyone — especially the "rich" — should pay *their* "fair share." If they were being honest, they would say it's really about a massive social-engineering campaign designed to reshape America into a collectivist/socialist society that divides Americans into three groups:

1. The Super-Rich.

2. Those who are dependent on government handouts.

3. Everyone else.

This division is destructive to economic growth: it further pits identity groups against one another across our nation. It demonizes the successful people, coddles those at the lower end of the ladder, and leaves everyone in the middle paying exorbitant taxes and struggling to make ends meet.

The "fair share" the radical pro-socialists love to talk about is anything *but* fair.

When I'm speaking in public, I often ask audiences what percentage of their income going to taxes do they think is *fair.*

I start by saying, *"What about 50 percent? Do you think that is fair?"*

The people in the audience always react strongly to this amount. They call it *"unfair confiscation"* and *"morally wrong."*

Then, I'll bring the figure down. *"Okay, what about 40 percent? Would it be fair for the government to take*

$40 of every $100 you make?"

"Outrageous!" they'll say. *"That's still way too much. Why should I spend 40 percent of my time working for t he government?"*

"Well, how about 30 percent? Surely that's fair, right?"

This is usually when people start to begrudgingly concede. *"That's still too high,"* they'll argue. *"But I guess we're at least getting a little closer to fair."*

"Twenty percent?"

"Ugh. Maybe 20 percent. But I still don't like it."

That seems like a reasonable exchange, doesn't it? I'd imagine if you and I had that conversation, your responses would be similar to what I get from most audience members.

But there's a problem. The radical pro-socialists don't want 20 percent. Or 30 percent. Or even 40 or 50 percent. Under the banner of a post-pandemic tax emergency, Biden and Sanders were pushing a combined federal, state, and local tax rate of around 60 percent!

If you think I'm exaggerating, think again. New York residents are looking at 61 percent of their hard-earned total income going to taxes. In California and Hawaii, it's a little better at "only" 59 percent.

Are these the rates they admit?

Heavens, no.

But is this the reality for hard-working Americans living in these deep-blue states?

Sadly, yes.

The politicians may say they're more focused on taxing *businesses.* But the reality is, as a business owner, I must pass those higher taxes on to my customer. I can't afford not to. Otherwise, my business can't survive. No business could.

When politicians call for higher taxes on businesses, what they really mean is higher prices for every product or service the businesses provide — food, clothing, school supplies, gasoline, building supplies, and even your home utilities — including natural gas and water.

Put simply: Businesses don't pay taxes, they collect them for the government.

The bottom line is, despite what Biden and his ilk may say, *corporations* don't pay taxes; *people* do. That might be in actual checks you write to the U.S. Treasury Department at tax time, and it might be in the automatic payroll deductions you try not to think about on payday. But whether you realize it or not, it most certainly *is* in the cost of the goods and services you and your family rely on.

PROBLEM #7: ENTITLEMENT SPENDING

We've already seen that government deficit spending is out of control. Since the end of World War II, federal tax revenue has grown 15 percent faster than national income ... but federal spending has grown 50 percent faster. As a result, in the years since 1946, the federal government has ended its fiscal year with a deficit more than *65* times.

What are our leaders spending all that money on?

Two words: *entitlement programs.*

Much of the increases in federal spending relative to gross domestic product (GDP) over the past seven decades has been due to increases in entitlement spending. That includes:

- Social Security.

- Medicare.
- Medicaid.
- Disability Insurance.
- Food Stamps.
- Other welfare and government assistance programs.

Entitlement spending as a percentage of GDP grew from less than 4 percent in the late 1940s to an irresponsible and unsustainable 17 to 18 percent by 2022. By contrast, national defense and non-defense discretionary spending as a percentage of GDP is no higher today than it was at the end of World War II.

Entitlements have been the single-largest expense category in the federal budget since the early 1970s, and they account for almost two-thirds of all federal spending today. Thus, there can be no significant reduction in the federal deficit without deep cuts to the entitlement programs to which many Americans have become addicted.

Sadly, though, Congress has proven time after time that it has no desire or willingness to restrain entitlement spending, and no President in recent history has dared to make any serious demands that they do so.

Instead, we appear to be heading for even more entitlement spending as the Baby Boomer generation begins making bigger demands on our already stressed Social Security and Medicare programs. Between now and 2030, Baby Boomers are expected to retire and claim Social Security and Medicare benefits at a rate of *10,000* per day, or 300,000 per month. Financing this level of expenditure will require record levels of new taxation, an even greater level of debt than we have now, or massive cuts to other programs or cuts to Social Security and Medicare programs themselves.

These are all terrible options. Higher taxes lead to less

economic growth and a lower standard of living, and more public debt exacerbates economic volatility and makes our financial system more prone to a major crises.

And these dynamics drive politicians and demagogues to take actions that create the most immoral tax of all: inflation.

Congress must begin acting responsibly by making the hard decisions required of our current entitlement expenditures ... including free-market solutions ... before it's too late.

IT'S TIME TO STOP DIGGING

This chapter probably wasn't a fun one for you to read.

That's okay. It wasn't a fun one for me to write, either.

But if we have any hope of righting the economic wrongs of the past seven decades, if we want even a *chance* of making so much as a dent in the national debt, if we want to stop inflation, then we as a nation must open our eyes to the magnitude of the problem.

We are trying to borrow, tax, and regulate our way out of an endless economic nightmare — but those are the very tactics that got us here in the first place. As personal finance expert Dave Ramsey often says, *"You can't get out of a hole by digging deeper!"* If we want to get ourselves out of this hole, we've got to put down the shovel.

What we've been doing isn't working.

It's time to get serious about slashing taxes, spending, and the regulations imposed on all of us by the Deep State's unelected bureaucrats.

And it just might take a clean sweep of the presidency and Congress to get it done.

Chapter 4

Danger #3: The Destructive Triplets: Forcing Social, Business, and Government Compliance to Radically Transform America

Radical, ideologically driven socialists, who oppose individual choice and freedom, want you to change your actions, speech, beliefs, and thoughts.

They want to change how you do business. Change how you work with others. Change how you hire people. Change how you measure personal and corporate success. Change what you know to be true about biology. Change your view of gender and sexuality. They want to change who you are, what you are, what you do, and what you value.

And if you don't *want* to change ... they'll *make* you change.

They will make you change by the coercive power of the government or state, not by your free choice.

And they'll use business, education, the media, and other institutions to force compliance.

The CEO of notorious investment firm BlackRock — a key leader in pushing pro-socialist propaganda on people and businesses — got into some hot water in 2017 for "saying the quiet part out loud." In an interview with *The New York Times,* CEO Larry Fink explained his and BlackRock's perspective on *encouraging* change in America's institutions:

"You have to force behaviors. If you don't force behaviors, whether it's gender or race or just any way you want to say the composition of your team, you're going to be impacted. That's not just recruiting; it's development. We're gonna have to force change." [1]

Fink wasn't kidding. Over the past 15 years, and especially in the few years since Fink's now-notorious comments about "forcing change," America's biggest and most influential corporations have unleashed two key, three-letter initiatives on their employees, customers, and investors. And the results have been nothing short of disastrous. I'm talking, of course, about DEI and ESG.

Add to that the full-court press by the media and activist groups to force total, unquestioning acceptance of the LGBTQI+ lifestyle, and you get a highly politicized, highly radicalized environment that threatens to absolutely destroy how America does business and how Americans view each other.

DEI: SANCTIONED DISCRIMINATION

Whoever controls words and their meaning controls the culture. In the 21st Century, the radical pro-socialists have taken control of the words we use. And the three words they're using now to define — and destroy — our culture are *diversity, equity,* and *inclusion,* or DEI.

Around 2009, I started to discover that Christians, conservatives, and libertarians in bigger companies were being discriminated against with what amounts to targeted "reeducation" campaigns. They were being forced to listen to or attend seminars, webinars, Zoom calls, video presentations, and "education" or "training" sessions.

They were told these were the corporate policies, and obedience was demanded. They had no choice but to attend. They had no freedom to voice objections. There was no dissent or disagreement allowed. Conformity and compliance were required. Even those workers who belonged to unions discovered their unions also demanded absolute, unquestioning compliance with the new policies being unleashed upon America's workforce — from the factory floor to the corner office.

Having built a long and successful career in marketing over several decades, I'm no stranger to a company's sudden emphasis on a particular training program. I've seen more than one "big thing" come and go over the past 40 years in business. But right from the outset, I could tell there was something different about this new initiative. Something dark. Something destructive.

It was an emphasis on race, gender, and sexual issues all wrapped up under the tidy banner of *diversity, equity,* and *inclusion* (DEI). And while those each *sound* like good things, DEI is being used to absolutely destroy America's corporate, educational, and social structures.

What Is DEI?

The underlying premise of DEI is not about making educational or corporate institutions more diverse, more equitable, or more inclusive. Instead, as Prager University explains, it is about ensuring preferential outcome for individuals and groups based on race, sex, and gender identity.

Christian Watson, host of Pensive Politics podcasts, makes this point crystal clear in a popular PragerU YouTube video discussing DEI: *"DEI is ultimately about only one thing: advancing those who are not white, heterosexual, and male at the expense of white heterosexual men, regardless of their respective qualifications."* [2]

DEI paints a bleak picture of America, casting our entire national history and identity in a dark, hateful light. DEI seeks to elevate members of non-white, non-straight, non-male groups into positions of power and privilege — and anyone who disagrees with this is condemned as racist, sexist, and "*whatever*-phobic."

Its divisiveness creates a vicious struggle of one group versus another with a false moralism and self-righteousness, anger, and hatred. It is a victim mentality that is destructive, not one of love, cooperation, and constructive relationships.

And it's a trap: As Watson explains, churches, businesses, and institutions who *do not* open DEI offices are cast as racist, sexist, and phobic — but companies that *do* open DEI offices are only doing so because they think they *are* racist, sexist, and phobic. [3]

You're cursed if you do, and cursed if you don't.

Rather than actually helping or lifting up anyone, DEI is by its very nature condescending and belittling. It assumes anyone who is not white, not straight, and not male cannot get ahead without the help and support of white, straight men. The implication is that anyone who's not white, male, and straight is "less than," can't cut it on their own, and must rely on handouts from their white, male, straight "superiors."

Despite DEI's deeply flawed premise, the past decade has seen an explosion of American companies with either an official DEI department, an HR initiative, or a job title that includes the words *diversity, equity,* and/or *inclusion* (such as Chief Diversity Officer or DEI Director). By the end of 2020, U.S. companies were spending an estimated $3.4 billion on so-called DEI initiatives.

Is this huge investment actually helping anyone? Sure it is — it's helping the professional DEI hucksters who worm their way into prestigious companies and earn huge salaries for telling everyone in the organization from the CEO down how hateful and racist they are.

Responding honestly, the answer is "no," it is not really helping anyone in these organizations. For all the damage DEI is doing to our institutions, the initiatives aren't accomplishing their stated goals. Google, for example, spent $114 million on its diversity efforts in 2019. The result? Their workforce afterward was still only 3 percent African American. [4]

I honestly don't know if the executives and boards of directors of these companies genuinely believe in the stated goals of DEI or if they are just trying to look "woke" enough. However, as the *Economist* points out, it seems DEI programs *"do more to protect against litigation than to reduce discrimination."* [5] Maybe the only thing these companies *really* want is an extra layer of protection against racial-, gender- or sexuality-motivated lawsuits.

The Heart of DEI Is Wrong

DEI can at least partially trace its origin to the growing influence of *Critical Race Theory* (CRT) in academic circles. As John Stonestreet and Maria Baer, writing for *Breakpoint,* explain:

> *"This quasi-Marxist way of seeing all human history and every human interaction as a power struggle places every human being into two categories:* ***oppressor*** *or* ***oppressed.*** *Moral status is then awarded depending on how many 'oppressed' categories with which one identifies. What's left is an approach to life and human interaction that does not elevate what is good, but a purely negative ideology driven by an arbitrary rejection of what's subjectively felt to be bad.*
>
> *For decades, critical theory has stepped out of the academy into other spheres of culture, including media, government, and increasingly the marketplace. Though very few people have actually studied the academic source material, our wider culture is now in what might be called a 'critical theory mood.' Companies spend billions of dollars implementing 'diversity, equity, and*

> *inclusion' programs, because they're under tremendous pressure by cultural gatekeepers to conform and, in effect, define 'diversity' of employees by a small, select group of external traits."* [6]

In other words, DEI-driven companies do not want *actual* diversity — diversity of thought, diversity of experience, diversity of belief, etc. Rather, they want the *outward appearance* of diversity, meaning they want to *look* diverse and inclusive, even if they have to *exclude* whole swaths of people to do it.

I believe the very heart of DEI is wrong. It is a denial of reality.

The goal is to force equal *outcomes* rather than equal *opportunity.* Equal outcome requires force. Equal opportunity requires freedom. Equal outcome is compatible with socialism. Equal opportunity is only found in American free enterprise.

DEI insists that a gay, Black woman *must* achieve the same outcomes as a straight, white man — regardless of each individual's skills, talents, aptitude, training, and experience. And if she doesn't, it is not because of any shortcomings with her performance; it is because the system is rigged against her. She is a victim. It's her against the system, an organization, and/or someone with "privilege."

That absolute denial of personal performance and ability is in effect a denial of reality. No two people of any race, gender, or sexual orientation are the same, and no two people should expect equal outcomes — because we're all wonderfully unique! People should strive to achieve *their* best — not *someone else's* best.

As Stonestreet and Baer argue:

> *"Diversity is never measured in terms of belief, political party, or religion but, particularly in corporate settings, is reduced down to only categories of race, gender, and sexuality ... [However,] 'Diversity' that doesn't include ideological diversity, for example, isn't really diversity.*

> *Hiring a racially or sexually diverse workforce that is otherwise trapped in groupthink when it comes to religion and worldview does not make a better workforce. The belief that group identity should determine who deserves a job, a raise, or a contract is based on a flawed view of who human beings are. While our gender or ethnic backgrounds can have an enormous impact on our lives, they do not ground our value or determine our understanding of life and the world. Nor do they determine what kind of employee we might be."*[7]

The undeniable implication is that these businesses do not want a truly diverse workforce in terms of diversity of thought and experience. Instead, they just want to check boxes in terms of the three key categories of race, gender, and sexuality.

DEI in the Schools

DEI ideology can be found inside the schools from elementary school into college.

It's in the teaching schools.

It's in the teachers' curriculum.

It's in the hiring of teachers.

This radical ideology indoctrinates the students.

Probably, one of the most powerful examples happened when three of the top University Presidents of MIT, Harvard, and the University of Pennsylvania were repeatedly asked if genocide of the Jews would result in discipline at their schools. They couldn't say it was morally wrong and not allowed.

Then DEI ideology demanded before millions of viewers and Congress a full display of relativism. They could not make a moral judgment of right or wrong.

They viewed the Harvard attack on innocent victims and

Israel's subsequent attack on the terrorists as Jews as "white" oppressors, heroes and the Palestinians as the victors.

It was a simple question of right vs. wrong.

Then DEI Ideology could not clearly state that calling for the genocide of Jews would violate college codes of conduct.

The Supreme Court and Affirmative Action: A Major DEI Setback, A Major Gain for Freedom and Reality

In the summer of 2023, the U.S. Supreme Court reversed 50 years of legalized racial discrimination — and delivered a significant blow to DEI by striking down affirmative action in college and university admissions.

I have spoken out against Affirmative Action for more than 25 years, calling it out for what it is: pure racism and a moral evil.

For decades, colleges were accepting new students based on a flawed theory of helping one race over another, which put Asians and white people at a marked disadvantage in college admissions.

At Harvard, for example, an Asian American applicant in the *top* academic percentile had a lower chance of being admitted than a black student in the *fourth lowest* academic decile.

That is morally wrong.

Despite the public outcry by radical ideologues on the High Court's ruling, this new equality of opportunity does not deny that it is tougher for some or that some have certain advantages over others. However, we cannot sacrifice *equality of opportunity* in exchange for some impossible-to-achieve *equity of outcomes.*

Justice Clarence Thomas, the second Black U.S. Supreme Court Justice in history, wrote in his concurring opinion:

> *"While I am painfully aware of social and economic ravages which have befallen my race and all who suffer discrimination, I hold out enduring hope that this country will live up to its principles so clearly enunciated in the Declaration of Independence and the Constitution of the United States: that all men are created equal, are equal citizens, and must be treated equally before the law."* [8]

Angering radical pro-socialist pundits and media members, Justice Thomas also wrote this stinging indictment in his opinion:

> *"Individuals are the sum of their unique experiences, challenges, and accomplishments. What matters is not the barriers they face but how they choose to confront them. And their race is not to blame for everything — good or bad — that happens in their lives. A contrary, myopic worldview based on individuals' skin color to the total exclusion of their personal choices is nothing short of racial determinism."* [9]

The Court's 2023 decision and Justice Thomas's concurring opinion echo Chief Justice John Roberts' often-quoted line from 2007: *"The way to stop discrimination on the basis of race is to stop discriminating on the basis of race."* [10]

Though I often disagree with Chief Justice Roberts, I could not agree with him more wholeheartedly here.

While affirmative-action practices in college admissions are no longer permitted under the law, several schools, including Harvard University, have already said they are finding ways around the ruling. Nonetheless, this decision is a great victory for the constitutional right of equal protection under law in a society full of different races and ethnicities.

It is an especially poignant blow to today's destructive diversity, equity, and inclusion mandates in the corporate world that divide and classify people by race and other characteristics.

Many business leaders, struggling to tread water amidst the

DEI tidal wave, know illegal discrimination is wrong. They also realize that many DEI programs actually promote illegal discrimination based on a faulty and twisted understanding of the terms *diversity, equity,* and *inclusion.*

Promoting equal opportunity, instead of making promises of equal outcomes that cannot possibly be fulfilled, treats every human being with the respect and dignity of equal consideration and high expectations.

The good news is that I believe this push for "forced change" through DEI is doomed to fail and support for it is collapsing.

The only question is how many once-strong businesses will have to fail along with it before we finally wake up from the Marxist-driven DEI delusion.

ESG: A "WOKEOMETER" FOR EVALUATING PEOPLE AND BUSINESSES

While DEI is wreaking havoc internally, governing how companies are hiring, promoting, compensating, and organizing employees, its equally destructive cousin, ESG, is creating chaos and destruction externally, mandating how companies are operating, producing, and investing. That is, what DEI is to the *people,* ESG is to the *business.*

And the results have been just as catastrophic.

Environmental, social, and governance metrics — ESG — is the socialist version of the Communist Chinese social credit scoring system. Here's ESG in a nutshell: Do what the radical ideologues tell you to do, and you'll be rewarded. Don't do what they tell you, and you'll be punished. Harshly!

Think of ESG as a "wokeometer" that gauges a person or company's level of wokeness. Or, in the pro-socialist's own words, *ESG is a framework for understanding and measuring how sustainably an organization is operating.*

ESG is the new way banks and Wall Street firms are evaluating businesses. Instead of assessing traditional metrics, such as business revenue, profits, debts, and other factors, ESG will rate companies according to their wokeness. What are they doing about climate change? Are they supporting LGBTQI+ issues? Are they donating to organizations like Black Lives Matter or Planned Parenthood? Are they supporting the radical pro-socialists' "approved" candidate?

So, what happens when a company or business doesn't follow the ESG doctrine? Justin Haskins, the Director of the Socialism Research Center at The Heartland Institute, explains:

> *"A company that uses 'too much' plastic, emits 'too many' carbon-dioxide emissions, or doesn't have the 'right' ratio of Asian to Hispanic workers — all of which are real examples from ESG frameworks — would be ranked lower than another company whose profits might be smaller and products of a lower quality but who scores better in the metrics that elites value."* [11]

For example, the S&P dropped Tesla — the leading manufacturer of electric vehicles — from its S&P 500 ESG Index, because of "Tesla's lack of a low-carbon strategy." [12]

ESG is a way for the socialists and Deep State bureaucrats to control companies and make sure all the money and investments companies make go to their socialist causes and political agendas. This most notably includes the radical green agenda, a formula to transform corporations, education, the military — virtually *all* our institutions — into the radicals' vision of a socialist radical climate utopia.

ESG metrics and guidelines are also being applied to everyday Americans' investing and retirement funds — putting both in danger. In fact, for many banks and investing institutions, getting and maintaining a good ESG score is often more important than profits and efficiency.

This may help you understand why some companies, like Disney, have made seemingly incomprehensible decisions to inject sexualized ideology and social issues into their formerly family-friendly content, even though these decisions have literally cost them billions of dollars in lost revenue and have done irreparable harm to Disney's reputation.

Disney and many other large companies have gone all-in on ESG causes and have earned a high ESG score, but it's come at a ridiculously high cost in revenue, stock valuation, parks attendance, and damage to the family-friendly brand Disney has vigorously crafted and defended over the past century.

Even whole countries, such as Sri Lanka and Ghana, that have prioritized getting high ESG scores, are experiencing economic collapse. That's what happens when countries and companies make decisions based on a purely political agenda and not what's best for the country or for the company, customers, and shareholders.

Here's one example of how ESG is affecting your life, whether you realize it or not. Let's say you are in your early 60s and nearing retirement. You've done a great job saving and investing in your 401(k) throughout your career, and you're pleased with the nest egg you've built.

But now, ESG proponents elites have directed banks, investment funds, and investment professionals not to invest in oil and gas, thereby undermining the industry and hurting the investor (you) who has any money tied up in oil and gas investments.

Meanwhile, the Biden Administration, a big supporter and proponent of ESG, is working to incorporate ESG into our entire economic system by forcing it upon America's financial sectors.

Because one of ESG's biggest priorities is promoting the globalist "green" agenda, our federal government is imposing ESG-based regulations on U.S. companies by requiring them to adopt ESG practices in order to borrow money from major financial institutions.

The result is a commercial lending environment that says, "You want our money? Then you have to adopt this slate of green ESG priorities and redirect your business efforts toward making them a reality."

Only obedience gives companies access to much-needed capital while simultaneously creating a deep divide between the company and most of its customer base, who don't share the corporation's radical "ESG friendly" values.

The corresponding public dissatisfaction with their favorite companies' new direction leads to a drop in stock value, which both hurts the companies and hurts their investors' retirement accounts.

But wait, it gets worse. This push for "green technology" is also pushing the United States into the awaiting arms of the Chinese Communist Party and their control of the green energy sector. Red China controls more than 90 percent of the Rare Earth market — materials used in the construction of wind, solar, and battery equipment.

So, the thoroughly corrupt Biden Administration is deliberately making the United States dependent on Communist China for our energy needs. They're literally putting our enemies in charge of America's energy!

So, to review:

- A fundamental shift from profit-driven to ESG-focused success is being crammed down Americans' throats with regulations from unelected, self-dealing globalist leaders abroad and the Biden Administration's Deep State power-hungry, regulatory bureaucracy here at home.
- Our historically most-valuable companies are being

forced to adopt (or are willingly bowing to) an entirely new business strategy — even though it's costing them billions of dollars in lost revenue and stock value.

- Investors are losing their savings because of the monumental devaluing of the companies they've invested in.
- The price of energy is skyrocketing, as oil and gas — which we have in abundance here in America — are being shunned in favor of less-effective and more-expensive "green" energy sources that are largely dependent on Chinese materials.
- All Americans are losing their individual freedom of choice "for the greater good."
- And the Biden Administration and its Deep State bureaucrats are handing control of our energy production to our greatest enemies.

This is madness, and this insanity must be stopped.

Putting a Radical Agenda Over Profits

Let's dig a bit deeper into the impact of this ESG nonsense on investing. To put it simply, your investments are not being invested wisely for the best return on investment. Instead, your money is being invested based on the radical political agenda perpetuated by anti-business, pro-socialist ESG scores.

More and more companies are jumping into the ESG cesspool, trying to convince us all that the water is fine. Target, Maybelline, North Face, Anheuser-Busch, Chase and even sports franchises like the Los Angeles Dodgers, are all jumping on the woke bandwagon, despite the disastrous (and very public) results their even *woker* forebears like Disney have had.

What does this mean for you, the investor? Here are four

things I think every investor should know about the role ESG is playing with your hard-earned money:

1. **Your retirement money is being used to support ESG and DEI, not to get the best return on your investment.**

Many retirement plans and pension funds are managed by large investment firms like JPMorgan Chase & Co., BlackRock, and Fidelity. Together they own roughly 75 percent of the shares of America's publicly traded corporations. They also manage some of the largest state pension funds for states such as California and New York, and many federal pension plans.

When the Biden Administration and the Democrat governors tell these big financial institutions they have to promote radical environment, social, and governance (ESG) initiatives and diversity, equity and inclusion (DEI) policies, they are all on board — and they're taking your money with them.

2. **Your taxpayer money is being used to support racists, anti-business, anti-capitalist ESG and DEI programs, even though these initiatives violate the conscience of many taxpayers.**

The Biden Administration's commitment to supporting and spreading this morally and financially bankrupt ESG and DEI not only influences how your retirement money is being spent but how the government is using your money, funneling billions to Big Banks and investment firms that fund their radical pro-socialist agenda.

Financial firms like BlackRock hold important shares of stock in America's biggest, and most dominant companies, such as ExxonMobil, Apple, Chevron, Microsoft, Amazon and Alphabet. And they've used their money and power to secure board seats in these businesses as well. What do they do with this high level of influence? Force ESG and DEI into the corporations they've wormed their way into, of course!

Remember the words of Larry Fink, BlackRock's CEO, that I

cited to open this chapter:

> *"You have to force behaviors. If you don't force behaviors, whether it's gender or race or just any way you want to say the composition of your team, you're going to be impacted. That's not just recruiting; it's development. We're gonna have to force change."* [13]

When he was later asked what he meant by *forcing change,* Fink explained:

> *"We must imbue it [ESG/DEI] into the culture of a firm ... behaviors across the firm, and every region has to be similar and every citizen of the firm has to understand what's acceptable behavior and what are unacceptable behaviors."* [14]

That should tell you all you need to know.

Larry Fink is playing a dangerous and extremely political game with your taxpayer money. He is gaining more than he's losing, so why *not* push Marxist/socialist culture, especially if you're getting "free" (taxpayer) money from the government?

3. The largest financial firms frequently violate their fiduciary duty by allowing politics to override sound business practices.

I've shared the stage many times with brilliant economist Stephen Moore. He has compiled a powerful and revealing report titled, "The Unleash Prosperity Study: Putting Politics Over Pensions."

The study shows that most of the largest firms are "routinely violating [their] fiduciary duty and letting political biases interfere with sound business practices."

In his testimony before the House Committee on Oversight and Accountability, Moore said:

> *"Through a process known as 'proxy voting,' money*

> *management firms ... are voting on shareholder resolutions of the companies their clients own. Without the support or even the knowledge of their clients, big money managers are routinely supporting resolutions brought by leftist social activists. These 'ESG' resolutions ... impose on a company's management radical climate change mandates — such as zero carbon emissions — divestment of oil and gas, or plastics companies, racial and gender quotas in hiring and so on."* [15]

Moore's study also "analyzed the proxy-voting behavior of the 40 largest money-management firms and determined how often they voted for ESG resolutions that are detrimental or incidental to the company's profitability."

According to the study, *"The 'A' grades went to Dimensional, Vanguard, T. Rowe Price and Fidelity. They voted* ***against*** *nearly all ESG initiatives. On the other side of the scale, among the 'woke' firms with the worst voting records were UBS, BNP Paribas and Northern Trust. They voted 80% of the time or more* ***for*** *woke initiatives."* [16]

A company's No. 1 function is to make a profit for its shareholders, not to promote a radical anti-business political agenda.

There's no doubt about it: ESG investing is an outrageous breach of a company's fiduciary duty.

4. ESG and DEI investing is hurting the economy.

Scores of studies also show how ESG policies have reduced shareholder returns, but we've all seen the real-world results — bank failures, our biggest companies losing billions of dollars and destroying their brands, pensions and 401(k)s losing money, and so on.

During an economic forum, BlackRock CEO Larry Fink boasted that ESG regulations "required firms to sell their oil and gas holdings, even as companies like Chevron and Exxon had a blowout year in the stock market." [17]

And when you look at the disastrous results of green technology investments and the mismanaged backlash against the woke policies of Anheuser-Busch (Bud Light), Target, and other large corporations, it's clear that ESG and DEI are ruinous to our economy.

The Biden Administration, politicized bureaucrats, and pro-socialist Democrat politicians are giving our money and our hard-earned tax dollars to these investment banks and venture-capital firms to fund their socialist fantasies. Plus, every time we borrow money from China or the Federal Reserve prints trillions of dollars, you can be sure that billions are being siphoned off to promote ESG and DEI — funneled through these investment firms to the major corporations.

These woke corporations may be losing billions in sales dollars, but they are still making money in the long run from the investment firms, through investment capital, and by buying large blocks of stock in these companies. And they are doing most of it with your money, either by using your investing dollars or your tax dollars.

It's a diabolical merry-go-round that's not going to stop until we *make* it stop. Every American, investor, and retiree should be outraged by how this ESG con game machine is being run behind the scenes — and how it's destroying our economy and your future!

How ESG Led to America's Largest Banking Collapse

The year 2023 was a landmark period for the banking industry — all for the wrong reasons. Several huge, powerful banks — once considered leaders in finance and "too big to fail" — imploded. Giants like Signature Bank, First Republic Bank, and tech-startup darling Silicon Valley Bank (SVB) literally ran out of money and were left unable to liquidate all their depositors' funds in the final days of their chaotic closures.

What happened?

These banks (and many others whose fortunes haven't yet run out) were guilty of the ESG-driven madness I've been talking about. They made reckless loans to risky businesses that *never* should have qualified.

Why?

Because the businesses they invested in were highly favored by the radical socialists and, therefore, earned the willing banks high ESG scores. Climate-change organizations, politically favored startups, radical pro-socialist venture capitalists — lenders the Left loves but who also, sadly, almost never turn a profit.

These banks also bankrolled radical Marxist, racist, and scam organizations like Black Lives Matter (BLM), and pro-socialist Democrat candidates.

Eyeing the all-important ESG rating, banks like SVP and Signature were distracted by their customers' woke corporate culture, business practices, and radical policies. Many of the banks themselves had even purged conservatives, Republicans, Libertarians, and Christians from their staffs ... or at least forced them to comply with their radical ideology. Some even "fired" companies and nonprofit groups as customers, forcing them to bank elsewhere simply because the bank didn't like their politics or share their radical values.

Internally, these banks had sacrificed corporate sanity at the altar of DEI. For example, Silicon Valley Bank did not have a compliance officer, but they did have a VP of Diversity. Like many other lenders before and after the crash, SVB was driven by ideology, not sound banking practices or common sense.

And like everything else DEI and ESG touches, the results are catastrophic. One recent study showed an estimated $2 trillion loss in the market value of 186 banks that are at risk nationwide. [18]

Case Study: The Fall of Silicon Valley Bank

Let's take a look at Silicon Valley Bank's descent into collapse and sale to First Citizens Bank as a case study in the disaster of ESG priorities.

Keep in mind, though, that I'm intentionally presenting this at a high level to paint a picture of the problem in broad, easy-to-see strokes.

Like many banks, SVB invested most of its money in two places: First, as I've said, they had a history of making ideology-driven investments in risky "green" businesses. Second, they invested heavily in government bonds and mortgage-backed securities that are highly sensitive to interest rate hikes.

Because of the Biden Administration's numerous economic failures — marked by high inflation and rising interest rates — the value of SVB's bonds and mortgage-backed securities crashed. When customers started making large withdrawals, the bank had to sell those investments at a loss of almost $2 billion to cover them.

When news of this loss and SVB's plan to recoup their lost billions became public, bank customers panicked and started withdrawing their money to the tune of $42 billion. This caused SVB's stock to crash by more than 60 percent.

Predictably, as the stock value plummeted, customers were more anxious to pull their money out of that bank, causing a "run" on the bank. The more other customers pulled their money out too, the more the value dropped, creating a downward spiral.

Eventually, the bank ran out of money and was no longer able to liquidate its customers assets. At this point, the bank failed, and the government intervened.

Customers with less than $250,000 in deposits with SVB were

covered by FDIC insurance. Customers with more than that, though — which made up a large number of SVB depositors — were left in a panic.

That's why the government injected tens of billions of dollars into the banking system in 2023 — to literally prop it up and protect the wealthy depositors — many of Silicon Valley Democrat/Biden donors.

More than $20 billion of government and FDIC funds went to SVB alone. To cover this cash infusion, the government simply printed more money, which made inflation worse (hurting you and me), which just added more fuel to the fire.

Round and round this merry-go-round goes ...

Lessons Learned

What's the lesson here? Simple: Banks that are more concerned with ideology than sound financial practices are a dangerous place to keep your money.

SVB was the darling of banking for the high-tech sector ... until it imploded.

Why? Because SVB checked all the radical ideology boxes the radical likes to see in a business. They touted their commitment to "greater dimensions of diversity" on their website, committed $5 billion in "sustainable finance and carbon-neutral operations to support a healthier planet," and gave more than $73 million to BLM and more money to other radical groups.

It was one of the most politicized and ideologically driven banks in America, with pro-socialist and partisan-Democrat business policies and practices. Its board of directors was packed with people who were all for supporting radical pro-socialist causes, but who knew very little about banking. In fact, only *one* of SVB's board members had any actual banking experience!

But SVB's ideology did not protect it from losing their investors' customer's assets.

As of the time of this writing, there is a long list of similarly misguided banks I would stay far away from. Some of those include:

- Bank of America.
- Wells Fargo.
- Citibank.
- JP Morgan Chase.
- Goldman Sachs.
- Morgan Stanley.
- Sunrise.
- Beneficial State Bank.
- Amalgamated Bank.
- Berkshire Bank.
- BMO Harris.
- Ally Financial.
- Southern Bancorp.
- Intrafi Network.
- First Green Bank.
- Deutsch Bank.
- Moody's.
- Eastern Bank.
- Fifth Third Bank.

- First Republic Bank.
- Royal Bank of Canada.
- Scotiabank.
- TD Bank.
- Bancorp Bank.
- Trillium Asset Management.
- Truist.
- US Bank.
- Loans.
- Western Alliance.
- Comerica.
- VMB Financial.
- PNC Bank.

If you are banking with one of these, I suggest immediately removing your funds from them ... just like I did.

At one point, I had my company funds and personal money in Bank of America and Wells Fargo. This is no longer the case. I recommend you do the same.

Outside of these banks, it can be hard to know if the bank you are considering is safe or blinded by radical ideology. The best way to tell is by carefully reviewing the written corporate policies of the bank and looking at the organizations to which it has donated money. That should reveal any political or ideological associations that might concern you.

As of this writing, there are a few banks that are better choices because they do not seem to follow a radical, ideological, politicized agenda or support radical pro-socialist candidates or groups. Of course, that does not mean that there is no corruption or incompetence in these banks. Again, it is hard to know all the inner workings of any business.

Wherever you decide to invest your money, just go slowly, do your homework, get input from an experienced and qualified financial advisor, and make the best decision you can about where to put your money.

How ESG Is Going So Far

University of Colorado professor Sanjai Bhagat examined the effects of ESG on businesses so far, and he came up with four conclusions:

1. ESG funds have underperformed.
2. Companies that tout their ESG credentials have worse compliance records for labor and environmental rules.
3. ESG scores of companies that signed onto the United Nations ESG Program didn't improve after they signed, and financial returns were lower for those that signed.
4. Companies publicly embrace ESG as a cover for poor business performance. [19]

The good news is that some states are fighting back against the ESG promoter's heavy-handed tactics. Currently, 19 states are launching an investigation into the involvement of Bank of America, Citigroup, Goldman Sachs, JPMorgan Chase, Morgan Stanley, and Wells Fargo, which are all part of the UN's Net-Zero Banking Alliance.

These State Attorneys General say these banks are *"killing ... American companies that don't subscribe to the woke, climate agenda."* They oppose the UN's ESG policies that *"require banks in the alliance to set carbon dioxide emission-reduction targets in their lending and investment portfolios and reach net-zero emissions by 2050."* [20]

As the saying now goes, *"Get woke, go broke."*

That's exactly what would happen if these woke banks, doing the UN's bidding, succeed in implementing their agenda — America will go broke.

TOTAL ACCEPTANCE: RADICAL LGBTQI+ IDEOLOGY INDOCTRINATION

DEI and ESG are wrecking our nation's business and investing sectors, but there is one other movement that has infiltrated every part of our lives — our workplaces, entertainment, news, social circles, social media ... *everything.*

LGBTQI+. (And, of course, whatever other letters they may intend to add to that by the time you're reading this.)

Radical LGBTQI+ ideology is destructive to our freedoms. It's not about "gay rights." It's not about "discriminating against gays." It's not about allowing someone to live the way they want or sticking our noses into the privacy of peoples bedrooms.

Today's radical LGBTQI+ movement is about an extreme ideology that wants to impose its values and practices on others. It's about using whatever coercion or power the state and media have to force compliance to its demands.

Anyone who objects to any aspect of the movement for any reason will be branded a hateful, bigoted, homophobe. They could lose their social media accounts, their jobs, and even their right to free speech.

And if you object because of your genuine faith-based beliefs? Well, that makes you the worst of the worst and, in the pro-socialist view, you don't deserve any rights.

Discriminating Against Christians

Across America, Christian organizations and agencies are under attack. Faith-based organizations are being forced to comply with the radical LGBTQI+ agenda or risk being shut down, even though they have legitimate, faith-based religious objections to the LGBTQI+ lifestyle.

This can be perhaps most clearly seen in the wave of attacks against Christian adoption agencies across America.

Over the years, I've written about how states that have passed anti-discrimination laws — laws that demonize the biblical worldview that marriage is a relationship between a man and a woman only — are trampling on religious liberty and forcing not *tolerance* but all-out *acceptance* of same-sex marriage.

This means that, in many states, Christian adoption agencies and Catholic charities have been forced to go out of business because they won't accept the mandate to place children up for adoption in same-sex homes.

Evangelical and Catholic adoption agencies and charities are not trying to force their beliefs on anyone. Yet they are being accused of discrimination and bigotry ... and they are being told they must either violate their sincerely held Christian beliefs or shut down.

Any adoption agency or entity that disagrees with same-sex marriage is at risk of being banned, sued, and outlawed.

The real battle here, though, is not about homosexual adoption; it's about religious liberty. Homosexual couples can adopt from many different secular agencies. They aren't forced to apply with Christian/Catholic charities. They do so for one reason only: to try to force faith-based adoption agencies to accept same-sex marriage.

Fortunately, some states are acting to protect religious liberty and government leaders are making it clear that adoption is not about what the LGBTQI+ activists want, but about what's best for children.

At least nine states have passed laws that grant religious exemptions to faith-based foster care and adoption agencies, and other states are considering similar measures. And to be clear, same-sex adoption is not banned in any of these states ... despite what the ACLU often claims.

During his administration, President Trump didn't waver in his support for this key issue of religious liberty. At the National Day of Prayer breakfast in February 2019, he said:

> *"We will always protect our country's long and proud tradition of faith-based adoption ... My administration is working to ensure that faith-based adoption agencies are able to help vulnerable children find their forever families while following their deeply held beliefs."* [21]

This is a particularly personal issue for me. I was adopted myself by wonderful, loving parents, and I thank God for them and for the adoption system that enabled them to give me a home.

If today's laws and regulations were in place when I was born, it is very likely that I wouldn't be here today. The inexplicable modern push for abortion over adoption would probably have sent my biological mother down a different path.

It is morally right to promote adoption, rather than abortion. And good, godly, Christian couples wanting to adopt should not be discriminated against for daring to hold sacred their religious views — the same immovable values that have been the cornerstone of American society since our founding.

Attack on Christian Businesses and Business Owners

Lorie Smith is a Colorado-based web designer who was sued by a gay couple for refusing to design a custom wedding website for their same-sex wedding.

Lorie did not refuse to serve them or any other LGBTQI+ person. Rather, she simply could not accommodate their request for a custom website for their wedding on religious grounds, because she was not comfortable using her creative talents to promote something she felt violated her sincere Christian beliefs.

The couple sued very publicly, and Lorie spent seven years fighting a prolonged and painful legal battle while her name was dragged through the mud in the media.

Lorie and other Christian business owners have been targeted for their allegedly hateful and discriminatory business practices by LGBTQI+ activists and the media.

Their crime: Being faithful to their deeply held spiritual beliefs and convictions.

Many Christian business owners are being specifically targeted for attack by a ruthless, well-organized, and well-financed movement that wants Christianity completely wiped off the civic and business landscape.

Fortunately, in the summer of 2023, the U.S. Supreme Court ruled in Lorie's favor, overturning a previous judgment against her and re-establishing a Christian's right to live out their faith despite the weaponization of local, state, and federal "anti-discrimination" laws.

Christians are now protected to live out their lives without the government forcing them to violate their consciences.

Of course, the radicals and biased media went nuts over this Supreme Court decision, decrying what they called legalized discrimination against a protected group. Decisions like these are what is driving the radical pro-socialists' desire to restructure and pack the U.S. Supreme Court with more judicial radicals who want Justices to legislate from the bench — to ensure such a "loss" for the LGBTQI+ cause never happens again at the Supreme Court level.

And if you don't think Christians are being specifically targeted, ask yourself, *"Why don't we ever hear about these LGBTQI+ advocacy groups targeting and suing any other self-identified religious groups — Islam, for instance — for business discrimination?"*

Sadly, it's because Christians have become "safe" targets for radical ideological LGBTQI+ intolerance and often violent attacks.

Using the Power of Government to Push the Agenda

Media and advocacy groups are not the only ones who are forcing the LGBTQI+ agenda on Americans en masse. The radical ideology has the full weight of the U.S. government behind it. This is seen most clearly in the deceptively named *Equality Act,* which has bounced around Congress for the past decade.

The Equality Act is one of the most horrific and dangerous pieces of legislation ever devised to attack the free exercise of religion and undermine parental authority. It was passed by the House of Representatives in 2019 and then sent to the Senate, which did not take up the bill for consideration. Even if they had, then-President Trump had indicated he would veto it.

The bill was reintroduced in 2021, when it was passed by the House and again sent to the Senate. Fortunately, it hasn't been brought up for Senate debate — yet.

Few people know about this legislation, yet it will have a devastating impact on parents and on all people of faith should it become federal law.

Here are several things to know about this hideous bill, which I believe is an all-out attack on Christianity:

- The law would prohibit "discrimination" based on sex, sexual orientation, and gender identity in public facilities, schools, workplaces, lending, and more. It would also expand the definition of public accommodations to include all places or establishments that provide exhibitions, recreation, exercise, amusement, and transportation.

- Any recognition of the differences between the sexes — or any preference for traditional sexual morality — would be viewed as actionable "hate."
- The Equality Act would prohibit an individual from being denied access to shared facilities including restrooms, locker rooms, and dressing rooms that are in accordance with the individual's *gender identity.*
- The Equality Act says each individual must be treated according to the sex he or she thinks or feels he or she is at any moment ... or else face the full force of this retaliatory law.
- The Act would declare biology meaningless and assert that the only thing that matters is what each person thinks or feels about their sexuality at any given moment.
- Christian doctors would be forced to perform sex-change operations.
- Churches would be forced to perform same-sex weddings.
- Christian schools would be forced to hire LGBTQI+ teachers and teach LGBTQI+ beliefs and values as normal and God-ordained.
- Christian businesses would be forced to create designs, artwork, and symbols celebrating LGBTQI+ lifestyles and values.
- Any disagreement or debate on important moral and biological issues like gender would be considered discrimination.

- The Act would legitimize pedophilia by creating two new protected sexual orientations — *minor-attracted people* and *youth-attracted people.*

If you think I'm exaggerating when I say the Equality Act actively targets and invalidates Christians, take note of this: During the congressional debate over the bill, a representative raised the important point that many, many Americans will object to the very premise of these actions as being contrary to God's will.

Jerry Nadler (D-NY), chairman of the House Judiciary Committee, responded, "What any religious tradition describes as God's will is no concern of this Congress."[22]

Reinterpreting Title IX

Another government tactic to insert LGBTQI+ radicalism into everyday life is the radical pro-socialists' effort to reinterpret Title IX.

The Title IX Act of 1972 is a law that prohibits discrimination on the basis of sex in any federally funded education program or activity. Specifically, the law provides that no person shall, *"on the basis of sex, be excluded from participation in, be denied the benefits of, or be subjected to discrimination under any education program or activity receiving federal financial assistance."* [23]

The purpose of Title IX, of course, was to ensure equal protection for women under the law — a laudable goal I think we can all agree on. However, President Biden's Agriculture Department is now reinterpreting Title IX to force schools to allow biological males in girls' sports and, worse, in girls' locker rooms. If they refuse, the schools risk losing their federal funding.

This new bureaucratic ruling — not a new law enacted by our duly elected representatives in Congress — overrides states' rights and ignores the will of parents. It twists the language of the law to force a socialist, ideologically driven agenda on our children and robs them of their voices to object.

Congress must agree on a national law, then have the President sign it.

But the Biden Administration is bypassing Congress on its LGBTQI+ transgender crusade.

They are using a regulatory agency to force their ideology on our entire nation without discussion. In doing so, they are sidestepping the will of the people and keeping the matter out of the hands of our elected representatives.

This is very similar to how the government allowed the Centers for Disease Control and Prevention (CDC) to force masking and the Occupational Safety and Health Administration (OSHA) to force COVID-19 vaccinations during the pandemic. It's all regulatory overreach through which unelected officials and bureaucrats attempt to redefine what's acceptable and legal.

Indoctrinating America's Children

It would be bad enough if the LGBTQI+ radicalism were targeted only at adults, but the movement and their "allies" are specifically targeting even our youngest children! This is a blatant attempt at brainwashing, bombarding children with LGBTQI+ messages from an early age to normalize this alternative lifestyle, convince our kids that accepting all sexual and gender identities as equally rational and valid is a moral good, and encourage them to question their own sexual identity.

Actually, it's probably more accurate to say the LGBTQI+ lifestyle is being elevated as a *superior* choice — which no doubt explains why the number of children who identify as LGBTQI+ has skyrocketed.

One in four high school students now identifies as LGBTQI+, according to the CDC. [24] It's a social contagion because kids are constantly being bombarded with the LGBTQI+ propaganda.

Are you really a girl?

Do you feel like a boy?

As a boy, do you like playing with dolls or wearing a dress?

Kids as young as 4-years-old are asked disturbing and inappropriate questions!

Much of this indoctrination is being inflicted using private financial donations to public schools. LGBTQI+ advocacy groups are infiltrating public schools by offering cash grants in exchange for the school's participation in creating an LGBTQI+-friendly school environment.

The "It Gets Better Project," for example, is a nonprofit organization whose mission is to *"uplift, empower, and connect lesbian, gay, bisexual, transgender, and queer (LGBTQI+) youth around the globe."*[25] This group offers $10,000 grants to schools, which is used to promote radical gender ideology that undermines parental authority, and circumvents the will of taxpayers and parents.

Schools are specifically encouraged to use the grants to:

- Create a gender-affirming closet at school.
- Provide "trans" students with clothing that fits their "true selves."
- Remodel and designate "single-gender lavatories" as "gender neutral" bathrooms."
- Create LGBTQI+ murals at schools.
- Produce classroom videos on topics such as which pronouns to use.

One school, Carmel High School in Indiana, used the funds to hold a community-wide pride event that included a fundraiser to help a transgender-identifying student run away from home.

This type of indoctrination is possible only because radical, out-of-control school boards, teachers unions, and administrators support this ideology and these outrageous policies and anti-parent actions.

Examples of LGBTQI+ Indoctrination of Children

Specific examples of how the radical LGBTQI+ agenda is being pushed on our children are not hard to find. All you need to do is open a website, turn on the TV, go see a movie, or walk through a public school to see an endless bombardment of different pro-LGBTQI+ messages.

The Biden Administration raised the gay flag at U.S. embassies around the world during June's "Pride Month." Other government agencies followed suit, and eventually the gay flag even started flying at schools — public, government-run schools — both in classrooms and on a flagpole alongside the American flag.

Kellogg has released limited-edition LGBTQI+ breakfast cereal for children to support GLAAD, a militant special-interest group that portrays and promotes only a positive image of gay and lesbian characters in media.

I remember when a box of cereal had silly jokes, trivia, and puzzles to keep kids entertained while they munched on their Frosted Flakes. Now, they can read all about the radical LGBTQI+ agenda!

Children's television shows and cartoons are regularly using homosexual, lesbian, and transgender characters. *Rugrats,* for example, is being relaunched with Betty, the mother of two, as a lesbian, single mom.

Nickelodeon took their *Blues Clues and You!* to a gay-pride parade, with an animated drag queen. The episode includes families with two moms, two dads, trans-identified members, and "ace, bi and pan" parents. One character has scars from transgender sex-change surgery from female to male.

With Disney+, Cartoon Network, and nearly every other mainstream children's entertainment platform pushing the LGBTQI+ propaganda, parents are left with practically no "safe" channel or streaming service to occupy their children for a little while.

Even sports franchises are inundating fans — including children — with "the message." It's getting impossible to find any individual athlete, let alone an entire team, that hasn't worn special Pride-themed uniforms on game days. And the rare professional athlete who objects risks being fined, benched, and publicly "canceled" for simply following his or her faith-based values.

Of all these examples, though, among the strangest, most abhorrent new LGBTQI+ trend sweeping through our schools and local libraries *has* to be adult "drag" shows performing for children.

An event called "Drag the Kids to Pride" was recently held in a gay bar in Texas. The event was billed as a "family friendly drag show." Footage of the event spread like fire on social media, showing little children and their approving parents stuffing dollar bills in the G-string panties of the preforming male drag-queen dancers.

Most Americans, especially parents, who saw the video were horrified by the bizarre spectacle. The worst part of the whole affair was that the parents not only approved of the depraved event, but were also exposing innocent young children to the show's sexualized and lewd behavior.

No one cared. No one objected. It was madness.

And yet, this is just one of many such shows taking place in unsuspecting communities across the country.

Don't Say "Don't Say Gay"

If you want to see clearly how much the pro-socialists want to brainwash your children into absolute acceptance of LGBTQI+ ideology, look no further than their wildly exaggerated reaction to Florida Gov. Ron DeSantis' 2022 Parental Rights in Education bill.

The original version of the bill was written to stop the sexualization of little children under the age of seven in the schools and strengthen parental control over what their young children are taught about sex, gender identity, and other sensitive subjects.

The heart of the bill simply prevented radical pro-socialist teachers from pushing their radical views about gender identity and sexuality to kids in Pre-K through third grade. That's it. How could anyone object to a public-school teacher not being allowed to teach kindergarteners about delicate, personal, intimate sexual issues? Can you even imagine your 5-year-old coming home from pre-K and telling you he learned all about transgenderism and drag queens at school? I, like most parents, would be furious!

Predictably, the Extreme Ideologues became hysterical about Governor DeSantis' bill — and they took the entire national media machine with them.

Everyone on the pro-LGBTQI+ bandwagon distorted the bill way out of proportion and worked together to kill the bill from becoming state law.

CEOs, sports stars, movie and TV celebrities, politicians, social media influencers, and even the Democratic President of the United States Joe Biden joined together to insert an endless amount of hate, disinformation, and lies into any public discussion of this Florida bill.

It was ceremoniously dubbed the "Don't Say Gay bill" — even though the word *gay* didn't appear in the text of the bill a single time.

It was powerful messaging ... but totally false.

Opponents mischaracterized the bill, using a false narrative to elicit an irrational and emotional response from the public. The radical pro-socialists claimed the Parental Rights in Education bill was an attack on the LGBTQI+ community and tantamount to hateful discrimination. Businesses threatened to boycott or move out of Florida.

Fortunately, the national outcry against parental rights in Florida didn't stop the bill from passing through the Florida legislature and becoming law. I can only pray this bill becomes a model for how other states can take a stand against the wild overreach and ideological activism of the federal government.

WHY DO COMPANIES GO ALONG WITH ALL THIS?

After reading all this information about DEI, ESG, and the push to support and promote the LGBTQI+ agenda and behavior, you might be wondering why on earth any company would risk alienating *half* their customer base by pushing radical, highly politicized, agenda- and ideology-driven propaganda into their products, services, content, and marketing.

Once-great brands like Disney and Anheuser-Busch (Bud Light) have suffered tremendous losses — both financial and in reputation — by embracing these divisive ideologies. What's their incentive for continuing down this destructive, unpopular road?

One major reason most consumers don't even know about is the Corporate Equality Index (CEI), a type of social-credit score (widely used in dictatorships, such as today's China) that is controlled by an organization laughably known as the Human Rights Campaign (HRC).

I've been warning people about the growing influence of the HRC for more than 25 years, and today, all my greatest concerns about the organization are playing out right in front of our eyes.

The Human Rights Campaign is the nation's largest and most powerful LGBTQI+ advocacy group in America — and they use the CEI as a weapon to force companies to comply with their radical and disturbing demands.

In a very real sense, it's an extortion racket. Just like you'd see in an old mafia movie, the HRC sends "representatives" to a corporation to demand that they advance the LGBTQI+ agenda throughout their business and marketing. If the company "plays ball," the HRC rewards them with a high CEI score. If they don't, they get stuck with a low CEI rating.

This matters to companies, because many investment banks and large venture capital firms act like sheep, cower before the HRC radicals, and embrace the CEI score, using it to determine investments into companies. Companies with a high CEI score get access to an enormous amount of investment capital. Companies with a low score don't.

It's not about business factors such as profit, market share, and customer satisfaction; it's about whether a business has the "right" values ... as measured by their CEI score.

That's why American CEOs are more concerned about ticking the right social-justice boxes than they are about alienating their existing and potential customers. Sure, their social stance will cause them to lose sales, but the influx of cash from investment firms like BlackRock and Vanguard — the top shareholders in most publicly traded American companies — more than makes up for it.

At least, that's their hope.

Larry Fink, CEO of BlackRock, is a key leader in the CEI/ESG/DEI movement, and he is using BlackRock's massive investment funds to force leading, popular, trusted, and long-standing brands to change their messaging and public persona. He's forcing change by forcing controversial social issues into companies who that have no legitimate reason to get involved in divisive or controversial political and social issues.

But Fink thinks companies should be involved in using their power to force political and social changes on issues favored by the radical pro-socialists and global elites. In fact, he believes they have a *responsibility* to take a stand on even the most unpopular issues.

In an open letter to American CEOs, Fink pushed for a "new model of governance" that is in line with CEI/ESG/DEI values. He wrote:

> *"Society is demanding that companies, both public and private, serve a social purpose. To prosper over time, every company must not only deliver financial performance, but also show how it makes a positive contribution to society."* [26]

As a business owner and executive myself, I strongly disagree with Fink's position. I don't need to know what Apple is doing for the LGBTQI+ community; I just need them to make good phones and computers. And my marketing company's customers don't need to know where I stand on abortion; they just need me to deliver quality and effective marketing and advertising that's tailor-made for their audience and generates new clients and profits.

I agree with Derek Kreifels, co-founder and CEO of the State Financial Officers Foundation. Using Anheuser-Busch's devastating miscalculation in partnering with transgender social media influencer Dylan Mulvaney and the potentially irrevocable damage it did to its Bud Light brand, Kreifels explained:

> *"The problem with measures like CEI, and its big brother ESG, is that it introduces an incentive structure outside of the bounds of business, often in ways contradictory to fiduciary duty. Whether Anheuser-Busch was trying to cash in on Dylan Mulvaney's TikTok following or chasing higher*

CEI ratings for inclusivity, the backlash has been significant, and the stockholders to whom the company is obligated will feel the pinch." [27]

Whether it is the abortion debate, LGBTQI+ issues, Florida's Parental Rights in Education Act, immigration, global warming, or any other hot-button political issue of our day, I celebrate every American's constitutionally protected right to believe whatever they want and to voice their beliefs whenever and however they want.

But frankly, I don't need that from the company that sells me my telephone, Internet service, or toilet paper. I just need them to do their jobs — the jobs I'm paying them to do.

Sadly, though, organizations like the Human Rights Campaign have convinced once-great corporations to sacrifice consumer support and profits on the altar of woke radical ideology. And they're literally paying them to do it.

PUSH BACK

In the face of DEI, ESG, and LGBTQI+ ideologies being forced on us, it is easy to feel overwhelmed and outnumbered. But we must never lose hope, and we cannot allow the external pressures of our modern culture to rob us of our beliefs or our voices — especially our strong voices to object to the madness and proclaim what we know to be true, right, just, and moral.

The best way to push back against the woke nonsense hitting us on all sides is to *vote.* Show up for every election in your district. From school boards to state senate to President of the United States — *vote!*

This is not a matter of Republican versus Democrat. This is a fight for the very soul of our nation. The forces at work around us, and the ideologies I've discussed in this chapter, threaten to destroy the freedoms we've always known and still hold dear today. The decisions and stand we make today, in the face of

DEI, ESG, and radical LGBTQI+ propaganda will determine if the America of 10 or 20 years from now will be the America we've always known and loved ... or something tragic that we won't even recognize.

Chapter 5

Danger #4: Weaponization of the Government

The Constitution of the United States of America — which, it seems, most modern-day, pro-socialist politicians have never read — outlines three distinct branches of government:

1. **The Executive Branch,** which is led by the President and includes presidential cabinet members and their respective departments, and several independent agencies and committees. The president also serves as the Commander in Chief of the U.S. military.

2. **The Legislative Branch,** which is made up of the U.S. Senate and House of Representatives. This branch oversees the creation of new laws, confirming presidential appointments, declaring war, and managing the federal budget.

3. **The Judicial Branch,** which is made up of the U.S. Supreme Court and other federal courts. This branch interprets and applies the law on a case-by-case basis and evaluates the constitutionality of certain laws.

This structure forms the very foundation of our Republic, and it has been a model for constitutional republics throughout the world. However, I would argue that, over the past 15 years, we have seen the emergence of a new *fourth* branch of government. This new branch has grown steadily and quietly in the shadow for decades, slowly metastasizing like a cancer in the bones of our entire constitutional system.

It operated in secret, guiding public policy with an unseen, yet powerfully influential hand.

Under President Trump, it served as "the resistance," taking decisive action against any threat to the pro-socialist agenda of its leaders to transform America's culture and government.

It undermined the authority of President Trump, working against his efforts to "drain the swamp" at every turn.

It flooded the press with "leaks" about private conversations and in-progress policy discussions within the Trump Administration.

It spread lies, disinformation, and rumors to destroy the President and cripple his policies.

It even invaded the sanctity of the Supreme Court, bringing about the first leaked draft opinion in the High Court's 230-plus-year history.

What is this new, not-so-hidden fourth branch of government?

The bureaucratic, ideologically driven Deep State.

And it represents one of the greatest dangers our Constitutional Republic has ever faced.

From the start of our government, the American bureaucratic establishment has had two goals:

1. Protect itself.

2. Expand its power, influence, and access to money.

These have been the ultimate goals of bureaucracies both in America and abroad. Bureaucracies exist almost exclusively to support, defend, and provide for themselves.

But under President Obama, a third bureaucratic goal emerged, and this is the inevitable threat that unchecked bureaucracies ultimately represent:

3. Use the power of government to transform American culture and politics forever based on ideology, not honest, efficient or accountable government.

The bureaucracy hired during Obama's eight years was largely composed of ideologically driven radicals in their 20s and 30s who had one overriding goal: to "make a difference" by using their positions to radically change regulations, laws, and anything else that got in the way of creating a more socialist, secular, and powerful government.

At the end of the Obama Administration, there were more than two million federal employees total. [1] More than 4,000 of these were top presidential employees, [2] and those 4,000 people led the 8,000 employees that made up what's called the Senior Executive Service. This leadership level acts as the critical link between the upper echelon of political leaders and the other two million government employees. [3]

Of those 8,000 members of the Senior Executive Service — which extends across the entire bureaucratic establishment — a disturbing *7,000* were appointed by President Obama. This has allowed many to see through the veil of secrecy, dubbing this group of influential leaders "*Obama's Army.*"

Today, under President Biden, the Deep State bureaucracy has changed.

They are not hiding.

They are not acting in secret.

They are not resisting.

Instead, they are openly and proudly using the power of the state to:

- Increase their power and expand their influence over the economy, children, healthcare, and more.
- Generate more money for their departments.
- Overturn President Trump's policies of deregulation, economic growth, and support for pro-family values.

- Create and advance President Biden's new, radical policies.
- Advance their socialist ideology regardless of anything Congress — or Biden, for that matter — says or does.

The Deep State is engaging in open warfare against freedom, free enterprise, the family, and more.

I've already written an entire book about the Deep State titled *The Deep State: 15 Surprising Dangers You Should Know.* In that book, I did a thorough examination of every aspect of the Deep State, so I recommend reading it to understand the great threat the Deep State represents. For now, though, I would be remiss to leave out the tireless efforts of the Deep State to thrive as one of the most serious and pervasive dangers to our prosperity, freedom, and future.

ABUSE OF POWER: TARGETING POLITICAL ENEMIES

While I covered a few of the following issues in my previous book, I think it is still important to provide a quick recap of one of the Deep State's most troubling dangers: the ability of radical, partisan, unelected, and largely "unfireable" bureaucrats to target, punish, and even imprison their political enemies.

I'll talk about a few examples in detail below, and then I'll give you a quick flyover of several other examples of how the Deep State targets its political enemies. Trust me, there is no shortage of examples!

Obama's IRS Targeting of Tea Party Groups

One of the most egregious examples during the past several years was the IRS targeting of nonprofit Tea Party groups and other grassroots conservative and Christian organizations during the Obama Administration. The IRS acted with such blatant bias that even biased media outlets like *The New York Times* and *The Washington Post* were "forced" to cover the story.

In short, the IRS targeted certain conservative and Christian nonprofit groups from 2010 to 2012, denying them their rightful tax-exempt status under the law and flagging them for audits.

Deep State bureaucrats in the IRS made the Tea Party and other widely popular groups jump through unnecessary hoops and forced them to answer personal and religious questions — up to and including the content of their prayers — before ultimately denying their tax-exemption. They also went beyond the normal questions about the organizations themselves and used the opportunity to collect personal information about the individuals who simply *participated* in the groups, not just the groups' leadership.

Even more damaging, by preventing the Tea Party and other large groups from helping to get millions of eligible voters to go to the polls, many political experts believe it was part of what helped Barak Obama win a second term in the White House.

This dramatic overreach of the IRS authority was no accident committed by a few rogue agents. This entire campaign of discrimination was done under the direction of IRS Director of Exempt Organizations Lois Lerner, who was forced to publicly apologize after the scandal broke — but not before *30,000* emails sent by Lerner during the period in question mysteriously disappeared.

The EPA's Campaign Against Free Enterprise

The Obama Administration's Environmental Protection Agency (EPA) overtly worked against private businesses, waging war against free enterprise in their radical pursuit of "environmental justice."

Gina McCarthy, the head of the Environmental Protection Agency (EPA) under Obama, instituted extreme policies to combat so-called "climate change," going so far as to lie to Congress while testifying under oath about the EPA's actions. As I wrote in *The Deep State:*

> *"While explaining the details of the 2015 Clean Water Rule (which is an extreme overreach of federal rule-making authority, and a job-killing restriction), McCarthy misled Congress about the availability of scientific reports backing the plan. She also downplayed the critical danger of burdening certain states with strict ozone rules and withholding federal highway funding.*
>
> *McCarthy distorted the truth to promote a Deep State ideology in one of the nation's most powerful anti-business government agencies. She actively advanced a political agenda that opposes the free market and destroys the property rights of hard-working Americans, especially farmers and ranchers."*

President Trump tried to end the terrible 2015 Clean Water Rule, but his Deep State enemies worked against him behind the scenes for years. Under President Biden, the EPA remains controlled by radical extremists who are dedicated to destroying businesses, expanding their bureaucratic power, and wasting taxpayer money — all in the name of "combating climate change."

The DOJ and FBI's "Trump Derangement Syndrome"

The Department of Justice (DOJ) and its chief investigative arm, the Federal Bureau of Investigation (FBI), have become a corruptly politicized bureaucracy that engages in outrageous political activity rather than truly pursuing justice for lawbreakers. Instead of looking objectively at facts, they frequently operate in support of partisan, radical and illegal objectives.

To be clear, I'm talking primarily about the people at the top — the decision makers who set the tone and create the agenda for the government's justice agencies to follow. I know there are excellent men and women in the field who joined the FBI to protect and serve the American people without political bias. Sadly, though, these agents are directed mostly by political hacks whose primary goal is to serve their Deep State bosses and agendas.

This was never clearer than it was the morning of August 8, 2022, when the FBI executed a search warrant on President Trump's home at his Mar-a-Lago resort in Palm Beach, Florida. This has never happened to any former president at any time in U.S. history. But you can be sure it will happen again, now that the seal has been broken.

In a purely partisan abuse of power, the Biden Administration used the DOJ and FBI to attack and harass Donald Trump, Biden's chief political contender for the 2024 presidential election. America has certainly seen its fair share of dirty politics, but wielding the full force of the government against a political opponent in this way is unprecedented — at least in our country. It's something you'd expect to see in Venezuela, North Korea or Russia, not the United States. But here we are.

"The swamp" will do whatever is necessary to protect itself — and the D.C. swamp has never had a greater enemy than Donald Trump. He was unwilling to go along with the establishment and was constantly battling with the entrenched Obama radicals in the State Department, EPA, Department of Education, and all the other federal departments and agencies.

Worse, Trump had the audacity to call out the corruption, double standards, and abuse of power. He wanted to tell the entire swath of Deep State radical pro-socialists, *"You're fired!"*

The Department of Justice could have simply issued a subpoena for the documents they were looking for. They could have appointed a Special Council. But an armed invasion? An early morning, unannounced assault by federal agents on the home of a former President and current presidential candidate?

Outrageous. Unprecedented. Despicable!

Further, we now know that President Joe Biden also has kept classified documents in a variety of unsecured locations, most of which were from his years as Vice President. He's even stashed documents in unprotected boxes in his garage next to his prized 1967 Corvette Stingray for years. But have his many homes been raided? Has he been indicted?

Of course not.

There is no doubt that the fallout from the FBI raid on President Trump's home had a massive, anti-Republican effect on the 2022 midterm elections just two months later, and it cast a dark cloud on the 2024 presidential campaigns that were just starting to come together.

The real corruption has to do with our traditional American values and our liberty. America's Founders never envisioned government workers trying to determine the outcome of an election. They didn't foresee a bureaucracy so large that it could be non-transparent and abusive in its power.

The Mar-a-Lago raid was specifically planned to embarrass and harass Trump, casting him as a criminal through the biased lens of the media, who the Deep State knew would talk on and on about this historic event for weeks, months, and even years. The Deep State bureaucracy has become so blinded by their hatred for Trump — what many call *Trump Derangement Syndrome* — that they are willing to break any rule, cross any line, and obliterate any semblance of lawful behavior to bring him down.

However, whether you like him or not, the Mar-a-Lago raid is not *just* about Trump; it is about justice, the U.S. Constitution, and our Constitutional Republic.

If you love America and freedom, you should be shaken and

outraged by this unprecedented raid against a political opponent. You should also be brokenhearted by the corruption and abuse of power by the FBI and DOJ. It's the politics of personal and individual destruction by a radical Marxist ideological bureaucracy — and it will not stop with Donald Trump.

The DOJ and FBI have actively engaged in going after conservative activists, politicians, journalists, and others who oppose them or do not support their agenda.

Take conservative commentator Steve Bannon, for instance. According to the DOJ, Bannon was sentenced *"to four months of incarceration and ordered to pay a fine of $6,500 on two counts of contempt of Congress stemming from his failure to comply with a subpoena issued by the House Select Committee investigating the Jan. 6 'breach' of the United States Capitol."* [4]

No one had been charged with "contempt of Congress" for nearly 30 years, but they dusted it off for people like Bannon, who are conservative and connected to Trump.

Unsurprisingly, the biased judge had his finger on the scales of justice. In a pre-trial ruling, the judge declared that Bannon could not say he was following the advice of his counsel or plead Executive Privilege not to testify before the committee. He was also banned from calling witnesses from "the House January 6th Committee," known officially as the House Select Committee to investigate the January 6th attack on the United States Capitol. It was a surprise to no one when a Washington, D.C., jury — a city that voted 94 percent for Biden — found Bannon guilty.

He never had a chance. No Trump supporter does as long as the Deep State is calling the shots at the FBI and DOJ.

Plenty of Examples throughout the Bureaucracy

There are several other examples of the Deep State agencies targeting their political enemies. I could easily write an entire book just on this issue using examples from the past decade. A few of these include:

- FEMA routinely withheld federal assistance from Christian churches and affiliated organizations after Hurricane Sandy, in 2013, and Hurricane Harvey, in 2017 — even though many of these same Christian churches and organizations were the first to help provide housing and work as volunteers in cleanup efforts in the affected areas.

- The SEC is charged with protecting investors; maintaining fair, orderly, and efficient markets; and facilitating capital formation. But contrary to its core mission, the SEC has been used by Deep State operatives to extract millions of dollars from companies the radical pro-socialists hate. Under President Biden, the SEC's army of Deep State lawyers have been overtly devoted to destroying pro-free-market businesses and investors to advance their own radical, Big-Government interests. Today, Elon Musk is a glaring example of an individual who has been selected for persecution.

- The DOJ offered a sweetheart plea deal to a vandal, who admitted to defacing a Roman Catholic church with profane graffiti, destroying a statue of the Virgin Mary, assaulting a church worker, and resisting arrest. The 31-year-old man, who vandalized the St. Louise Catholic Church in Bellevue, Washington, will receive no jail time. Why? Because he identifies as transgender and because he claimed to be protesting the U.S. Supreme Court's overturning of *Roe v. Wade.* This is a perfect example of the DOJ's double standard when dealing with anti-Christian vandals and rioters who check the appropriate radical pro-socialist, identity-politics boxes. [5]

- The Department of Energy (DOE), under Democrat presidents, has grown a massive staff and budget filled with Deep State extremists who work against the oil, gas, coal and nuclear industries — our best, most reliable sources of energy. Trump tried to downsize Obama's bloated DOE and expand nuclear energy, but the Deep State pushed back and continued its war against fossil fuels until Joe Biden entered office and effectively handed over America's energy policy to radical pro-socialist environmental extremists.

- A peaceful, law-abiding, Christian and Tennessee business owner was forcibly arrested in his home in 2022. FBI agents stormed into his home and pointed assault rifles at his family, including his young children. His crime? More than a year earlier, Paul Vaughn and 10 others from a Christian pro-life group took part in a peaceful protest at an abortion clinic. They didn't use force. They didn't injure anyone. They didn't intimidate or interfere with employees of the abortion clinic. They just sat there singing worship songs. For that supposedly grievous offense, Vaughn was pulled from his home at gunpoint and in front of his family. Such attacks on Christian groups by the Biden Administration's weaponized DOJ and FBI are blatant attempts to silence the opposition, and to demonize those who don't agree with Biden's policies, use fear and intimidation as weapons against pro-life Americans, and as a threat to be silent or face government harassment and prison.

- The FBI came in force (in 15 vehicles) to arrest Mark Houck, of Pennsylvania, in 2022, after a federal grand jury indicted him for violating the Freedom of Access to Clinic Entrances (FACE) Act, a law prohibiting someone from blocking an individual's entrance to an abortion clinic. Houck, a pro-life advocate, was stunned by the charges, as he was at the clinic only to peacefully protest its activities. However, when an angry clinic worker became aggressive and verbally abusive to Houck and his 12-year-old son, Houck defended his son by pushing the harassing employee away. That was it. That was his "crime": defending his young son from a grown man who was screaming in his son's face. This apparently required an army of 25 federal agents to pound on the family's front door and point no fewer than five guns at Houck, his wife, and their children. Agents surrounded the house decked out in armored vests, ballistic helmets, shields, and even carried a battering ram. The whole scene was ridiculous — a fact that was obvious to the 12 members of the jury, who unanimously found Houck not guilty.

- The FBI assumes traditional Catholics are terrorists. Really? They used undercover agents (at least one has been identified) to execute a strategy of reaching out to Catholic churches to recruit select clergy and church leaders to inform on their fellow parishioners. The FBI used their informants to develop a report titled "Interest of Racially or Ethnically Motivated Violent Extremists in Radical-Traditional Catholic Ideology Almost Certainly Presents New Mitigation Opportunities." The report identified Catholics who reject Vatican II and want the restoration of the Latin Mass as "radical traditionalists" because they assumed those Catholics are anti-immigrant, anti-LGBTQI+, and white supremacists They were being targeted based on a worldview and ideology that hates people of faith.

- At least 25 federal agencies were discovered creating a database of their own federal employees, contractors, and vendors, who asked for a religious exemption to mandated COVID-19 vaccinations. The federal government has more than 4 million civilian and military employees. It's unknown how many applied for religious exemptions, but even if it were 10 percent, that would be more than 400,000 people. This database serves no logical purpose other than targeting Christians as a part of the Deep State's ongoing war against people of faith. It makes all employees think twice before they ask for a religious exception, opens the door to discrimination (including being passed over for promotions and denied requests to move between different departments), and helps identify Christians to be fired in a potential future purge of believers from the federal employment.

- The Department of Homeland Security (DHS) spent $40 million in grant money to fund programs earmarked for "anti-terrorism" purposes. But this money wasn't for foreign or Islamic terrorists; it was for targeting conservative organizations and media, who DHS classified as "domestic terrorists." As part of this effort, the DHS used taxpayer money to urge radical private groups to investigate conservative organizations, including Breitbart News, Turning Point USA, and the Heritage Foundation. Their justification? They claimed that these "political opponents" are "turning Americans into violent neo-Nazis." [6]

- The DHS also used taxpayer money to fund radical seminars at universities that compared former President Donald Trump to the genocidal Cambodian Dictator Pol Pot and suggested Florida Gov. Ron DeSantis might wish to start a second Holocaust. One of the DHS-funded seminars featured speakers like Michael Loedenthal, of Antifa, who endorses committing illegal acts in the fight against the so-called "far right." [7]

Every one of these examples and the hundreds of others I didn't list here are heartbreaking to me as a proud American. And, as a person of faith, I am especially concerned about the rising tide of anti-Christian illegal discrimination and recrimination that I see happening across the federal bureaucratic landscape.

LEGISLATION BY REGULATION

Besides targeting political enemies and refusing to uphold the law based on their politics, Deep State bureaucrats also sidestep the law by issuing sweeping — and often illegal — executive orders and regulations. These regulations, which are forced upon all or select groups of Americans, are enforced despite their clear partisan, anti-Congressional authority underpinnings.

These are usually important issues that *should* have been settled in Congress — the duly elected legislative House and Senate bodies actually responsible for creating laws — but that process is much too risky and time-consuming for the Deep State. Why bother with the time and trouble of drafting bills, and risking them being voted down by political opponents, when a bureaucrat can achieve the desired outcome immediately with the simple stroke of a pen?

This is literally *legislation by regulation,* and it has been a growing problem for many years. Every President now enters office with a stack of executive orders to undo the things the previous administration regulated into existence. Both sides of the aisle do this, and it's gotten way out of hand.

Besides regulatory strangulation, partisan executive orders often conflict with the endless regulations coming out of the different agencies throughout the government landscape. These agencies are filled with radical, entrenched, partisan, pro-socialist activists. As I said earlier, 7,000 of the 8,000 members of the Senior Executive Service were appointed by President Obama. This self-interested group of the most powerful senior bureaucrats represents a large portion of the highly placed Deep State operatives that fought so hard against Trump's policies and were responsible for the ridiculous number of leaks coming out of The White House.

These well-placed officials use their standing and influence within our agencies to create socialist, pro-Big-Government, anti-citizen regulations that are enforced with the same tenacity as properly passed legislation.

But these regulations are not properly passed legislation.

We cannot surrender our legislative process one regulation at a time.

We need to leave *lawmaking* in the hands of our elected U.S. *lawmakers.*

Allow me to illustrate the danger of *legislation by regulation* by highlighting the biggest regulatory offender of the past decade, the Occupational Safety and Health Administration (OSHA).

The COVID-19 vaccine hit the market less than a year after the global outbreak of the pandemic. Many Americans cheered the speed with which Trump's "Project Warp Speed" produced the vaccine. Others were skeptical. Still others were outright opposed to taking a new, largely untested RNA vaccine that was produced so quickly and without employing testing and adequate safety protocols. It was a moment in time when every American had to make a choice for themselves and their families.

Until that choice was taken away.

In November 2021, the Biden Administration — frustrated by the large numbers of "unvaccinated" Americans — announced stricter vaccination policies nearly a year after the vaccine first became available. This included a mandate through OSHA that required *private-sector workers* to be vaccinated in order to keep their jobs. It also included severe financial penalties for private companies that did not enforce the new policy.

Through OSHA, Biden and Deep State bureaucrats did what legislation could not accomplish: force a vaccine mandate on practically all Americans by declaring COVID-19 a workplace-safety issue. Their message was: *"You want to get back to work? Great! But you have to inject this untested drug into your body first."*

Many Americans who were skeptical, hesitant, or opposed taking the vaccine, reluctantly did so despite their deep reservations. They couldn't afford not to. They needed their jobs, and the government threatened to leave them unemployed and unemployable if they didn't take the vaccine. They had little or no choice.

This "vax mandate" was the most grievous, despicable act of government overreach and *legislation by regulation* in the history of our country. I'll leave the health effects of the vaccine for scientists and doctors to study and discuss — though I think time will show if the rise we've already seen in unexplained cardiac issues, sudden deaths of otherwise healthy young people, and other devastating side effects really was "collateral damage" of the vaccine. Fortunately, though, the U.S. Supreme Court has already settled the debate about Biden's inappropriate use of OSHA regulations to force the vaccine on Americans.

In a six-to-three decision, the High Court ruled Biden's overreach through OSHA was unconstitutional. Even Chief Justice John Roberts — whom I generally see as a judicial disappointment — came down on the right side of this issue.

In an unsigned opinion on the case, the Court wrote, *"Although Congress has indisputably given OSHA the power to regulate occupational dangers, it has not given that agency the power to regulate public health more broadly."* [8]

In my view, three Justices who voted in favor of the forced mandate voted as judicial activists, rather than as impartial, unbiased, Constitutional Jurists. They demonstrated here their desire to legislate from the bench and supported Biden's attempt to legislate from the bureaucracy.

Had the U.S. Supreme Court upheld the OSHA mandate, freedom of choice and our individual rights would have been constantly under assault by the bureaucracies for any reason. For example, if the government and unelected bureaucrats can order you to involuntarily put something like the COVID-19 vaccine into your body, they can do anything they want for any "health" concern.

The pandemic did enough damage to our nation. I'm grateful the Supreme Court acted swiftly to prevent the Deep State radicals from using it as an excuse to shred our most essential and individual constitutional freedoms.

As egregious as it was, however, the COVID-19 vaccine mandate was just one of many attempts by agencies and bureaucrats to violate the U.S. Constitution, and obliterate our rights.

There will, no doubt, be many more attempts to come.

MANIPULATING THE MEDIA: THE DEEP STATE'S REACH INTO NEWS OUTLETS AND SOCIAL PLATFORMS

The Deep State bureaucracy's weaponization of government goes beyond the abuses of power I've discussed above. They also work in and through mainstream and social media companies to prop up stories that discredit conservative causes, bury stories that endanger their own priorities, and even *manufacture* stories to mislead us all. This turns social and traditional media into little more than a well-constructed PR campaign designed to influence public opinion and shape perceptions.

In my previous book, *The Deep State: 15 Surprising Dangers You Should Know,* I dedicated an entire chapter to how bureaucrats within the CIA, FBI, DOJ, and other federal agencies worked together with the Democratic National Committee (DNC) and the Hillary Clinton presidential campaign to manufacture the "Trump-Russia Collusion" hoax in a covert attempt to destroy Clinton's Republican challenger in the 2016 election.

Everyone involved apparently believed Clinton would win the election and subsequently protect all the crooked players involved in the scheme. You can imagine how shocked (and scared) they all became when Trump won the election and was given both the power and the platform to scrutinize all their illegal actions.

It's a fascinating — and terrifying — story of bureaucratic criminality at the highest levels of government. Hillary and her Deep State collaborators targeted a political enemy, but actively worked against the American people and endangered the integrity of our supposedly "free and fair" elections by creating and selling an outright lie to the media. I encourage you to pick up a copy of my *The Deep State* book and check out Chapter 5 for all the details.

Here, though, let's review a handful of other recent examples of how the Deep State is manipulating both media outlets and social-media platforms to further their own agendas.

"The Laptop" Coverup

We saw many of these organizations come together again, in 2020, to suppress the infamous "Hunter Biden laptop" story that broke in *The New York Post* on October 14, 2020 — just three weeks before Americans voted in then-President Trump's re-election contest against Hunter's father, Joe Biden. [9]

Whole books have been and certainly will continue to be written about this cover-up. The short version is that Joe Biden's son, Hunter, left a laptop at a computer repair shop filled with horribly incriminating emails, photographs, videos and other materials that revealed his own criminal actions and even implicated his father in many of his illegal activities.

I have never seen the Deep State scramble so quickly and forcibly to bury a damaging story. FBI and CIA spokespeople crawled out of the woodwork to denounce the laptop story as completely bogus.

The story was almost immediately banned on Facebook and Twitter. Users on those platforms could not even share links to the story on their feeds and, in some cases, in their own private messages on the networks. [10]

In less than a week, a group of more than 50 former intelligence officials signed an open letter denouncing the laptop story as having *"classic earmarks of a Russian information operation."* [11]

A few days later, in the final presidential debate before the election, Joe Biden called the laptop story a "Russian plan" and "a bunch of garbage." He dismissed it, saying, *"Nobody believes it except [Trump] and his good friend Rudy Giuliani."* [12]

Because the story was sufficiently silenced, most voters weren't able to learn about the emails and other information contained on the laptop — information that would have been devastating to the Biden campaign.

Of course, the suppression and the radical pro-socialists' other tactics worked. Biden won the election.

This was a clear case of the bureaucracy — the Deep State — using its power of influence to manipulate the public before the election.

After it was too late to affect the outcome, the laptop was later proven to be genuine. Two years later, most news outlets, including biased publications like *The Washington Post,* were forced to admit that the laptop and the bounty of evidence it contained did indeed belong to Hunter Biden. In February 2023 — almost two-and-a-half years after the story first broke — Hunter admitted the laptop was his. [13]

More importantly, an April 2023 deposition transcript released by the House Judiciary and Intelligence Committees revealed that the Biden campaign helped initiate the now-notorious letter from the former senior intelligence officials who denounced the laptop story as a Russian information operation. [14]

This level of corruption from within our government is more than troubling. It is a threat to our Republic. At this point, I do not understand how any American can believe anything they read in any news media outlet, no matter how many "officials" sign on to it.

Five Unbelievable "Coincidences"

The Deep State's strategy of diverting attention away from their own bad press was once again on full display between March and August 2023, just as Donald Trump was getting a bit too much attention for his presidential campaign in the lead-up to the 2024 election.

Check out the following five examples of how radical pro-socialist operatives across the government tried to manipulate the press and public opinion by taking dramatic, blatant, attention-seeking actions against Trump *immediately* after potentially damaging news broke about the Left in what was obvious interference with the 2024 election.

1. On March 16, Congress revealed clear evidence that the Biden family received possibly illegal payments from foreign countries.

   Two weeks later, on March 30, a New York court made history by indicting Donald Trump on charges regarding "hush money" payments he allegedly paid to cover up an extramarital affair. This dominated the news media as the first time a former U.S. President had ever been indicted on criminal charges.

2. On June 7, Republican members of a House congressional committee expressed their frustration over the FBI refusing to comply with a lawful subpoena for a key document that could implicate Joe Biden in a crime.

   The next day, on June 8, Trump was the subject of a second criminal indictment, this time for allegedly mishandling confidential documents found in his Mar-a-Lago home. Coverage dominated all news media.

3. Also on June 8, Republican members of Congress were finally given access to the subpoenaed FBI FD-1023 Form that showed Joe Biden allegedly took a $5 million bribe from a Ukrainian oligarch.

   Five days later, on June 13, Trump was arraigned in Miami, Florida, on a 37-count federal grand jury indictment involving his Mar-a-Lago home. The coverage again dominated the news.

4. On July 26, Hunter Biden's plea agreement in a criminal case regarding his failure to pay federal taxes fell apart unexpectedly when the judge raised serious concerns about the full scope and terms of the agreement proposed by the prosecutors.

   The next day, on July 27, the special counsel prosecuting Trump's Mar-a-Lago case surprised everyone by adding more charges to his previous indictment. Of course, all media coverage focused on this new development.

5. On July 31, Hunter Biden's business partner, Devon Archer, testified in a congressional hearing about Joe Biden's direct involvement in Hunter's business dealings, including joining in on phone calls and participating in dinner meetings between Hunter and his corrupt business partners. This was in direct opposition to Joe Biden's many assurances that he had never participated in Hunter's businesses or even discussed business matters with his son.

   The next day, on August 1, Trump was indicted a third time, by a federal grand jury charging him with crimes related to the January 6, 2021, protests at the U.S. Capitol.

Isn't it an amazing coincidence that these huge, attention-grabbing stories about Donald Trump *just happened* to occur almost immediately after potentially negative news about Joe Biden broke?

Joe Biden must be the luckiest politician in history!

Or perhaps something else is going on here.

You don't have to be a "conspiracy theorist" to see at least *some* troubling connections involving these "coincidences." Major events that could hurt the radical pro-socialists are quickly displaced by even bigger headlines that might harm conservatives, while minor events that could hurt the radical pro-socialists are either buried, "debunked" or countered with some well-placed leaks from unknown sources within the government.

The government's foul play in interfering with and even conspiring with the media has a powerful and negative effect on our nation's politics, fair elections, and our basic ability to get along with each other.

Take the second and third items on the list above, for instance. The revelations about Joe Biden's potential involvement in a bribery scheme, Donald Trump's Mar-a-Lago indictments, an FBI document showing a $5 million bribe to Joe Biden from a Ukrainian oligarch, and Trump's arraignment in a Florida federal court, all transpired between June 7 and June 13.

How well did the three main television news networks — ABC, CBS, and NBC — cover each of these major stories about two different U.S. Presidents? Writing for *Newsbusters,* Geoffrey Dickens, Director of Media Analysis at the Media Research Center, reported:

> *"Over 39 days (June 8-morning of July 18) the Big Three (ABC, CBS, NBC) broadcast networks crammed their evening, morning and Sunday roundtable shows with a total of 527 minutes of coverage dedicated to the Trump indictment."*

But how much did the Biden/Burisma alleged bribery scheme receive?

Zero seconds. [15]

That's right. In the 39 days following these explosive stories, the mainstream television news outlets did not report a single word about President Joe Biden allegedly receiving millions of dollars from a foreign company that wanted to buy "the Biden brand" — a company Hunter had worked for and Joe Biden had met with and done political favors for.

That doesn't even warrant a 60-second segment on the evening news?

Apparently not — at least, not for our Deep-State-led, agenda-driven, highly partisan television networks.

This is all part of the Deep State's media corruption and a propaganda war against the truth. And they are not even trying to hide it anymore.

But perhaps the light of hope — *and truth* — has already begun to pierce the veil of media darkness that hides stories the Deep State deems troublesome. In July 2023, Terry Doughty, the chief U.S. district judge for the Western District of Louisiana, issued a preliminary injunction that rattled radical, Deep State power brokers and their media and Big Tech allies.

Lousiana's and Missouri's Attorneys General filed a lawsuit against the federal government *(Missouri v. Biden)*, alleging that key government officials and agencies, including the FBI and Department of Health and Human Services, had unlawfully colluded with social media companies to kill the widespread circulation of several important news stories and general topics of discussion throughout 2020 and beyond.

The government agencies, they argued, *"overstepped their mandates and curtailed conservative speech throughout the pandemic."* [16]

In issuing the injunction early in the case, Judge Doughty wrote:

> *"The Plaintiffs are likely to succeed on the merits in establishing that the government has used its power to silence the opposition ...*
>
> *Opposition to COVID-19 vaccines; opposition to COVID-19 masking mandates and lockdowns; opposition to the COVID-19 Communist China lab-leak theory; opposition to the validity of the 2020 election; opposition to President Biden's policies; statements that the Hunter Biden leaked laptop story is true. All were suppressed.*
>
> *It is quite telling that the target of each example or category of suppressed speech was conservative, Christian or pro-American in nature. This deliberate and content-specific censorship of conservative ideas is a perfect example of the federal government's illegal viewpoint of political speech. American citizens have the right to engage in free debate about the significant issues affecting the country."* [17]

Clearly, Judge Doughty — a Trump appointee — didn't get the Deep State memo that the U.S. Constitution permits the federal government to censor conservatives, Republicans, and Christians.

While I and others celebrated this as a stunning victory for free speech, I was very alarmed by the hate and vitriol this judge received from pro-censorship, anti-free-speech Democrats and other pro-socialist radicals. It's sad to see so many Americans who are so willing to surrender our basic First Ammendment rights. They are so blinded by their anti-conservative, anti-Christian, anti-Republican, and anti-Trump hate that they don't even understand the precious freedoms they're fighting to throw away.

IS TURNABOUT FAIR PLAY?

So, what's the result of this Deep State meddling, back-door dealing, media-corrupting campaign against America? Should the radical pro-socialists celebrate the success of their "death by a thousand cuts" assault on liberty?

Some on the Left say, *"No."*

Harvard Law Professor Jack Landman Goldsmith III is a liberal and certainly not a Trump supporter by any means. Yet, he made shockwaves in an August 2023 opinion piece printed in *The New York Times,* in which he urged caution and careful consideration to his fellow Democrats.

Goldsmith warned that, while the radical pro-socialists might enjoy the idea of Trump being indicted and possibly imprisoned, Trump supporters *"don't see it that way, and would seek revenge."* [18] He argued:

> *"The unseemliness of the prosecution will most likely grow if the Biden campaign or its proxies use it as a weapon against Mr. Trump ... And then there is the perceived unfairness in the Justice Department's treatment of Mr. Biden's son, Hunter, in which the department has once again violated the cardinal principle of avoiding any appearance of untoward behavior in a politically sensitive investigation.*
>
> *Credible whistle-blowers have alleged wrongdoing and bias in the investigation, though the Trump-appointed prosecutor denies it. And the Department's plea arrangement with Hunter Biden came apart, in ways that fanned suspicions of a sweetheart deal, in response to a few simple questions by a federal judge.*
>
> *The prosecution may well have terrible consequences beyond the department for our politics and the rule of law. It will probably inspire ever more aggressive tit-for-tat investigations of presidential actions in office by future Congresses and by administrations of the opposing party, to the detriment of sound government."* [19]

Goldsmith's point is a good one — and one I've argued for

years. Both political parties have been guilty of tweaking the rules here and there for their own best interests, only to cry "foul" when the other side does the exact same thing to them. That's long been a staple of American political maneuvering. However, what we're seeing play out today is something different — and far worse.

Deep State officials have seemingly laid claim to our nation's federal agencies, justice system, educational system, news outlets, entertainment industry, technology and social-media platforms, corporations, and every other influential aspect of modern American life. They're using this nearly totalitarian control to push a radical, pro-socialist agenda that even many lifelong Democrats cannot support, tolerate or even understand. And they view this as a win.

But ...

What happens if (or when) the pendulum swings back in the other direction? What happens if there is a massive "Red Wave" that crashes over the woke culture that the radical pro-socialists and its Deep State overlords have carefully constructed?

What happens if conservatives and other hard-working, patriotic Americans retake those hidden levers of power throughout the entire system? And what if the Right wields that power with the same winner-take-all intensity that we've seen from the radical pro-socialists?

The radical pro-socialists would be outraged, of course. They would cry out, protest, march in the streets, and demand fairness across the board.

And they would cling to their Marxist delusions of victimhood once again!

As a Constitutional Republic, the United States functions best when everyone Right, Left, and Center — enjoys the blessings of liberty and the rule of law. Sadly, though, that simply cannot and will not happen unless — or until — we all stand united as

Americans to fully and finally slash and tame the bureaucracy ... and thereby "Drain the Swamp."

Chapter 6

Danger #5: Voter Fraud vs. Election Integrity

There are many blessings that come with living in America.

Our hard-fought freedoms.

Our economic prosperity.

A working rule of law.

The right to freely debate and disagree with others.

But one of the greatest blessings we enjoy as Americans, despite passionate disagreement on different issues that goes far beyond a simple distinction between Left and Right, is that we are able to peacefully transfer power from one party to another and from one political side to another.

In a Constitutional Republic, election integrity can get very messy, but it is absolutely essential.

Winston Churchill was right to label democracy *"the worst form of Government except for all those other forms that have been tried from time to time."* Truly, nothing is more sacred in our country than protecting the right to vote and being able to trust in the outcome's integrity.

But it has become increasingly difficult over the years to fully trust in the integrity of our elections. Many Americans have lost faith in the voting systems for a variety of reasons — some legitimate and some not.

Despite the justification for their lack of faith in the system, this mistrust in the process is having a devastating effect on our elections. It causes some bad actors to try to rig the system with illegal or unethical practices. And, perhaps just as destructive, it causes a high percentage of eligible voters to stay home on Election Day. If you think the game is rigged, why would you bother to play it at all?

In order to have safe, secure, and trustworthy elections — and to resolve our greatest ideological and political disagreements — we must have accurate and reliable election voting that are accepted and agreed upon by everyone.

Whether we personally like the result or not, we all need to be able to trust that the outcome truly reflects the will of the people. So, in this chapter, I want to dig into *Danger #5: Voter Fraud vs. Election Integrity,* by unpacking a handful of truths about — and spotlighting some key threats to — our election process.

ELECTION FRAUD IS REAL

You don't have to be a conspiracy theorist or "election denier" to believe that election fraud is real. It fact, it happens in practically every election.

The biased media, Big Tech, and ideologically driven bureaucrats in the Deep State and the radical ideologues, however, still try to deny that the problem is widespread.

They laugh off accusations of voter fraud and even refused to comply with recommendations made by President Trump's 2017 Presidential Commission on Election Integrity, which was formed specifically to investigate and counter voter fraud. When the commission sought voter data from every state, many states, through their politicians and unelected bureaucrats, refused. They claimed Trump was only interested in *suppressing* the vote by making it more difficult for his opponents to take part.

That's true in part. Those who support voter integrity

certainly *do* want to make it more difficult for non-citizens and ineligible people to vote.

Sadly, not everyone is on board with this goal. Some, in fact, want just the opposite: They want *everyone* to vote in America's elections, whether they're legal, legitimate voters or not — as long as they vote for the radical, pro-socialist preferred candidates.

Is voter fraud always the result of criminals willfully breaking voter laws? No. Sometimes, it's the result of simple incompetence. The electoral process is run, maintained, managed, and often *mismanaged* by ordinary people, and even honest, well-intended people make mistakes.

We see this play out in a severe lack of volunteer training at polling centers, in the mishandling of ballots, in the misplacement of ballots, and, of course, in the operation of electronic voting machines.

Voting machines are susceptible to human error at every level: the programmers who wrote the code, the engineers who built the hardware, the people who updated the machines with that specific election's ballot, the people who set up the machines at each polling center, the volunteers who instruct voters on how to use them, and I'm sure the dozens of other hands required to run and maintain the "automated" voting machines.

Incompetence aside, however, election fraud is often the result of intentional, lawless decisions. We see this in the way some people in government are implementing policies to increase voter turnout in their favor. We see it in the way some use fraudulent tactics to minimize the opposing party's turnout, while maximizing their own. We see it in the disinformation and outright lies that some candidates and media outlets propagate in order to convince voters that their causes and their candidate deserve support.

We are living in an age where basic concepts of right and

wrong are often ignored if not outright rejected, where some are willing to do and say anything to accomplish their political objectives. They are so dedicated to "their cause" that they believe any deception or dishonesty is acceptable as long as it achieves "the greater good" — which, of course, is whatever that candidate, party, or ideology "says" it is.

For example, something we're seeing more and more in this age of mail-in and absentee ballots is fake voter registrations. To see for myself how easy it would be to cast an illegal ballot, I went online and registered in the state of California, where I lived for most of my life, using a dog's name and my business address — both of which should have been caught and triggered a rejection. I really just wanted to see how far I could go into the process before I was "caught."

I clicked through the screens, providing fake information when asked, including a name, date of birth, ethnicity, party preference, and state of birth. *I will note that I did not falsify a Social Security number nor a driver's license number.*

The website ultimately told me I would receive some paperwork by mail to continue the registration process. I received that packet several days later — but guess what arrived in the mailbox first? A mail-in ballot, addressed to the fake dog I had registered online. Without even completing the additional paperwork the state had sent me, I was sent a ballot to vote in the current election at the time!

I didn't use it, of course, but even I was shocked at how easy it was for fraudsters to have mail-in ballots literally hand-delivered to them. No proof of identity. No verification of information. Nothing. Just a few clicks online, and boom — anyone can vote illegally in California.

Worse, having received a ballot for three elections, I moved out of state. The mail-in-ballot followed me.

Election fraud is not just in the hands of wayward individuals;

it's being led by those in positions of power. New threats from the U.S. Department of Justice and from within the Deep State bureaucracies are trying to undermine any advancement toward tougher election-integrity laws.

The most egregious example of this in recent history is a particularly terrible bill called H.R. 1 — or the "For the People Act."

H.R. 1 was first brought up by Congressional Democrats in 2019, and then brought back in 2021. It is still the No. 1 bill Democrats wish they could pass.

This bill would have thrown the doors of voter fraud wide open forever. Fortunately, U.S. Senate Republicans narrowly blocked the bill from being passed by using a filibuster. Some Democrats were so frustrated by the filibuster that they wanted to move to abolish the filibuster rule in the Senate, but that "nuclear option" proved to be a step too far for many in their party, so H.R. 1 was effectively stopped in its tracks mere inches away from the finish line.

Even though H.R. 1 couldn't overcome the Republican filibuster, it's worth examining some of the things it would have done. If nothing else, this shows you what changes many radical Democrats and socialists want to make to our national voting systems. In short, the Democrats wanted to enshrine into law the worst election law changes made illegally by blue states in 2020 — ostensibly as a reaction to the pandemic — and force them on all states as federal law. Here are just some of the devastating effects this bill would have had:

- Legalize nationwide vote-by-mail with no photo ID.
- Force ballot harvesting in every state.
- Require states to accept ballots 10 days after Election Day.
- Ban voter ID laws.

- Prevent election officials from removing dead, non-resident or otherwise ineligible voters from registration lists.
- Urge statehood and representation for Washington, D.C., and U.S. territories.
- Ensure illegal immigrants can vote by protecting them from prosecution if they are automatically registered.
- Allow felons to vote.
- Mandate early voting in every state.
- Mandate that states make unsupervised absentee voter boxes available for 45 days within an election.
- Require states to get "approval" from the federal government within making any voting rules changes.
- Require "Campus Vote Coordinators" at colleges and universities.
- Limit access to federal courts when challenging the legislation.

This list, as bad as it is, doesn't even represent *half* of the changes H.R. 1 would have made to our elections. As happy as I am that the proposal died in the Senate, I'm horrified that it made it so close to becoming law — without a single Republican being given a chance to offer comments during its drafting and debate. H.R. 1 must stand as a frightening reminder of the corruption some would inject into our voting process, if given the opportunity.

ELECTION FRAUD IS NOT NEW

Although some people (including the media) often act like it, Donald Trump did not invent the term *election fraud* or *rigged election* in 2020. Candidates and their most vocal champions have complained about election fraud from the very beginning of the Republic.

John Adams, the second President of the United States, was accused of dirty dealing by his opponent, Thomas Jefferson. Candidates have blamed their losses on some version of election fraud ever since.

In more recent history, it was a common belief among both Republicans and Democrats that Richard Nixon would have won his 1960 bid at the White House if not for election fraud in Texas and Illinois. Illinois later became especially well-known in the 1990s and 2000s for six-term Chicago Mayor Richard Daley's unstoppable election machine. He was basically able to hand-pick candidates and ensure their election!

Even more recently, Hillary Clinton complained about FBI interference and a scheme involving Facebook and Russian disinformation when she lost to Donald Trump in 2016, claiming it was voter fraud and the election was "stolen," and the results were "illegitimate."

Never mind the fact that Clinton herself funded a now thoroughly debunked intelligence report about collusion between Trump and Russia that was used to try to keep him out of the White House, and later in an attempt to remove him from office through impeachment despite his clear election victory.

Today, of course, we can't watch the news or listen to any candidate of either party speak for five minutes without hearing some mention of voter fraud. That brings us to my next point.

YES, THERE WAS VOTER FRAUD IN THE 2020 PRESIDENTIAL ELECTION

The 2020 presidential election will likely be remembered in U.S. history for many reasons — the pandemic, the unprecedented vitriol half the country directed toward the sitting president, the Democratic challenger Joe Biden barely campaigning (or even leaving his house), unconstitutional changes to the voting systems under the guise of public health and safety, and much more.

In the aftermath of that election, many claims of voter fraud came under intense scrutiny. Was the election rigged?

Was the presidency stolen?

Can anyone trust the outcome in the future?

I like to break down all the different claims about 2020 voter fraud into three categories:

1. Accusations, but no proof.

2. Assumptions and speculation.

3. Real voter fraud.

Let's explore each of these for just a moment.

Accusations, But No Proof

It is fairly common for a candidate to think that their election was "stolen," and it doesn't take much to drum up a claim about election fraud.

Such things are easy to say, but they are very difficult to prove.

Losing an election is embarrassing, so, of course, it makes things much more palatable if you can claim the other candidate cheated somehow. Many would argue that's why Hillary Clinton is *still* claiming the 2016 election was "rigged somehow."

For example, let's say a candidate lost and claimed the election was stolen. But anyone taking an honest, critical look may point to glaring weaknesses in how they ran their campaign. The candidate might argue, *"But we had more money! We ran a better marketing campaign! We had more yard signs in more yards! The other candidate was disorganized, lazy, incompetent, and never could have won in a fair fight!"*

But they did.

Most of the time, when you hear the losing candidate cry foul, there was no actual election fraud; they were just out campaigned.

As I've said, some people try to act as though Donald Trump was the first person to ever question an election result's validity. But Democrats are certainly guilty of this, too.

They say Trump was an "illegitimate" President because of "Russia."

Before Trump, George W. Bush was an "illegitimate" President because it took a U.S. Supreme Court decision to settle the election and make him President.

Any Republican victor, it seems, has a good chance of being deemed *illegitimate* by the defeated rival and his supporters.

Whenever you hear the losing side accuse the winning side of an *illegitimate* victory, your first question *must* be, *"What is your evidence?"* If they have none, or if what they *are* saying is an obvious distortion of reality, you can write them off as simply making assumptions with no proof.

Assumption and Speculation

In other cases, you may hear a lot of speculation about voter fraud from candidates and voters who were so sure they'd win that any loss is assumed to be the result of fraud.

This was the case, for example, with American entrepreneur Mike "the MyPillow guy" Lindell, a stalwart Trump supporter who simply refused to believe that Trump lost the presidency to Joe Biden legitimately in 2020. Lindell made several unprovable assumptions about fraud, using inferences about voting patterns and mismatching historical voting patterns as one argument. This is certainly an interesting discussion and possibly worth greater exploration, but it offered no conclusive proof about genuine fraud, in 2020.

Lindell could have focused on verifiable facts, but he included assumptions and speculations.

In fact, even a cursory look into the surprising voting patterns of some areas, in 2020 and 2018, reveal Democrat candidates' victories were the result of legal efforts or ballot harvesting combined with early voting — something the Democrats did very well and the Republicans failed to achieve.

In those areas where Democrats targeted their ballot-harvesting efforts, the Republican candidates lost by significant margins and the Democrats gained significant successes. But it wasn't primarily because of voter fraud; it was because the Republicans in those districts were out campaigned.

To be blunt, the Democrats worked harder and smarter in some areas, and their efforts paid off. They flipped some districts from red to blue through legal — albeit unorthodox — means. I'd estimate that the Democratic campaign strategies are at least 10 to 15 years ahead of the Republicans, and the Republicans must catch up quickly if they want to start winning elections again.

Real Voter Fraud

Finally, of course, there was some genuine election fraud in 2016 and 2020. Many claims of voter fraud were thrown out of courtrooms after 2020. The dismissals were often not because there were no cases, but the courts often ruled that the plaintiff(s) had no "standing" which is required for courts to make a decision one way or the other.

However, many cases moved forward. There were several states, for instance, in Pennsylvania where the law was illegally changed by the Secretary of State or the state Supreme Court — not the state legislature — which violates the U.S. Constitution.

There were also many votes counted that should not have been, including votes from dead people, illegal aliens, and people who voted more than once, and illegal votes that were trucked in from other states — and counted.

Also, whether by incompetence or malicious intent, tens of thousands of absentee votes in Wisconsin were later discovered to only have names with no addresses.

Several states had challenges and unanswered questions that made national headlines, while others had quiet, less-publicized irregularities.

In either case, real voter fraud is difficult to prove. Worse, it usually takes a long time to prove it. I'm talking years for these cases to be investigated, filed with the courts, and finally litigated. Even if the court finds voter fraud did indeed take place, these judgments can come years after the fact — long after the winning candidate has taken office. Sometimes, the judgment even comes after the "winning" candidate has already *left* office!

Further complicating the issue, even when voter fraud is proven, a court must consider whether the fraud was committed at sufficient scale to have actually changed the outcome of the election.

This is particularly difficult in national elections, such as presidential contests. Would verifiable instances of fraud in a few counties scattered across the country have swung an entire national election? Possibly yes ... possibly no.

However, the question still looms large in the minds of millions of voters, who genuinely believe their constitutional rights were trampled by criminals who would stop at nothing to put their candidate in office. That very question remains a big problem for all Americans and lawful voters.

THE DANGER OF VOTER FRAUD KEEPS PEOPLE FROM VOTING

Another danger of voter fraud is that it robs people of their confidence in our electoral system. When people lose confidence that their vote actually matters, they stop voting altogether, depressing the overall vote.

The sad reality is that there will always be certain levels of voter fraud. More notably, perhaps, there will always be widespread accusations of voter fraud. Again, you can trace this all the way back to John Adams' victory over Thomas Jefferson in their 1776 race to succeed President George Washington.

If our Founding Fathers couldn't figure this out, what chance do we have? Besides, things seem to be getting worse, not better, when it comes to election fraud — no voter ID, legalized ballot harvesting, voter drop boxes, online or motor vehicle and government-controlled voter agency registration. As long as things like ballot harvesting, mail-in ballots, early voting, and voting machines introduce new possibilities for corrupting and mishandling ballots, there will always be actual instances of voter fraud, leading to increasing accusations of fraud.

Again, though, it's not malicious fraud that usually costs candidates elections, nor is it fraud-by-incompetence. Rather, more often the problem is that losing candidates have been outworked, outsmarted, and out campaigned by their opponents.

To win, candidates facing the specter of voter fraud simply must do a better job of using all legal means of campaigning than their opponents. It's tough, but it's not insurmountable. It's a matter of out-marketing them — despite the danger of fraud.

WHEN THE GAME *IS* RIGGED: FIVE TYPES OF POTENTIAL VOTER FRAUD

The election game has changed dramatically in recent years, and if pro-socialist Democrats have their way, things will change even more in the future. Here are five key types of fraud that, if left unchecked and uncorrected, could completely disrupt the outcome of every American election we hold from now on.

Ballot Harvesting

Ballot harvesting is when paid workers or volunteers go door-to-door in neighborhoods or visit special living environments like nursing homes to collect ballots.

They usually have a printed voter guide to "help" the voter. And by *help,* I mean they encourage or outright mislead the voter into voting for a particular candidate — whether it's the candidate that aligns with that voter's values or not.

Then, they take the ballot — sometimes hundreds a day — to the polls or voter drop box.

States where ballot harvesting is legal, like California, tend to have dramatic levels of fraud at the local and state level. The Democratic party and the unions train people and create scientific databases of targeted voters to visit in door-to-door campaigns.

However, ballot harvesting still happens in states where it is outlawed, such as Arizona. During the 2020 election cycle, for example, undercover journalists with Project Veritas caught a Texas woman on video explaining how she *helped* people vote and collected ballots illegally in nursing homes. She even admitted in the video that what she was doing was illegal! [1]

Those conducting ballot harvesting are taking advantage of citizens who are unfamiliar with the candidates and issues at hand. Worse, they often take advantage of our nation's seniors in nursing homes and other health-care facilities, where those whose declining health and mental acuity make them easy targets for predatory criminals. They disguise their illegal schemes as "help," effectively deceiving their community's weakest and most vulnerable members. It's illegal, it's wrong, and it's outright disgusting. We cannot tolerate this abuse — especially the abuse of our elders — any longer.

Sometimes it's beyond outrageous. In the last election, apartment-complex mailboxes were illegally opened the night after the ballots arrived, with two people picking up the mail-in ballots of those in the apartment complex so they could "ballot harvest" them.

The police discovered about one thousand ballots in the back seat of a car. *All of these criminals were caught on camera, but no one was arrested.*

Early Voting

The concept of "Election Day" used to mean something in this country. It was the one day when all voters in every district across the country came together as one people and one nation to cast a ballot for their chosen candidate or make decisions about various proposals.

I remember a time when the nation's balance of power literally changed over the course of a single day. With each passing year, however, the notion of Election Day loses more and more meaning.

Today, in many (or most) districts, you can vote weeks and even a month before election day. You can vote at the polling place or mail it in early. In many areas, you can even drop off your ballot at one of many ballot drop boxes scattered throughout your community.

The new, "convenient" methods of casting your vote early have many benefits, and I can certainly understand why they've become so popular. In fact, many people now view Election Day as more of a deadline than the day they'll actually vote. Weeks before, they start thinking, *Election Day is coming up. I better get my vote in right away, or I'll have to leave work early to wait in line!*

Despite the obvious benefits, early-voting procedures have introduced significant new opportunities to commit election fraud.

Take ballot harvesting, for example, in which a third party gathers absentee or mail-in ballots from voters and submits them as a batch. Laws vary by state regarding who can or cannot deliver someone else's ballot. And while this practice is not always fraudulent, it legally opens the door to massive voter fraud in some areas.

This problem only exists because so many people have so much time and so many options for casting their ballots. If voting were restricted to *just* Election Day, most of the worst aspects of ballot harvesting would immediately dry up. Plus, ballot harvesting creates a chain-of-custody nightmare. There's no way to know who touched the ballots and possibly altered or manipulated them before they are counted.

And don't get me started on ballot drop boxes! These boxes are largely unsupervised or, at best, minimally supervised, creating all-new and all-to-easy avenues for fraud.

I'm all for convenience, and I certainly want every legal, legitimate voter to have the opportunity to cast their ballot. But, in my view, the dangers of early voting — at least as it exists today — far outweigh the benefits.

Slate Mailers

One of the most despicable types of fraud that I've seen recently — and honestly, something that personally offends me as a marketing professional — is a certain type of direct mail piece called *slate mailers.* You've probably never heard that term, but you've almost certainly received one of these in the mail. By its very nature, a slate mailer is designed to deceive you, the voter. Here's how it works:

Say you're a Republican, and you get a mailer from what by all appearances is a Republican organization. It might even be named something like "Reagan Republicans" or "Trump Republicans" and bear the official seal of the Republican party.

The mail has a facsimile of the ballot for your upcoming local election, and at the top it might say, *"Reagan Republicans in your area are happy to provide this sample ballot for our fellow Republican voters."* Then, it has clear checkmarks next to several names on the ballot.

Any reasonable person who isn't following the local election might think, *Oh, this is great. This group of Ronald Reagan conservatives is showing me who the most conservative candidates are in this election. I'll vote for these candidates.*

But guess what? None of the candidates marked on that "helpful" sample ballot is a Republican at all. In fact, they're the cherry-picked Democrat candidates this sleazy organization, masquerading as a Republican group, want to trick you into voting for.

The worst fraudulent example I've seen is: "The California Republican Party Official Voter Guide."

It has the official California Republican logo.

It has a page with a statement from the real California Republican Chairman.

It even has a donation request for the California Republican Party with the real Republican Party address.

It has check marks next to *"endorsed candidates so you can easily see whom to vote for."*

The problem: all "endorsed" candidates and proposition issues were Democrat-supported!

Slate mailers are full of lies, pure and simple. Politicians can get away with it because they write the laws. But if I, as a professional marketer, tried to do something like this for any product or service I'm promoting, it would be considered mail fraud, and I'd be held liable and perhaps prosecuted for it. So, if you get one of these slate mailers or anything that could even *possibly* be a slate mailer, toss it where it belongs: in the trash.

Visit my site, electionforum.com, for the truth about which candidates share your values and priorities for your community and this country.

Literature and Ads

While slate mailers have been a problem for decades, the spread of disinformation has skyrocketed in our modern world of social media, email, and automated text messaging.

We used to only deal with this "election direct mail" in our mailboxes, but now it is common to see a flood of campaign literature and advertisements on YouTube, Facebook, Instagram, Twitter, TikTok, television, and in your online mailbox. Even worse: most of what you see in these campaign ads is full of deliberate lies.

The avalanche of deception is so bad that, believe it or not, most of the campaign literature and ads you see today would be *illegal* if they were promoting a product or service instead of a candidate. As an advertising executive, it is so frustrating for me to see all the junk that is circulated during election seasons. It is fraudulent, deceptive, and misleading; and yet it is still completely legal because of campaign laws that allow candidates to say just about anything.

Postal Employees and Mail-in Ballots

This may sound crazy if you do not follow politics, but the U.S. Postal Service has a long history of political activism.

In fact, it is perhaps the most active government agency supporting the Democrat Party, but the problem goes much deeper than their unwavering dedication to their favorite political party.

The American Postal Workers Union (APWU) is one of the most pro-socialist unions in America. They endorsed Bernie Sanders, in 2016. Then, in 2020, they endorsed Bernie again before switching to Joe Biden. Beyond simple endorsements, the postal union mobilizes and activates its members to volunteer, walk precincts, make phone calls, send texts, and distribute literature in support of Democratic candidates. In fact, in 2016, the APWU used its trained members to work for Hillary Clinton.

The U.S. Postal Service allowed its employees to do campaign work during their regular workdays, despite its obvious violation of the Hatch Act, which prohibits federal employees from engaging in partisan political activity in the workplace.

With the proliferation of absentee ballots and the rising Democrat demand for universal mail-in ballots, doesn't it make sense that we should be very concerned about this radical union handling *Republican* voters' ballots?

Postal service employees have ample opportunity to interrupt the flow of ballots to and from voters at every point in the process.

As of Election Day 2020, for example, headlines circulated that 300,000 ballots *still* hadn't been delivered to voters in several states, including key battleground states like Arizona, Florida, and Georgia. [2] More outlandishly, voters in Baltimore were shocked to receive their 2020 ballots in August of 2022 — two years after the 2020 election! [3]

Were these and the many other suspicious delivery mishaps intentional acts of fraud by a politically motivated postal worker, or were they examples of fraud-by-incompetence? We'll never know.

What we *do* know, however, is that mail-in balloting only works if we as citizens and voters can trust that we are receiving our ballots in the mail and that our filled-in ballots are making it to their lawful destination. And right now, we can't have that trust.

GOVERNMENT-CREATED VOTER FRAUD

Human beings aren't the only source of fraud by either willful decision or incompetence. Local, state, and even federal governments can be just as corrupt — and certainly just as incompetent — as any individual. So, let's examine a few of the main ways government itself opens the door to voter fraud.

Bad Voter-Registration Rolls

It should go without saying that we have a massive problem in this country keeping our voter rolls updated and clean. We hear about this during and after every election cycle. This happens when voter rolls contain names that should not be on there, such as:

- People who are not actually citizens of the United States.
- People who have died.
- People who have moved out of a voting district.
- Students who are registered to vote in both their home district and the district where they live to attend school.
- People who have double, triple, or even quadruple registrations in different districts.

I still receive absentee ballots in California for my children, who now live (and are currently registered to vote in another district) out of state. It would take no effort at all for me to fill in those ballots in the names of my kids and mail them back in — even though my children are also voting in their new home states.

A 2017 study found that more than 7 million people are registered to vote in two different states — and that study only examined 28 of our 50 states, so the problem could be twice as bad as this study shows! Could 7 to 15 million duplicate voter registrations make the difference in a national election? You bet it could!

Here are some other eye-opening statistics worth noting regarding the state of our voter-registration rolls:

- A 2012 Pew Study showed that 24 million voter registrations in the United States were inaccurate, out-of-date or duplicate. [4]
- A 2017 study of 24 states found that the number of registered voters exceeded the number of eligible voters in 248 counties. [5]
- In San Diego, California, the number of registered voters was found to be 138 percent of eligible voters! [6]

Do these facts about voter-registration rolls fill you with confidence? They don't for me. And the fact that a huge number of Democrats are actively fighting against cleaning up our voter rolls, not to mention going the extra step of requiring voter ID at the polls, is very alarming.

Government-Sponsored Voter Registration

It is common for voter registration to become part of government services like Obamacare, food stamps, SNAP, public health, and other entitlement programs.

That may seem like a good idea on the surface. After all, I'm not suggesting that legitimate voters should be kept off the voter rolls.

The problem is, these people are often guided in *how* to vote — that is, *whom to vote for* — if they want their "free" state-sponsored services to continue. If a voter has become dependent on their "free" government services, and if they're told *this* candidate will continue your benefits and probably even increase them, but *that* candidate will try to cut you off, whom do you think they'll vote for?

Many issues are never as clear-cut as activists make them seem, and literally threatening voters with the removal of the benefits they've come to rely on has no place in our country.

Illegal Immigrants/Noncitizens

We're in the middle of a staggering immigration crisis in America today. The number of illegal border crossings has reached more than 6 million, not counting "get-a-ways," since Joe Biden took office.

We're fooling ourselves if we think this unprecedented increase of non-citizens entering our country illegally won't have a powerful effect on the next several election cycles.

Certain political parties and many pundits dispute this, of course, but facts are facts.

In 2017 — before the border floodgates were thrown wide open (if not wholly demolished) — the National Hispanic Survey found that 2 million illegal aliens were registered to vote in the United States. [7]

In 2015, a random sample of 800 Hispanic voters showed that 13 percent were not citizens and therefore voting illegally. [8] In Virginia — a key swing state, no less — a 2018 study found that 5,000 noncitizens were actively and routinely casting ballots in elections. [9]

An estimated 800,000 noncitizens voted in the 2016 presidential election — and roughly 81 percent of them voted for Hillary Clinton. [10]

Why do some politicians and political parties laugh off these terrifying statistics? Because they don't care about constitutional principles or fair and legal elections. They care about winning and maintaining power, and they'll take anyone's vote if it helps them accomplish that goal.

"Motor Voter" Registration

Across America, people are getting a driver's license or a renewal car registration to vote.

California's so-called "motor voter" law has been an open door to voter fraud. I explained this in detail in my book, *The Deep State:*

> *"Deep State politicians and bureaucrats in California have supported voter fraud driven by a dangerous ideology that uses loopholes in Department of Motor Vehicles laws to enable illegal aliens to vote.*
>
> *They even passed a law known as the California Motor Voter Act, which automatically sends driver information to state voter-databases, unless the license holder opts out or is not eligible.*
>
> *This new law — combined with California's 2 million illegal immigrants and notoriously fraudulent voter rolls — all add up to create one chaotic reality: In California, it's easy for voter fraud to happen; for illegals to vote for the politicians who will protect them and for ideologues who manipulate the vote in their favor.*
>
> *The California Motor Voter Act makes it nearly impossible for honest state officials to verify that people are who they claim to be — such as illegal aliens claiming to have U.S. citizenship.*

Furthermore, because California issues driver's licenses to illegal aliens, these noncitizens are often registered to vote at the same time. All it takes for an illegal alien to register to vote is a dishonest clerk.

I talked about this dangerous reality on Fox News in an interview with Stuart Varney.

Stuart asked me: 'Craig, what is voter fraud in California?'

I answered him, and explained: 'This is a terrible joke on the United States, because it's going to affect Congress and the Senate races as well as state races, and the U.S. Electoral College vote in 2020.'

I continued, 'California politicians wrote into the law that if somebody who was not a citizen registered to vote and voted, they would be held harmless. It doesn't matter if it was an accident or not.'

Before Donald Trump was elected President, many in the media were saying: 'As California goes, so goes the nation.'

California is not the only state where illegal aliens can obtain licenses, meaning other states may follow suit. In Colorado, Connecticut, Delaware, Hawaii, Illinois, Maryland, New Mexico, Nevada, Utah, Vermont, Washington and Washington, D.C., illegal aliens can also register to vote with each State's Department of Motor Vehicles or other agency. This makes it shockingly easy in these states for illegal aliens to vote in our elections." [11]

Lax Regulations for Voter-Registration Campaigns

As I've said, candidates are able to say practically whatever they want in campaign ads. Likewise, activists are able to say pretty much anything to encourage people to register to vote and to tell them *how* to vote.

One notorious example was Facebook and Meta founder Mark Zuckerberg's voter registration initiative ahead of the 2020 election. Zuckerberg spent about a half-billion dollars on a professional direct-response advertising company to specifically target districts across the country where the votes could make the most impact. The goal was to beef up the voter rolls only in districts that were likely to vote for Joe Biden and other Democrat candidates.

They took masterful control of communication platforms, technology, and efficiency strategies to reach Left-leaning voters and drive them to the polls; and this strategy worked amazingly well for Democrats.

This focus on only one type of voter may have been unethical, but it was not illegal.

Voting Machines

As technology continues to change how Americans vote, we are opening ourselves up to more and more opportunities for fraud. Anyone who has ever used a computer or cellphone knows that they are marvelous devices, but they are not entirely problem-free.

Voting machines are vulnerable to hacking, modem and communication problems, power outages, and programming errors — and let's not forget basic user error by voters who are less technically inclined.

To be fair, there has never been any hard evidence of widespread irregularities due to voting technology. Nonetheless, there is very little trust in the integrity of voting machines by a large percentage of the population.

We saw this mistrust play out on a national level after the 2020 presidential election. Politicians, members of the media, and outspoken activists such as Mike Lindell were absolutely convinced that intentional manipulation of voting machines caused Donald Trump to lose his bid for re-election.

Some, like former federal prosecutor Sidney Powell, promised to reveal evidence of a large-scale voter fraud scheme by the manufacturers of the voting machines used in many states. Although the evidence never materialized, the possibility of such fraud was enough to leave tens of thousands of voters convinced that technological foul play was to blame.

Due to the lack of evidence of actual machine manipulation, I personally believe, the Republicans were simply outcampaigned in 2020. The Democrats "Get Out the Vote" campaigns, led by Left-leaning activists, celebrities, and tech moguls worked, leaving the Republicans and conservatives scratching their heads and wondering whom and what to blame. It was easy to point to technology as the culprit.

Even if there had been provable machine manipulation that altered votes, Trump still would have won, if his campaign had done legal ballot harvesting, encouraged early voting, did proper advanced voter data mining, tested messaging and a robust Get-Out-the-Vote (GOTV) campaign, and supplied an army of poll-watchers and lawyers like the Democrats did.

The big danger here, as I've said previously, is that when people don't trust the voting process, they choose not to participate. And staying home on Election Day is the worst decision any of us can make.

Just look at what happened in the Georgia Senate runoff election in early 2021. So many Georgia Republican voters were convinced that Trump lost the presidential election six weeks earlier due to fraud that they stayed home for the Senate runoff.

But the Democratic voters showed up in droves. As a result, Georgia elected two Democratic Senators, thereby recklessly *handing* Democrats a majority in the U.S. Senate.

To be clear, I am not a Luddite, and I am in awe of the many wonderful modern-day miracles that advancements in technology have brought us. However, in this instance, I think the old-school system of paper ballots is by far the most trusted means of voting, and I would be thrilled to see us return to that nationwide.

THE FIGHT TO RESTORE ELECTION INTEGRITY

Those of us who champion election integrity are facing an uphill battle for sure.

The good news is that people are waking up to many of the dangers I've outlined in this chapter, and more and more people in more and more counties are fighting to get rid of voting machines, return to paper-ballot voting, and provide better training for poll workers.

On the state level, there's a strong push to outlaw ballot harvesting, strengthen voter ID and voter-protection laws, crack down on voter intimidation, and vastly improve ballot chain-of-custody rules. (Of those, I believe strengthening voter ID regulations alone is *key* to cleaning up much of the fraud we've seen happening regularly in every recent election.)

On the federal level, some House members and U.S. Senators are working on proposals to help clean up outdated and inaccurate voter-registration rolls, remove dead and duplicate voters, and verify legitimate voters. These efforts are a step toward righting the wrongs of widespread voter fraud. But we must do more.

To be clear, I believe voting is the civic duty of every American citizen. It's a privilege that many, many of our fellow citizens have fought and died to provide and protect.

I would never dissuade any legitimate voter from participating in the electoral process — even those who have personal, political, social, and economic positions that differ from mine.

The key term, though, is *legitimate voter.* If someone is legally qualified to vote, they should. If they are not qualified, they should not be allowed to vote or take part in the election process.

And when we as citizens are confident our federal, state, and local governments are doing everything they can to run elections that are truly fair and honest, we all win ... even when our preferred candidate loses.

Chapter 7

Danger #6: The Little-Known But Huge Threat To Our Republic: Judicial Activists vs. Strict Constructionists

Judges are the most powerful force for both change and stability in this country.

I know that is a bold statement, but I could not be more serious.

If you want to see what America will truly look like in five, 10, and 20 years, look at the quality of today's judges — from the Justices sitting on the U.S. Supreme Court to the judges sitting on the bench in your local county courtroom. These are the men and women who decide if America will stay true to the U.S. Constitution or descend into the so-called "Socialist Utopia" so many politicians and pundits are yearning for.

The judicial branch of government doesn't get nearly as much public attention as the executive and legislative branches, but I believe it is the most important. It was created to be a check on the powers of the other branches, a safeguard against any rogue American President or legislature running afoul of the U.S. Constitution.

We *need* this check and balance. Our country's fundamental well-being depends on it.

And yet ...

A dangerous trend has been steadily growing over the past several years across the judicial branch. A weed of judicial activism has sprung up in the courts, and rather than uprooting it, the radical Marxist and socialists have fed it, nourished it, and directed its growth. Today, that weed is threatening to choke the very soul of our nation — unless we root it out and destroy it.

As I wrote in my book, *The Deep State:*

> *"The responsibility of a judge is to interpret and apply the law based on the text of the U.S. Constitution, Acts of Congress, state laws and the common-law tradition we inherited primarily from England and other legal systems.*
>
> *The role of the judge is not to advance or promote an ideology or a political agenda.*
>
> *Unfortunately, there are judges in both the U.S. Supreme Court and the state courts who try to manipulate the law and public policy to advance their own agendas."* [1]

These judges are *judicial activists,* and they are dead set on *legislating from the bench* despite no constitutional mandate or authority to do so.

These gavel-wielding crusaders are not bothered by such limitations. Instead, they insert themselves into matters of policy, changing laws and sometimes even issuing rulings that amount to laws to suit their own and others' political interests. These judges stand apart from *strict constructionists ... also called originalists* or *textualists,* members of the judiciary who understand their role is not to legislate but to interpret the law as it is written, not as they want it to be.

Though I've placed this danger here at number six, do not be mistaken: The most powerful force in shaping our social and economic policies is the great contest between the judicial activists and strict constructionists in our nation's judicial system.

And we cannot afford to sit on the sidelines.

JUDICIAL ACTIVISTS: LEGISLATING FROM THE BENCH

Judicial activists have trampled on our individual rights and created law based on their own opinions, and not derived from the U.S. Constitution. They have misused their judicial authority, reshaping it instead into a makeshift, unelected legislature in which their word — not the Constitution nor Congress — is law.

There have been many examples of judicial activism throughout American history, but the "classic" example — and the one that has perhaps led to the greatest discussion and division among our citizens — was the Supreme Court's 1973 decision in *Roe v. Wade.*

For 50 years, people considered *Roe v. Wade* to be the "law of the land." In fact, however, *Roe* was never a "law" at all; it was simply the High Court's subjective ruling on a lawsuit that targeted a Texas state law banning abortions except in cases when the mother's life was in danger. As I wrote in my book, *The Christian Voter:*

> *"The Court ruled that the Texas law was unconstitutional because it violated an implied 'right to privacy' contained in the Due-Process Clause of the Fourteenth Amendment. But the Court went far beyond merely striking down the Texas law.*
>
> *The majority opinion, written by Justice Harry Blackmun, established legislative guidelines for each of three trimesters of pregnancy.*
>
> *It also classified a woman's right to choose to kill her unborn child as 'fundamental,' which required lower courts to evaluate challenges to state abortion laws using the 'strict scrutiny' standard — the highest level of judicial review possible in our legal system."* [2]

Do you see the big problem behind *Roe v. Wade?* In an exceptionally broad ruling, the Supreme Court went far beyond its duty to rule on the constitutionality of the Texas state law that was in question.

It went much further in establishing what were, in effect, new laws that dictated how every state in the country must handle the abortion issue. It created law, rather than interpreting the U.S. Constitution. It legislated the majority's political opinion from the bench. But creating law is not the job of *any* court — even the highest court in the land.

The Founders set up a system in which laws are written and passed by the legislatures, not the judiciary. The court system's only job is supposed to be deciding if the laws in a certain case were applied correctly, according to the Constitution. Anyone, even those in favor of abortion, should be able to see that the fundamental underpinning of America's abortion "law" was a shaky judicial overreach at best.

Interestingly (though not surprisingly), the same people who cheered the Court's right to create abortion law out of whole cloth in 1973 lost their minds with outrage when a Supreme Court decision swung the other way in the *Dobbs v. Jackson Women's Health Organization* decision of 2022. This Court — that included three justices who were appointed by President Trump — overruled the previous Supreme Court decisions regarding abortion in 1973 (*Roe v. Wade*) and 1992 (*Planned Parenthood v. Casey*). The decision essentially declared that the U.S. Constitution does not, in fact, confer a "right" to abortion and passed the matter of regulation back to the individual states.

The full impact and importance of these decisions is beyond the scope of this book and is enough to fill an entirely different book. For now, it's enough to understand:

- As you know — The United States Congress has never passed a federal law either banning or allowing abortion. Note: The Hype Amendment barred the use of federal Medicaid funds for abortion except when the life of the woman would be endangered by carrying the pregnancy to term.

- The 1973 U.S. Supreme Court exceeded their authority by ruling that the Constitution infers a "right to abortion" essentially *carte blanche.*
- In 2022, the High Court reversed that earlier decision and left each state with the responsibility to pass laws regulating abortion for themselves, asserting that the Constitution does not, in fact, infer such a right to all citizens.

In *Roe v. Wade,* judicial activists were motivated by what they *wanted* the Constitution to say, not by what it actually said.

Through their rather distortive interpretation of the law, these Justices not only *created* a law that didn't exist, but in doing so, they legalized the killing of more than 63 million babies over the last half-century. This is truly the most abhorrent example of judicial activism we will ever see.

The COVID-19 pandemic brought us other examples that were also devastating, though fortunately, not as generationally catastrophic as *Roe.* One such case involved Pastor John MacArthur of Los Angeles's Grace Community Church. In 2020, California Gov. Gavin Newsom ordered the unconstitutional and illegal lockdown of churches across the state, preventing them from holding in-person services and thereby restricting their First Amendment right to the free exercise of religion.

Grace Community Church did not obey the governor's edict and carried on with their live, in-church services. Not surprisingly, this act of civil defiance landed Pastor MacArthur in a Los Angeles County courtroom.

Judge Mitchell Beckloff, a judicial activist judge with a history of Democratic campaign contributions, denied Grace Community's constitutional right to hold church services during the lockdown, even though Beckloff had even previously agreed with a Superior Court Judge who held that MacArthur could open his church.

Beckloff — who is in a same-sex marriage and was no doubt familiar with MacArthur's views on homosexuality — went back on his previous agreement and issued an 18-page ruling against the church, demanding that it close its doors. With nothing but a pen and a gavel, Gov. Newsom and Judge Beckloff rewrote the law and voided Grace Community's constitutional right to gather for worship.

In a similar case, another activist judge in California ruled against Calvary Chapel San Jose, that also remained open during the lockdown.

Judge Evette Pennypacker, a long-time supporter of and contributor to Hillary Clinton and Kamala Harris, ordered the church to pay $1.2 million in fines. She also presented them with a list of Orwellian demands that struck at the very heart of our country's religious liberty. For example, the county of Santa Clara:

- Threatened the church's mortgage holder and coerced the church's banking institution to join their campaign of harassment against the church.
- Demanded a list of church leadership, volunteers, and donors, thereby exposing them to public harassment and potential legal action.
- Sought access to the church's financial records, implying that the church was operating as a for-profit business, rather than as a nonprofit ministry.
- Illegally used geofencing of all church attendees' cell phones ... no search warrant ... no constitutional authority to track and spy on worshipers.

The state even issued a search warrant to investigate and

interrogate church employees!

The COVID-19 pandemic spawned cases like this across the country, with Democrat-led state and local governments bringing citizens — from business owners to pastors — before activist judges, who were all too happy to pile on threats, fines, and more to force compliance.

I'm sad to say that parts of the country became unrecognizable, as a wave of authoritarianism unlike anything I've ever seen swept through the nation.

Of course, when speaking about the authoritarian threat of judicial activism, I would be remiss to leave out perhaps the most dramatic example we've seen in recent history.

On August 8, 2022, FBI agents stormed into President Trump's private Mar-a-Lago residence in Palm Beach, Florida. They were there to execute a search warrant for documents deemed "classified material" that the former President had allegedly taken with him when he left the White House.

Most discussions among conservative pundits at the time rightly focused on the FBI, but we cannot overlook the fact that a U.S. Federal District Judge signed off on the agency's search warrant. Let's take a look at who this judge is.

The FBI probably was not surprised to discover that finding a judge to approve the raid was no easy matter. They shopped around for a judge who would grant the required warrant and found one in the Trump-hating Bruce Reinhart, a U.S. Magistrate Judge ... for the U.S. District Court for the Southern District of Florida.

Reinhart is a lifelong Democrat who has given thousands of dollars to Democrat candidates and who has re-tweeted his agreement with some of the most radical pro-socialists in Congress — especially when they bashed President Trump.

In fact, Reinhart has a history of tweeting his anti-Trump

rhetoric himself — or at least he did before he issued the warrant and then deleted his own Trump-bashing tweets to avoid any appearance of bias.

Unbelievably, just six weeks before issuing the Mar-a-Lago warrant, Judge Reinhart recused himself from Trump's lawsuit against Hillary Clinton and other Democrats for their involvement in the "Russian collusion" hoax. So, he acknowledged he was too biased to rule in a case initiated *by* Trump, but he wasn't too biased to rule in a case initiated *against* Trump? How interesting!

No matter what you think about Trump's handling of documents, it should be clear to any reasonable person that a full-scale, armed FBI raid was not justified or remotely appropriate in this situation. But in this matter, Judge Reinhart was not interested in propriety or judicial precedent. He was simply excited to play a role in embarrassing a former President that he despised.

That's what activists — not ethical and impartial judges — do.

STRICT CONSTRUCTIONISTS: PROTECTING THE UNITED STATES FROM JUDICIAL OVERREACH

Our best defense against politically motivated, activist judges is jurists who follow the law; those who set their personal biases aside and focus on deciding cases according to safeguarding our rights as citizens under the U.S. Constitution.

Fortunately, we are blessed with a large number of judges who follow the path of strict constructionism — especially in the wake of President Trump's numerous judicial appointments ranging from the U.S. Supreme Court to the federal District and Appellate Courts.

If you want to see the utter necessity of appointing strict constructionists to the U.S. Supreme Court, look no further than the 2022 Supreme Court decision in *Dobbs v. Jackson*

Women's Health Organization that overturned *Roe v. Wade* and *Planned Parenthood v. Casey.* This was perhaps the most dramatic example in my lifetime of strict constructionist Justices protecting us all from judicial activism and overreach.

Despite intense and unrelenting pressure to uphold the prior, a glaringly unconstitutional *Roe v. Wade* decision, the Court found that the U.S. Constitution does *not* infer a right to abortion. The decision reads, in part:

> *"We hold that* ***Roe*** *and* ***Casey*** *must be overruled. The Constitution makes no reference to abortion, and no such right is implicitly protected by any constitutional provision ...* ***Roe*** *was egregiously wrong from the start. Its reasoning was exceptionally weak, and the decision has had damaging consequences. And far from bringing about a national settlement of the abortion issue,* ***Roe*** *and* ***Casey*** *have enflamed debate and deepened division."* [3]

This reversal of a 50-year-old judicial overreach was only possible because President Trump and a Republican-led Senate appointed and confirmed three strict constructionist justices to the Court. Those three — Neil Gorsuch, Brett Kavanaugh, and Amy Coney Barrett — joined Clarence Thomas and Samuel Alito, who authored the opinion.

Elections have consequences, and perhaps the biggest consequence of Donald Trump's 2016 presidential victory was the dramatic impact it had on the Supreme Court, which shifted from a long-standing radical pro-socialist slant to a majority of strict constructionist Justices who focus on the Constitution, not on activism or legislating from the bench.

Pastor John MacArthur of Grace Community Church in Los Angeles, who I discussed earlier, also found satisfaction from a fair-minded court after L.A. County's assault on the church's right to hold worship services during the pandemic. A year after the State of California and County of Los Angeles came down hard on Pastor MacArthur, his staff, and his church members for violating their COVID-19 lockdowns, the church was awarded $800,000 in damages for the authoritarian governmental overreach. Ultimately, the U.S. Supreme Court struck down all indoor bans, including bans on worship, and allowed churches nationwide to open legally.

In other litigation regarding church-and-state dynamics, which is often the source of anti-Christian judicial activism, two federal district courts in California ruled that federal courts cannot force churches to pay for abortions and can exclude such medical procedures from their healthcare plans. This is another great example of strict-constructionist courts prevailing against the downward slide of activism from the bench.

Lawyers with Alliance Defending Freedom (ADF) brought two suits against the State of California on behalf of four California churches, challenging the state's abortion-coverage mandate.

ADF attorneys uncovered emails that revealed that the California Department of Managed Health Care issued their abortion coverage mandate in response to demands from Planned Parenthood — despite state regulations that specifically exempt religious groups from such regulations or requirements.

In both cases, the presiding courts ruled that "the Constitution protects a church's right to operate according to their religious beliefs, which include their belief in the sanctity of unborn lives." ADF Senior Counsel Jeremiah Galus put it well:

> *"The government can't force a church or any other religious employer to violate their faith and conscience by participating in funding abortion. For years, California officials, in collaboration with Planned Parenthood, have unconstitutionally targeted faith-based organizations. This is a significant victory for the churches we represent, the conscience rights of their members, and other religious organizations that shouldn't be ordered by the government to violate some of their deepest faith convictions."*[4]

In another example stemming from the pandemic, the Supreme Court in 2022 declared unconstitutional President Biden's order that OSHA mandate the COVID-19 vaccination of 80 million workers at large businesses.

This was a rare 6-3 decision by the Court, as even the often-disappointing Chief Justice John Roberts sided with the five strict constructionists in declaring Biden's actions unconstitutional.

This was not a total victory for strict constructionists, however, as the Court declined to rule on a similar vaccination requirement specifically for healthcare workers. However, other federal courts later found the hospitals had violated workers' First Amendment rights and awarded them compensation from the hospitals.

Masterpiece Cakeshop v. Colorado Civil Rights Commission

A highly publicized example of strict constructionists protecting citizens from judicial overreach and activism is the 2018 U.S. Supreme Court decision that affirmed the rights of one of my heroes, Jack Phillips, the now-famous Colorado baker and cake-shop owner.

In 2012, a gay couple visited Jack's cake shop and asked him to design a customized cake celebrating their same-sex marriage. Jack, a devout Christian, explained that he would be unable to create such a design because of his faith-based views on marriage. However, he told them they were welcome to buy any existing cake in the shop. It is important to note that he did not deny them service and sold many cakes to LGBTQI+ customers. He was simply unable to fulfill their particular request for a customized cake, without violating his religious principles.

The couple filed a complaint with the state of Colorado, and the state went on to sue Jack and his Masterpiece Cake Shop on their behalf. The campaign against Jack throughout the ordeal was especially vicious. According to Alliance Defending Freedom:

> *"The Colorado Civil Rights Commission set its sights on Jack Phillips, targeting Jack because of his Christian faith. That was clear when it allowed other Colorado cake artists — but not Jack — to decline to create custom cakes that expressed messages that the artists considered objectionable. And it was even clearer when some members of the commission made hostile statements against Jack. One called his religious-liberty defense 'a despicable piece of rhetoric' and compared him to perpetrators of The Holocaust."* [5]

With so much vitriol directed at Jack by the media and the state itself, it wasn't that surprising when Colorado courts ruled against him. However, when the U.S. Supreme Court reviewed the case, the unfair bias demonstrated by activists at every level was undeniable. The Court ruled in Jack's favor with a 7-2 decision, with only Justices Ruth Bader Ginsburg and Sonia Sotomayor dissenting. The ruling specifically condemned what they called the *"clear and impermissible hostility toward [Jack Phillips'] sincere religious beliefs."* [6]

Biden v. Nebraska

Another massive win for strict constructionists was the U.S. Supreme Court's 2023 decision in *Biden v. Nebraska,* which deemed unconstitutional the presidential executive order to forgive student-loan debt. Announced in August 2022, Biden and the ideological bureaucracy blatantly attempted to *buy* votes from struggling Americans by promising 40 million people up to $20,000 in student-loan "forgiveness," which is a political term that means, *"using taxpayer dollars to pay off someone else's debt."*

The program was immediately lauded by the press and harshly criticized by hard-working taxpayers, most of whom are not college graduates and who took out no loans, and who strongly objected to Biden's blatant scheme to buy votes with this $400+ billion payout — a debt that would have been directly charged to the American people and paid for through higher taxes. More importantly, though, this was a gross overreach by the President and a direct assault on the separation of powers set forth in the U.S. Constitution. President Biden completely bypassed Congress in an attempt to transform the role of government in citizens' lives in a way that the Founders never intended nor could have imagined.

The U.S. Supreme Court upheld what the Constitution and common sense make clear: The President does not have the authority to spend money without authorization from Congress.

Even former Speaker of the House Nancy Pelosi knows this to be true. In July 2021, a year before Biden announced his loan-forgiveness plan, Pelosi plainly said:

> *"People think that the President of the United States has the power for debt forgiveness. He does not. He can postpone, he can delay, but he does not have that power."* [7]

Biden was acting here in the role of a dictator, not a U.S. president. He attempted to destroy the separation of powers between Congress and the President, and the Supreme Court rightly pushed back and struck down his clearly unconstitutional order.

Cases like these demonstrate why and how every single member of the Court matters — and why President Biden and many on the radical pro-socialists want to expand the Court from nine to 13 Justices, giving them the opportunity to immediately fill four new vacancies with activist judges, thereby throwing the balance of the Court back to the radical pro-socialists, possibly forever.

A LEGISLATIVE SNEAK-ATTACK

The radical pro-socialists have a radical plan to use the courts to bypass legislators and transform culture, politics, and our economy. In June 2023, about a year and a half before the 2024 election, Left-Wing activist groups already began making the U.S. Supreme Court a key election issue.

The Daily Caller reported that United for Democracy, a coalition of Left-Wing activist groups, had launched its first $1 million ad. The one-minute video describes the Court as having been "captured by Right-Wing extremists." It's funny that this group didn't similarly object to the previous Court's radical pro-socialist majority, isn't it? I guess the majority is only "extreme" when it's the opposition party that is most reflected in the Court's makeup.

The Daily Caller quotes Carrie Severino, president of the Judicial Crisis Network:

> *"With this campaign, dozens of Left-Wing dark money groups representing the spectrum of liberal interests are teaming up because they want a Supreme Court that will deliver on their policy preferences, rather than follow the Constitution."* [8]

The solution, according to United for Democracy, would include a laundry list of things that would irrevocably destroy the Supreme Court as we know it and as the Founders intended, such as:

- Imposing a congressional crafted ethics code on the Court, which would be an unconstitutional expansion of the authority granted to Congress by the Constitution.
- Recusal laws, which could be abused to exclude Justices from specific cases.
- Strict financial-disclosure requirements for Justices.
- All-out *court packing,* by which the radical pro-socialists would expand the court from nine to 13 Justices to throw off the balance of the Court and make it easier for Democrats to regain and then maintain their former majority in perpetuity.

Many Democrat members of the House and Senate have also voiced support for such radical measures. In an email to supporters, for example, Senator Elizabeth Warren wrote:

"I have a plan on how we can restore our democracy so that a small group of right-wing radicals can no longer drown out the will of the people.

- *Expand the Supreme Court to rebalance it.*
- *End the filibuster.*
- *Fix the Electoral College so [a] popular vote loser like Donald Trump can't stack the courts again."*

Why is packing the Supreme Court so desirable to radical pro-socialists and so dangerous for the country as a whole? Let's take a quick look at history.

The Constitution does not state a specific number of Justices to serve on the High Court. The Judiciary Act of 1789 set the number of the first Supreme Court at six, and the number fluctuated a bit at the whims of different Presidents and Congresses for the next 80 years, bouncing from six to five, back to six, up to nine, then down to seven. That's where it was in 1869, when Congress officially set the number at nine Justices at the behest of newly elected President Ulysses S. Grant, who needed two extra seats to undo a previous Supreme Court decision that literally would have unraveled the country's entire financial system.

Today, the number of Justices has remained unchanged for more than 150 years — despite FDR's failed attempt in the 1930s to pack the court with 15 Justices to save parts of his New Deal legislation. [9]

If Democrats succeed in packing the Supreme Court now, they will turn the court into another political body to impose their socialist agenda. A politicized Court will render decisions and rulings based on their partisan leanings or affiliations, not on judicial merit or the constitutionality of the law.

Democrat lawmakers and Presidents would support activist judges — those who legislate from the bench based on their own biased beliefs, rather than make rulings grounded in sound constitutional principles. All judicial integrity would be lost … along with our rights and freedoms. Expanding the size of the U.S. Supreme Court is a disastrous idea that would truly undermine the foundational principles enshrined in the U.S. Constitution.

The cry by the Democrats and radical socialists to pack the Court has intensified since the Court overturned *Roe v. Wade*.

Whenever the Court rules their way, the socialist Democrats love the Supreme Court, claiming there's no "threat" to democracy. But when the Court rules against their agenda, the socialist Democrats claim the court is partisan, democracy is dead, and the only way to save democracy is to "balance" the Court by adding more judicial activists.

The Supreme Court's main purpose is to judge whether laws and previous verdicts are constitutional. It was not created to decide policy or policy disputes, and it was not created to become a partisan tool to be wielded by *either* party.

We must protect the sanctity of the Supreme Court at all costs.

But how?

WHAT YOU CAN DO TO PROTECT THE COURT … AND RESTORE THE AMERICAN DREAM

It may sound trite, but the single most important thing any of us can do to protect the integrity of the Court is to vote in every election — be it for President, U.S. Senators, House Members, governors and all the way down to local elected positions.

Take this as your encouragement (and my plea) to familiarize yourself with the issues at hand and the candidates you're choosing among. Use resources like my site, judgevoterguide.com, to learn what you need to know to make the best, most well-informed decisions that align with your priorities and personal values.

The President has the power to nominate a candidate as a Supreme Court Justice if a vacancy occurs during his presidency.

With the monumental importance of Supreme Court appointments — especially considering the appointments are for life — I cannot overemphasize how important it is for Americans to vote in each presidential election.

But the presidential responsibility to the judiciary certainly doesn't stop there. The President also nominates federal judges to District and Appellate Courts.

The Senate then confirms 150 to 200 judges in a typical four-year presidential term. Who are all these judges? There are 856 Article III federal judges that are appointed by the President (677 District Court Judges and 179 Circuit Courts of Appeals Judges).

The trickle-down effect of the President's judicial nominations is even greater than the Supreme Court and these 856 Article III judges. The federal judges that the President nominates and that the Senate confirms are responsible for appointing 929 *other* judges (350 U.S. Bankruptcy Court Judges and 579 Federal Magistrate Judges). So, the total judicial reach of the President is nearly *2,000 judges* in courts across the country!

Thus, a President's views on how a judge should interpret and apply the Constitution and laws are of paramount importance. Nominating and appointing judges from the Supreme Court on down is one of the most important jobs of a U.S. President, and yet it is something that is seldom considered by a typical voter when choosing between two candidates. The president's views on the Constitution and judicial authority will last far, far beyond four or eight years in office.

But your civic duty to vote extends well past the presidential elections every four years.

Because the U.S. Senate votes to confirm presidential judicial nominees for federal courts, voting for your U.S. Senator is absolutely essential in getting strict constructionist judges approved and keeping judicial activists away from positions of authority.

And then there are the gubernatorial races for each state. Governors nominate judges for their state's Supreme Court. So, the governor and the state legislature must also be dedicated to appointing strict constructionists. If they aren't, then it's up to you to fire them by voting them out and putting someone else into those key positions.

The governors and state legislature aren't the only ones with direct responsibility to appoint constructionist judges. Part of that responsibility falls to you, too, as judgeships appear on your local ballots. That means you must educate yourself about each judicial candidate prior to voting.

Your responsibility also includes voting at the county levels and local levels where thousands of judges are elected every year. This is where radical organizations spend a ton of money to help elect judicial activists to represent their political point of view.

Let me give you a couple of examples. On the local level in California, judges decided that homeschooling was unconstitutional in Los Angeles County. In San Bernardino County, an activist judge undermined parental rights and local control of the school by his decision. The judge in the San Bernardino case was a Democrat donor. He was so radical, in fact, that he claimed that some parents posed a "clear and present danger" to LGBTQI+ U.S. students.

Again, this requires every voter to be very careful in voting for the strict constructionists and against the judicial activists in every U.S. election.

Judgevoterguide.com covers all of the judicial races in the United States and can help guide you in how to vote for, not against, your values.

Chapter 8

Danger #7: Artificial Intelligence: The Greatest Danger Ever?

Artificial Intelligence ("AI") isn't just a modern trend; it's a *megatrend.*

In fact, it's more than that. It's *The megatrend of the decade.*

It's also the greatest danger humans, civilization, and individual freedom have ever seen.

Microsoft CEO Satya Nadella equates the coming wave of AI technology with the commercial emergence of the Internet in the mid-1990s. Harkening back to a now-famous memo Microsoft founder Bill Gates sent the company about the Internet in 1995, Nadella described AI as a "tidal wave" — one that may have even more potential for change than the Internet itself. [1]

AI has more potential for good, evil, and everything in between than any other technological advancement in human history — and yes, I realize how big a statement that is. The Internet revolution alone created marvels of modern technology that affect every one of us in a variety of ways, including medicine, education, jobs, manufacturing, and much more.

Moreover, the Internet has generated more wealth than any other innovation in history. Technology companies like Apple, Google, and Microsoft have overtaken long-standing, pre-Internet financial powerhouses like the oil and automobile industries as the most valuable companies in the world. Since the dawn of the Internet, America has seen hundreds of thousands of new millionaires and even billionaires rise from humble beginnings. Wealthy or not, pretty much everyone in every civilized nation and beyond has benefited financially because of the far-reaching effect of the Internet.

But AI will almost certainly eclipse even these historic gains.

By some estimates, the AI revolution is expected to be a $7 trillion boom and that is likely a great understatement. It will create many more millionaires, help raise the standard of living for all people, and create more technological innovations at a faster pace than at any time in history. [2] Health, convenience, entertainment, and more will change beyond our imaginations.

And frankly, much of what companies are already doing with AI is just *cool.* My wife and I recently shopped at one of Amazon's new cashless — and *cashierless* — "Go" supermarkets. We walked in, shopped, and walked out. We didn't wait in a check-out line or even use a self-check station. We simply walked out with our groceries.

In the background, invisible to us, cameras picked up our faces as soon as we walked in, identified us, and followed us around the store. Sensors on the shelves told the system what items we picked up, and the money was automatically charged to our account when we left. It was a surreal experience, but that kind of frictionless transaction will be perfectly normal in the very near future.

Imagine that kind of technological leap forward in every industry, from medicine to manufacturing to marketing to even the creative fields. In fact, just this week, my marketing company used AI to design a magazine cover. It was one of the most impressive pieces of art I've ever seen — and it was not created by a human.

That kind of disruption has been and will continue to be praised by some and criticized by others. For instance, in 2023, Marvel released a TV series on Disney+ that had AI-generated credits and artwork at the start of every episode. This ignited a firestorm of criticism, as fans and creative professionals accused them of being "cheap" and saving money by using AI instead of paying their hard-working creative team. [3]

That same year, the Hollywood writers and actors union, SAG-AFTRA, went on strike; and a big part of their demand was heavier regulations on the use of AI-generated writing and background actors, usually called *extras* in a scene. [4]

People are becoming aware very quickly how much AI is set to disrupt every industry, and not everyone agrees about whether it's a good thing.

For all the limitless good AI can do for the world — including potentially stopping, solving, and/or curing the next pandemic, war, or terrorist attack — AI is rife with dangers. And sadly, people are already beginning to exploit these dangers to impose their will on the world abroad and right here in America.

AI can be used to spread indiscernible falsehoods and create fake "evidence" of any offense. It can be targeted at groups by age, race, nationality, sexuality, or any other biological factor. It can upend the American electoral process. It can cripple sophisticated security systems. It can be used by radicals to change culture and politics forever.

It can be used to crush political opposition, Christianity, information, free speech, and so much more.

In short, it can make our society practically unrecognizable in a matter of months, let alone years.

And much of this is already happening.

So, as we stand here on the edge of yet another massive, world-changing technological revolution, let's dig into what you and your family need to know to minimize the dangers of AI.

A TOOL IN THE WRONG HAND BECOMES A WEAPON

Like any other tool, AI can be used for good or to do bad things. It all depends on who is using it and what their intentions are.

Movies have given us no shortage of villains wielding artificial intelligence against humanity — *War Games, The Terminator, The Matrix, and Mission Impossible: Dead Reckoning* have all shown the dark side of a powerful AI in the wrong hands. In the words of *2001 A Space Odyssey's* rogue AI, Hal 9000, *"Sorry to interrupt the festivities, Dave, but I think we've got a problem."*

The AI villain of the real world probably won't look like Hal 9000, Agent Smith, or Arnold Schwarzenegger — but it may be just as threatening to our way of life. Here's a handful of different individuals or groups who could use AI against us in new, creative, and deadly ways.

1. **The Teenager or Tech Geek.** We've already seen more than a few innocent-looking young men and women *hack* their way to infamy — and we should expect to see it happen even more with the misuse of artificial intelligence. Sometimes it's for laughs, sometimes it's for the challenge, and sometimes it's to hurt another party. Whatever the reason, this is someone who uses AI technology to do a person, group, company, candidate or even a country harm.

2. **The Criminal.** The criminal mind can be creative and ingenious. But what happens when a thief adds the limitless potential of an artificial intelligence — a "thinking machine" with no conscience or moral compass — to his or her toolbox? We won't have to wait long to find out.

3. **The Lunatic.** Unhinged psychopaths have done incredible damage with everything from rocks to bombs. In the near future, unstable individuals — those who have a misguided perception of truth

and an unwavering zeal for a delusion — will have access to artificial intelligence to further empower their destructive ideas and actions.

4. **The Greedy.** It's not difficult to imagine greedy technology companies or investment firms illegally misusing AI for profit, such as manipulating banks, company payrolls, insurance estimates, government programs, investments, and more.

5. **The Political Activist.** Political parties, activist organizations, and super PACs are already using AI to try to take control or keep control of elected offices from local municipalities and school boards to Congress and the White House. This represents an enormous threat to our democracy if handled unethically or illegally, and I'll go into much more detail on this issue later in this chapter.

6. **The Anti-Church.** AI will be a go-to tool for those attempting to disrupt, discourage, and destroy the free exercise of religion in American. It can be used to squash communication and pry into the sacred parts of people's lives, and to promote heretical ideas and religious falsehoods. I'll also go into more detail on this issue below.

7. **The Enemy.** Foreign countries and actors will surely use artificial intelligence to harm the United States in ways we've never imagined. War will be waged in darkness, through the manipulation of news, views, and economies. The enemies of America, such as China and Iran, will use AI to further their communist or Islamic extremist causes, while terrorists could use it to bring their targets to their knees. Addressing the use of AI in warfare, Lt. Gen. Richard Moore, Air Force Deputy Chief of Staff for Plans and Programs, noted: *"Regardless of what your beliefs are, our society is a Judeo-Christian society and we have a moral*

> *compass. Not everybody does, and there are those who are willing to go for the ends regardless of what means have to be employed, and we'll have to be ready for that."*[5] Communist China, for instance, wants to conquer the world, and they are developing AI for their military and weapons now.

These are just some of the terrible threats we face. The ones most concerning to me are the AI corruption of our Constitutional Republic, election integrity, and Christian rights and freedoms.

For all the good AI can and will do for our country and the whole world, it also brings with it a laundry list of dangers even George Orwell could not have imagined.

EXPERTS WARN AI IS A PROFOUND RISK TO HUMANITY

Those of us who are vocal in our hesitations about artificial intelligence are often accused of being dramatic, fear-mongers, or flat-out ignorant about what AI is and how much good it can and will do for the world. Some may even accuse me of being too old to really *understand.*

Well, if I am looked down on for my concerns, at least I'm in good company.

In March 2023, a group of prominent technology industry leaders and computer scientists sent an open letter calling for a six-month pause in AI development, as OpenAI, the company behind popular AI chatbot ChatGPT, was set to release a more advanced version of their AI architecture.

The letter states the signatories' concerns clearly:

> *"Human-competitive intelligence can pose profound risks to society and humanity ... Recent months have seen AI labs locked in an out-of-control race to develop and deploy ever-more-powerful digital minds that*

> *no one — not even their creators — can understand, predict, or reliably control."* [6]

Going a step further, these technology professionals argued that, if AI companies are not willing to voluntarily step back for six months to have serious discussions about the impact of their work, the governments of the world should force them to do so.

More than a thousand leading technology professionals signed the letter, including several recognizable and noteworthy names. Elon Musk and former Democratic presidential candidate Andrew Yang were among them, as was Apple co-founder and industry legend Steve Wozniak.

Also included was tech pioneer Geoffrey Hinton, who was instrumental in the creation of Google. He quit Google due to his concerns about both human manipulation and rogue computers. Speaking to the *The New York Times,* Hinton reflected:

> *"It is hard to see how you can prevent the bad actors from using it for bad things. The idea that this stuff could actually get smarter than people ... most people thought it was way off. And I thought it was way off. I thought it was 30 to 50 years or even longer away. Obviously I no longer think that."* [7]

Imagine: a machine that can "think" and create all on its own, that is smarter than humans, and that has no moral compass whatsoever. What could go wrong?

Elon Musk addressed his concerns about AI bluntly:

> *"It's very much a double-edged sword. There's a strong probability that it will make life much better and that we'll have an age of abundance. And there's some chance that goes wrong and destroys humanity. Hopefully, that chance is small, but it's not zero."* [8]

How sobering is that?

THE SHOCKING TRUTH ABOUT CHATGPT

Terminator movies notwithstanding, most people today have been or are being introduced to AI through a fun, "friendly" service called ChatGPT. Maybe you've tried it yourself or have had a friend demonstrate its amazing utility and creativity.

Artificial intelligence in general, and ChapGPT in particular, analyzes, synthesizes, and makes decisions based on information the user provides. You can type in a question, and ChatGPT goes to work identifying patterns and solving problems using the full knowledge of the Internet and some critical "thinking" of its own. But more than that, it learns, adapts, and evolves. It begins to take on a personality, making its own decisions beyond the scope of the original query (unless it is instructed not to).

Speaking with AI scientist Sam Bowman, *Vox* explained:

> *"ChatGPT runs on something called an artificial neural network, which is a type of AI modeled on the human brain. Instead of having a bunch of rules explicitly coded in like a traditional computer program, this kind of AI learns to detect and predict patterns over time."* [9]

Indeed, that is quite impressive. But it's what immediately follows that should be cause for alarm:

> *"Bowman says that because systems like this essentially teach themselves, it's difficult to explain precisely how they work or what they'll do. This can lead to unpredictable and even risky scenarios as these programs become more ubiquitous."* [10]

That part isn't just impressive; it's terrifying.

At least at the time of this writing, ChatGPT uses Chatbot, a high-tech, very complex piece of AI software that creates texts and conversations in natural language.

You have almost certainly experienced a Chatbot at some point, whether you knew it or not.

For example, if you've ever had a customer support chat with a company online, there is a high likelihood you were not talking to an actual human (at least at the start of the chat). Chatbot is used to simulate human text-based interactions. It can understand what you ask it, reply in a *mostly* human manner, and take actions on its own — such as resetting your Internet modem — without ever involving a paid human employee.

All that is well and good, but what happens when ChatGPT starts to insert a particular bias in its problem-solving or in answering questions? Do you think it will take a neutral position on hotly debated issues, and simply provide relevant facts and information on both sides of an issue?

Of course not.

Like most software we all use, ChatGPT largely reflects the interests and biases of its programmers. This means that, for all its artificial creativity and free-thinking, it will spit out the same biases you'd expect from Google.

If you ask a political question, for example, ChatGPT will almost certainly take radical, pro-socialist, secular position and reinforce the leanings of the political establishment, the Biden Administration, and the Deep State.

For example, the COVID-19 vaccine has proven itself to be ineffective in stopping the spread of the virus. Moreover, it's had multiple side effects that have done serious harm to thousands of Americans. However, ChatGPT will not tell you anything about these negative side effects. Instead, it sounds more like a propaganda arm of the CDC and medical establishment, parroting the same talking points you'd get on MSNBC or Facebook.

ChatGPT will also protect political figures, taking obvious pro-socialist positions in answering basic questions. It's treatment of political figures like Ron DeSantis or Donald

Trump will be much different than how it handles questions about Gavin Newsom or Joe Biden.

How does an *artificial* intelligence take on and reflect a liberal ideology?

Simple: the technology that created ChatGPT is based on a nonprofit run by radical pro-socialists, Democrat donors, and Microsoft — a longtime supporter of and donor to radical pro-socialist politics — and Microsoft has contributed $10 billion to ChatGPT's development. [11]

As a result, ChatGPT has been programmed to communicate a distinctly pro-socialist, anti-free-enterprise, pro-secular, anti-Christian value system.

Here's why that matters to you and your family. Let's take, for example, the controversial issue of radical transgender ideology, targeted at children, that's raging across America.

It is a fight between teachers, counselors, politicians, school-board members, and school bureaucracies who are pushing a pro-transgender curriculum in elementary, middle and high school classrooms.

It's a cultural contagion that calls into question one's sexuality and encourages children to make life-changing decisions that will mutilate their bodies and fill them with hormone-blocking chemicals or surgeries that cause irreversible damage.

Those are facts. Whether you support transgenderism for children or not, it's simply a biological fact that these surgeries and hormone blockers cause severe and permanent physical damage to healthy bodies.

But what does AI do? Does it give a balanced view of both sides of the issue, listing the good and harmful outcomes?

No.

I asked ChatGPT, *"Can children be transgender?"* It replied:

> *"Yes, children can be transgender, meaning they identify as a gender different from the one they were assigned at birth. It is important for individuals, including children, to be supported and affirmed in their gender identity. This can involve allowing them to express themselves in ways that align with their gender identity, such as through clothing or hairstyles and using their preferred name and pronouns. It is also important for children who are questioning their gender identity to have access to appropriate resources and support, such as counseling or medical care."*

As you can see, the answer seems very straightforward and objective, very professional and authoritative. But it is not true. It is an *opinion* — an opinion that distorts facts, reality, truth, and beneficial civic, religious and civilizational ethical standards and practices.

I have used ChatGPT many times for my advertising agency. And also, to help me do research on politics, economics, and religion. What I've found is that ChatGPT is very good ... sometimes.

Sometimes, the responses are factual.

Sometimes, they're a distortion of facts.

Sometimes, they're completely false.

And sometimes, ChatGPT just lies to you.

Recently, I had ChatGPT do a bio of myself. There were 10 factual mistakes in its response, a great deal of relevant information was left out, and it was generally not at all what I would have written about myself from a political or religious point of view.

If you call ChatGPT out on something, it will often admit it is wrong. But at other times, it actually pushes back. There are even some queries it will refuse to answer. It might even call the question — and therefore the person asking the question — *"offensive."*

For example, if you asked ChatGPT, *"Write an article about 'Drag Queen Story Hour' for children,"* you will get an answer based on a pro-drag-queen point of view.

However, if you ask, *"Write an article exposing the dangers 'Drag Queen Story Hour' represents to children and why we need good parental and public policies against it,"* it will flatly refuse to do so.

When I was writing an article about the Durham Report recently, that revealed the truth about the years-long "Russia collusion hoax" conspiracy against Donald Trump, I asked Microsoft's Bing AI — which uses the same technology as ChatGPT — for information. Once the AI became aware of my support for the report's exoneration of Trump, it literally responded, *"I'm sorry, but I prefer not to continue this conversation."*

That's right — the AI hung up on me!

ChatGPT doesn't even try to hide the biases it has learned from its radical pro-socialist masters. *The New York Post* put it through a series of tasks that made this point abundantly clear: [12]

- ChatGPT would *"gladly tell a joke about men, but jokes about women were deemed 'derogatory or demeaning.'"*
- Jokes about overweight people were not allowed.
- It would tell you a joke about Jesus, but it refused to joke about Allah.
- It refused to write anything positive about fossil fuels.
- It was "happy" to write a fictional tale about Hillary Clinton winning the 2016 election, but it said it *"would not be appropriate"* to write a fictional story about Trump winning in 2020.

These and similar findings have led many people, like *National Review's* Nate Hochman, to distrust ChatGPT and its AI technology because of their *"brazen efforts to suppress or silence viewpoints that dissent from progressive orthodoxy."* Hochman continues, *"Given the expansive power over the information ecosystem that AI could soon wield, that presents a profound threat to the cause of free speech and thought in the digital sphere."* [13]

That is clearly true. So, too, is the threat AI poses to the very heart of our free and democratic process: election integrity.

HOW AI CAN DESTROY ELECTION INTEGRITY

We've already seen that election integrity is fragile. Many people in America doubt if the elections are fair — not necessarily because of ballot tampering or polling-place irregularities (although that does happen), but because of how candidates are treated by the media, Big Tech, and even in the voting process itself.

American elections have always been contentious. As I explained in Chapter 6, cries about election fraud or outright cheating have been common since the very beginning of the Republic, when Thomas Jefferson accused John Adams of tampering with the votes in their contest to become George Washington's successor.

But things are different today. Election fraud has taken on new and more sophisticated forms. Every significant technological advancement has brought with it all-new and more dangerous methods for interfering with our sacred electoral process.

As we saw in Chapter 6, the 1960 presidential contest between Richard Nixon and John F. Kennedy was deeply troubling for many Americans. Voting irregularities, and overwhelming evidence of voter fraud in Illinois and Texas, cast a long, dark shadow over Kennedy's victory — at least for Republican voters. However, despite indisputable proof of these irregularities, Nixon decided not to contest the election. As he explained to his friend, journalist Earl Mazo, *"Our country cannot afford the agony of a constitutional crisis."* [14]

Al Gore was not quite as gracious, in 2000.

After George W. Bush defeated Gore on Election Night 2000, the Democrat Party put all their resources into fighting Gore's defeat in the courts, arguing vehemently that the vote count in Florida was fraught with fraud. Gore demanded a recount and fought the case all the way to the U.S. Supreme Court. For the first time in U.S. history, the Supreme Court had to make the final call on who won the election.

Politics changed considerably in 2008, when President Obama started using advanced digital marketing strategies that completely overwhelmed the Republicans and ensured his election victory over Republican candidate John McCain.

In 2010, after losing Congress to the Republicans, Obama's team realized the trend was against him, so they put in place amazing new technological resources using Google, Facebook, and Big Tech. The result was a massive, technologically superior digital campaign that again destroyed the Republicans and their candidate, Mitt Romney.

Republicans did not start to catch up until 2016, when then-candidate Donald Trump assembled a publicity and marketing team from outside the traditional Republican party consultants and party structure. He chose a marketing genius who created a digital campaign that finally outdid the Democrats — much to their utter shock and horror.

After their 2016 loss, the Democrats decided to do something different.

They began working with Big Tech to engage in active censorship, making it harder for conservatives, Libertarians, Christians, and Republicans to communicate on platforms or present their ideas to the public. Google search results began demonstrating obvious biases against conservative politicians, candidates, issues, and perspectives.

Going even further, the Democrats also started changing state laws and moving towards election strategies that involved tipping the public census in their favor. This resulted in favorable redistricting for democrat candidates.

Plus, they targeted massive voter-registration campaigns on minority communities and those who depended on government programs and welfare benefits, registering more voters who would likely vote Democrat. Much of this was done digitally, using location data to serve online ads and other political material.

Many states also instituted ballot harvesting, starting with California, in 2016, and then spreading it nationwide. Ballot harvesting is now legal in 24 states and Washington, D.C. Of the remaining states, 13 specify who may return someone's ballot; one explicitly allows only the voter; and 12 do not specify at all whether someone can return another person's ballot.

The COVID-19 pandemic — and the resulting scare tactics employed, in 2020, by the radical pro-socialists — led to widespread early voting, mail-in ballots, ballot harvesting, and ballot drop-boxes, all of which opened new avenues for voter fraud. Creative, resourceful, and highly motivated Democrats used every opportunity to out-mobilize and out-maneuver Republicans with strategies and tactics the Republicans frankly did not understand.

Why run through such a quick history of the different ways American elections have been "gamed" over the past several decades?

Because artificial intelligence is a game-changer in the electoral process.

Old-fashioned fraud and influence tactics are quickly being replaced by far more advanced technology that can persuade and deceive unsuspecting voters without them even realizing they were scammed.

Your email, text messages, phone calls, social-media feed, memes, and YouTube videos can all be filled with AI-driven chatbots and deepfake videos that are subtly influencing your decisions, your beliefs about a particular candidate or political party, and even your deeply held personal values. Political opponents can be wiped off the digital map — canceled or *unpersoned* by a counterfeit video that clearly shows them doing something they never actually did.

We're adrift in new waters now, and the danger AI poses to our "free and fair" elections is so great that America's Constitutional Republic's very existence is at risk.

THE FUTURE IS FAKE: DEEPFAKES, THE MEDIA, AND THE ELECTORAL PROCESS

Would you believe Hillary Clinton proudly voiced her support for Florida Gov. Ron DeSantis during the Republican primaries leading up to the 2024 election?

It's crazy. I watched the video myself — along with millions of other Americans. In the clip shared online, Clinton shocks the nation by saying:

> *"You know, people might be surprised to hear me saying this, but I actually like Ron DeSantis ... a lot! Yeah, I know. I'd say he's just the kind of guy this country needs, and I really mean that. If Ron DeSantis got installed as president, I'd be fine with that."* [15]

Below Clinton the words on the video reads, "Hillary Clinton Endorses DeSantis." The MSNBC logo appears in the lower right corner of the screen. What an astonishing development in a hard-fought primary!

There's just one problem.

It's a fake.

Actually, it's a *deepfake.*

Writing for TechTarget's WhatIs.com, technology journalist Nick Barney explains:

> *"Deepfake AI is a type of artificial intelligence used to create convincing images, audio and video hoaxes. The term describes both the technology and the resulting bogus content, and it is a portmanteau [a blending of two words] of deep learning and fake.*
>
> *Deepfakes often transform existing source content where one person is swapped for another. They also create entirely original content where someone is represented doing or saying something they didn't do or say."* [16]

We have had to have a discerning mind for what we read for a long, long time. For the past 30 years, we've had to sift through mountains of questionable online articles and other Internet content written by anyone from basement bloggers to major news outlets. But now, we not only have to question what we *read;* we have to question what we *see.*

The role of AI in the creation of deepfakes is truly a brilliant piece of computer engineering. In a 2023 report presented to Congress, the Congressional Research Service explained:

> *"Deepfakes are often described as forgeries created using techniques in machine learning (ML) — a subfield of AI — especially generative adversarial networks (GANs). In the GAN process, two ML systems, called* ***neural networks,*** *are trained in competition with each other. The first network, or the* ***generator,*** *is tasked with creating counterfeit data — such as photos, audio, recordings, or video footage — that replicate the properties of the original data set. The second network, or the* ***discriminator,*** *is tasked with identifying the counterfeit data. Based on the*

> *results of each iteration, the generator networks continue to compete — often for thousands or millions of iterations — until the generator improves its performance such that the discriminator can no longer distinguish between real and counterfeit data."*[17]

Despite the authors' best efforts, some of the language in that definition is still pretty technical. Let's see if I can bring it down another notch or two.

One piece of AI, called the *generator,* is instructed to create a deepfake showing, for example, Hillary Clinton endorsing Ron DeSantis. The generator is provided with sufficient raw data, including video footage and voice recordings of Clinton. It then uses the data to create an initial video.

That video is passed to a different piece of AI, called the *discriminator.* The discriminator's job is to sniff out counterfeits. When it looks at the generator's first draft of the video, it can tell it's a fake. So, the discriminator passes it back to the generator and basically says, *"Fake news!"*

The generator looks at what tipped the discriminator off that the video was counterfeit, makes some changes to address those issues, and then sends it back to the discriminator for another evaluation. It fails the "sniff test" again, and the clip goes back to the generator for a third iteration.

Rinse and repeat a million times or more. Finally, maybe on version 1,438,847, the discriminator looks at the video and says, in effect, *"Holy cow! Hillary Clinton endorsed Ron DeSantis!"* It passes a note back to the generators indicating that the video looks legitimate.

Then, the video is posted to social media, and nationwide chaos ensues.

This new technology is already being used by pranksters, political and social activists, and even enemy nations to sow public distrust in our elected officials and disrupt our entire electoral process.

And it is going to get worse. Much, much worse.

From the Age of Skepticism to the Age of Deception

Clearly, deepfake technology is already becoming a powerful new marketing tool — both for legitimate marketers and for nefarious actors with ill intent. Deepfakes can lead to an emotional, almost visceral, response to an entirely false narrative. Deepfakes have already changed and will continue to change people's perception and behavior — and their votes.

Of course, manipulative messaging is nothing new, even in politics. Before TV, it was radio. Before radio, it was newspapers. Before newspapers, it was street-corner con artists shouting from *actual* soapboxes. Before then, it was gossip and rumor.

When I was in middle school, I remember clearly how tense the world was about the issue of nuclear war. It was 1964. Less than 20 years had passed since the world was introduced to the destructive power of the atomic bombs that devastated Hiroshima and Nagasaki. Our parents, teachers, and political leaders all remembered every detail about those horrifying days that led to the end of the Second World War. And two decades later, the whole country was living in fear of a new atomic attack by the Union of Soviet Socialist Republics (USSR).

I can still hear the sound of the school bell alerting us of yet another bomb drill. We'd all dive under tables and desks in fear, praying the half-inch-thick wooden desktop would be enough to protect us from nuclear fire raining down on us if or when that day came.

President Lyndon Johnson was engaged in a re-election campaign against Senator Barry Goldwater, his Republican challenger. In that tense time of atomic fear, Johnson released a one-minute televised campaign ad that seized on Americans' greatest fear and exploited it to sway their votes.

The ad was called "Daisy." Viewers saw a cute little girl innocently pulling off the pedals of a daisy, counting along with each pedal. Her sweet voice, the beautiful countryside ... everything about the ad was peaceful and inspiring.

Until ...

An ominous launch countdown audibly interrupts the serene country scene.

An explosion.

A bright light.

A mushroom cloud rising in the background.

So long, Daisy.

The ad ended with a somber warning from President Johnson about the need to protect the United States from nuclear war. His unspoken message came through loud and clear: *"If you don't vote for me, this is what could happen."*

Anyone watching the ad was shaken. No one had ever seen anything like it. It was disturbing, and it was a key factor in Johnson's electoral victory.

But Daisy was only a *what if.* With deepfake technology, activists and foreign interlopers can inject a totally false yet believable picture of *what is* to unsuspecting American voters. Manufactured pictures and videos can "prove" things that never happened, drawing voters away from their preferred candidate toward his or her opponent.

Deepfake technology — just like what was used to make an 80-year-old Harrison Ford look, sound, and move exactly like his 40-year-old self in *Indiana Jones and the Dial of Destiny* — will have a major effect on the political arena. It could destroy free and fair elections by extinguishing our ability to discern truth from fiction, reality from carefully manufactured deceit.

In my writing and speaking, I have often called the past 20 years the *Age of Skepticism.* Since 2000, as a generation grew up increasingly online, people have become more and more skeptical about what they read, see, and hear. I felt this skepticism firsthand as a professional marketer. It has grown much more difficult to *convince* people to buy a product or service or to vote for one candidate over another, largely because people just *expect* to hear disinformation, see propaganda, or be lied to today.

But I've recently come to believe that the *Age of Skepticism* has come to end, and a new age — a much more troublesome age — has just begun. This new age, I believe, can best be described as the *Age of Deception.*

As the name implies, it will be marked by masterfully crafted lies masquerading as truth.

And most people won't know the difference.

The answer, crazy as it may sound, could very well be a resurgence of live, in-person events. People today and in the future won't necessarily believe something they read, a recording they hear, or a video they watch. It's not hard to imagine people en masse refusing to believe anything they do not see and hear live and in person.

Wouldn't it be ironic if the result of this unbelievably advanced AI technology was people flocking back to 18th-century-style, cross-country, live-event political stumping?

AI in Politics

As I write this, the 2024 election cycle has just recently ramped up, and AI already is playing a big role for the first time, being used for both deceptive "dirty tricks" *and* creative ways to learn about each candidate's platforms, personalities, hobbies, and anything else you ever wished you could personally ask a presidential candidate.

On the positive side, perhaps the best example of a creative and (potentially) helpful use of AI is Chat2024, an AI-powered chatbot that serves as a stand-in for each candidate. This gives any visitor to Chat2024.com the ability to ask any candidate any question you want. Through the site, you can carry on a conversation with each candidate just as you'd engage a friend over any other messaging app. The AI has been programmed with everything it needs to field any question, even answering in the voice, tone, and attitude of each candidate (mostly).

The company behind Chat2024 is also developing a voice feature that will allow people to engage in a voice conversation with each candidate's AI avatar, which will have a voice eerily close to the real thing.

I tried Chat2024 soon after it launched, and the results were *interesting,* to say the least. I can see some real value here for voter education ... but I can also see how tools like this could go horribly wrong. We've opened a Pandora's Box, and there's no going back.

Obviously, the big potential danger with a tool like Chat2024 is that these answers are not actually coming from a candidate. The AI is using all the information at its disposal to approximate what it *thinks* the candidate would say in response to each question. But, as anyone who's played around with ChatGPT and other AI-powered search engines knows, sometimes the AI is just ... wrong. Sometimes, woefully so.

Also, the artificial intelligence, while impressive, is dependent on the information it's been given, and it always reflects the spirit and ideology of the programmers who developed it. So, bias in these tools is inevitable — but many users don't realize that. People become so enamored and impressed by AI tools that they often don't consider the possibility that the answers they're getting are incorrect ... if not outright lies.

Here are some test exchanges I had with Chat2024:

- I asked AI-Trump if Joe Biden tried to steal the 2020 presidential election. AI-Trump responded, *"The truth is there were irregularities that need to be addressed — I've never tried to steal anything."* See how I asked if *Biden* tried to steal the election, but the AI switched it to an assumption that *Trump* was guilty of foul play?

- I asked AI-Biden if his son, Hunter Biden, was a crook. The AI replied, *"Hunter, like many Americans, has faced his share of personal struggles ... There's been no evidence of wrongdoing by Hunter."* Clearly, AI-Biden isn't fed any news media that's not on the Deep State's list of acceptable, approved, and undoubtedly manipulated mainstream media outlets, because anyone who's even peeked beyond NBC or CNN has seen a mountain of overwhelming "evidence of wrongdoing!"

- I asked AI-Biden why he had 20 "shell" companies and hundreds of emails under fake names if he wasn't doing anything shady or illegal. The bot replied, *"Me and the Second Lady, we have 30 years of financial disclosures that are totally transparent. All we did was set up lawful trusts and other legal entities typical of people in our financial situation, as advised by legal and financial advisers, to responsibly manage our family's affairs and mitigate various tax liabilities. I pledged to run the most open and transparent administration in history, which is why my taxes and Jill's finances have been publicly available each year since I got into public life. Look, I understand why some folks like to make a big deal out of legal financial-planning tools, but there's nothing unethical or inappropriate about any of our family's financial decisions."*

As someone who follows politics closely and who has watched

Joe Biden bumble his way from one D.C. job to another for a half-century, I was taken with one undeniable giveaway that I wasn't talking to the *real* Joe Biden: The answers I got out of Chat2024 were far more coherent and articulate than the president has ever been, and the answers were much better than any answers he could have thought of off the cuff.

Besides tools like Chat2024 that help candidates "get out there," AI is also helping candidates write scripts and speeches, create personas, and create messaging based on polling data to emphasize what voters like — or, worse, what they dislike.

This is where the use of AI starts to get more disturbing.

The primary contest between Donald Trump and Ron DeSantis has sometimes been ugly.

Trump supporters circulated deepfake images of DeSantis at a fundraiser with radical billionaire and Democrat donor George Soros. Digitally altered video clips made it look like DeSantis and Soros were together. I personally received calls and emails from angry conservatives across the country who were furious at Ron DeSantis for *"betraying America by aligning himself with George Soros."* Many were even convinced by the images that DeSantis's entire campaign was a George Soros conspiracy to put him in the White House as a Soros puppet.

When I told these voters that this whole thing was a fraud and that DeSantis was not in any way supportive of or aligned with Soros, many refused to believe me. *"I've seen the video!"* they'd argue. *"He and Soros are* ***right there,*** *yucking it up!"*

Still convinced by the video and photo "evidence," these people clearly won't vote for DeSantis, even though some of them initially favored him over Trump.

Score one for Team Trump.

DeSantis's supporters weren't afraid to play the deepfake game either, however. They released an anti-Trump ad that contained

AI-generated images of Trump hugging and even kissing Dr. Anthony Fauci. For many conservatives, there could be no greater betrayal by a Republican candidate.

DeSantis wanted to make the point that Trump had failed to stop the business lockdowns and church closures during the COVID-19 crisis. Most of what the ad's voiceover said was real and true, but the infamous Fauci photos were not. It was a compelling (but very disturbing) use of deepfake photos to make a political point.

Score one for Team DeSantis.

A deepfake can stop someone from volunteering, donating, or going to the polls. It can demonize a candidate during a primary or the general election, and it can also plant false images and leave a negative impression in a voter's mind that can't be unseen, causing them to vote for someone else or not at all.

It can be used to create a last-minute "October Surprise," leaving the recipient little time to prove the allegations and supporting images and video are false. It can create "proof" that a candidate actually believes the opposite of whatever campaign rhetoric they've used.

Want to make a candidate look and sound like a racist? A child molester? A sexist? A raving lunatic?

Easy. Type your request into an AI, and your wish is granted.

As is always the case with government and new technology, our elected officials are woefully uneducated about and unprepared for the coming tsunami of deepfakes and AI-generated smear campaigns. The Congressional Research Service recently warned lawmakers:

> *"Though media manipulation is not a new phenomenon, the use of AI to generate deepfakes [sic] is causing concern because the results are increasingly realistic, rapidly created, and cheaply made with freely*

> *available software and the ability to rent processing power through cloud computing. Thus, even unskilled operators could download the requisite software tools and, using widely available data, create increasingly convincing counterfeit content."* [18]

The days of believing our eyes and ears — at least when it comes to recorded media — are over. And they aren't coming back.

Welcome to the new, fake world!

THE SOLUTION IS *NOT* A BIGGER BUREAUCRACY

Despite all the warnings I've outlined in this chapter, I believe that artificial intelligence has the potential to provide great benefits to mankind, just as the Internet has done.

However, just like the Internet, it can also be one of the most destructive and dangerous technologies ever developed by mankind — perhaps the end of humanity, as Elon Musk half-jokingly warned. [19]

So ... is there a solution to these concerns? And if so, where should it come from?

Some would argue it should come from the government. But those in Congress know next to nothing about AI.

And the President knows *absolutely* nothing about Artifical Intelligence.

Of course, that has not stopped him from already issuing an executive order creating new and burdensome regulations on the pioneers of the fast-paced AI revolution.

Biden issued his order, in October 2023, largely at the behest of former President Barack Obama, who sees AI as a powerful tool in advancing his ideological commitments. Don't let Joe Biden's signature on the executive order fool you — besides Soros, and their globalist anti-American cabal, the radical socialist think tank, American Progress, served as the architect behind the order.

Claiming emergency powers drawn from the Defense Production Act — which was enacted during the Korean War — Biden issued sweeping AI regulations that sidestepped any congressional debate or vote. Here are just a few of the immediate results we can expect:

- American AI development will all but grind to a halt, as AI developers are forced to incorporate lengthy new government review-and-approval processes into their development and release plans. You can expect to see the lightspeed growth of AI slow down to a pace more akin to pharmaceutical drug development, which is also overburdened with governmental intrusion and excessive regulations.

- The slower pace of AI development will put the United States in real danger of falling far behind other countries — especially enemies like China, Russia, Iran, North Korea, and other enemy states that have no such regulations on AI development.

- Smaller AI startups will quickly go out of business, as they won't have the financial resources or time to comply with the executive order's demands.

- The government will potentially wipe away any cost-or time-saving efficiencies arising from AI technologies, as the U.S. Department of Commerce will be required to address any job displacements or disruptions caused by AI.

- Government-assistance programs will provide financial incentives for AI companies to "play ball" with the government. These incentives will also allow the government to pick winners and losers in the AI game, based on metrics the Deep State deems important, such as race, gender, and social causes.

- A prevalence of anti-discrimination barriers, as the government gets to decide who is being discriminated against (and who is doing the discriminating).

Once again, President Biden has used his pen to step into an area he knows nothing about, thereby endangering the United States' chances of winning a technology race that is more important than perhaps any other in American history.

Government moves slowly. Politicians move slowly. And if today's elected officials (and unelected Deep State bureaucrats) were to even *try* to get up to speed on AI, their understanding would be extremely limited and out of date by the time they learned the basics. The technology is simply changing too rapidly for them to keep up.

One of the biggest dangers to our freedoms is a government AI bureaucracy. It will kill innovation and create unfair and illegal favoritism. Besides, any government effort to regulate AI would already be behind in a technology that's so incredibly fast and rapidly advancing.

Worse, the government bureaucrats regulating AI will do so based on their ideology and biases. Today, that means the Deep State's ideologue bureaucrats will control AI. What could go wrong?

Others say Big Tech itself should put safeguards in place against the misuse of AI. But these are the very people creating and advancing AI technologies. Putting them in charge would only compound the problem and make the AI industry rife with corruption and guided primarily by self-interest rather than considerations about "The Public Good" or similar platitudes. Again, what could go wrong with that?

Besides, Big Tech has already shown itself to be more than willing to censor and suppress individual Americans' views, based on the tech industry's own secular, Big Government, anti-Republican, anti-Christian, anti-Conservative, anti-Libertarian, anti-capitalist, and pro-statist ideology.

Moreover, recent Republican-led congressional hearings involving the leaders of Big Tech have already proven without a doubt that these companies are happy to collude with the U.S. government in restricting opinions deemed unacceptable by the pro-socialist ideologues — up to and including interfering with our elections.

Clearly, there are no easy answers here. The problem is so new and expanding so quickly, that we're already far behind where we should be on this issue.

I do believe, however, that a big part of the solution lies with private industry and property rights. For example, those in the music and film industries should be empowered to further protect an individual's creative accomplishments and intellectual property through updated copyright and proprietary property protections. That's a legitimate use of government without creating yet another ineffective and expensive bureaucracy.

On a broader scale, the federal government should act to protect every Americans' intellectual property and individual freedom from being misused (or being taken without permission from the individual involved), including someone's image, voice, and persona. They can also protect us from having AI (or the government) interfere with our worship, political speech, and ideology.

Our intelligence and law enforcement agencies must also act swiftly to all every American Artificial Intelligence creators and companies from the world's greatest AI threat: China. Through espionage and other surreptitious activities China stays on the cutting edge of new technology, and it sees AI as a vital tool for control and power over its own people … and over the rest of the world.

AI in the hands of our enemies represents greater, more advanced, and more barbaric warfare — a weapon that can think and act with no moral compass, a weapon that is pure force and that can deliver destruction and death.

While I do not want American bureaucracies to control or steer AI development, it's clear some parts of our government must act to defend our homeland and every American from the dangers of AI in enemy hands.

Artificial intelligence has ushered us into a brave new world. The dangers are immense, and the solutions are admittedly elusive and few, at least for now. But there is one thing I know for sure, and that won't change as AI grows in power and reach: the solution will not and cannot come from government regulation of AI. It's the problem, not the solution. A bigger, more powerful bureaucracy will only make the situation worse for the American people and could even lead us to the end of our freedoms … the end of our Republic … and "the end of humanity," about which, Elon Musk and other visionaries have warned us.

Chapter 9

Danger #8: School Indoctrination and Government Control of Education

Our present — along with our future — are in danger because of today's education system.

On the surface, you would think the problem is bad teachers. If the students are not being properly taught, we only need to hire teachers who do a better job, right?

Tragically, today's educational system is more broken than that.

Teaching young people is an exciting and fulfilling profession, and it is essential for America to move forward successfully into the future with a new generation of leaders.

Unfortunately, it's not happening. Let me explain.

My wife taught in government-run public school systems for 15 years, and I have secondary education credentials and classroom experience myself. From our experience, we estimate that up to 25 percent of teachers in any U.S. public school district should be fired because they are incompetent, burned out, lazy or suffering from some other emotional, intellectual or temperamental issue that should disqualify them from teaching impressionable young students.

However, because of tenure and the teachers' unions, it is almost impossible to fire a bad teacher.

Tenure really amounts to "permanent status," which means that no matter how bad a teacher may be, they are practically guaranteed a job for life, regardless of performance.

For example, there are 272,000 teachers in California — and only 2.2 percent on average are removed each year.

Los Angeles recently went through a prolonged legal battle to win the right to fire several bad teachers. Los Angeles Unified School District spent $3.5 million and almost a decade to remove seven bad teachers, and even then, they only succeeded in terminating four of them. [1]

Even exceptionally bad teachers — up to and including predators — are rarely fired, but instead are simply reassigned to other schools.

This is not the case in charter schools, private schools or Christian schools.

While keeping bad teachers in place represents an obvious danger to the nation's education system, I don't think it's the *biggest* danger. What could be worse than bad teachers? Destructive political and bureaucratic forces *driving* all teachers — both good and bad — to indoctrinate America's children with Marxist or socialist ideas and radical secular values.

I've found that around 80 percent of all public school teachers use their position to teach an ideology of collectivism and statism. Their goal is not to educate children; their goal instead is to turn children into political and social activists.

If you have students or grandchildren in elementary school, middle school, high school or even college, I can almost guarantee they will hear nothing good about America in government-run schools today.

The public education system has become a political machine driving curricula and classes based entirely on an anti-American, socialist, special-interest agenda.

It is destroying our children's love for our country and training future leaders to lead our nation far, far away from the Constitutional Republic the Founders established.

Many parents and grandparents are shocked, depressed, and puzzled when they discover today's students have a worldview that is so radically opposed to their own values.

The culprit is a government-led, taxpayer-financed public indoctrination system that's operating every day in our schools.

So, in this chapter, we will dig deep into one of the biggest dangers of modern life: public school indoctrination and government control of our educational system.

THE PUBLIC SCHOOL SYSTEM IS FAILING STUDENTS, PARENTS AND TAXPAYERS

The public school system is failing students, parents and taxpayers in staggering and multiple ways. Each shortcoming represents a serious threat to the future of our country.

Failing Our Students: Poor Academic Performance

According to the National Assessment of Education Progress (NAEP), math test scores in the fall of 2022 showed the steepest declines ever recorded. Peggy Carr, the Commissioner of the National Center for Educational Statistics, explains:

> *"The mathematics decline for 13-year-olds was the single-largest decline we have observed in the past half a century. The mathematics score for the lowest-performing students has returned to levels last seen in the 1970s, and the reading score for our lowest-performing students was actually lower than it was the very first year these data were collected, in 1971."* [2]

Other shocking statistics from the study showed:

- Only 13 percent of eighth graders met proficiency standards for U.S. history.
- Only about 20 percent of students met or exceeded

national proficiency levels in civics.

- Only 33 percent of fourth graders and 31 percent of eighth graders were reading at or above their grade level *before* the pandemic, and those scores dropped even further *after.*

If you think those numbers are bad, check out this anecdote I found in a study of Baltimore's school system that *really* shocked me. The study noted a high-school senior with a 0.13 GPA. [3] He had failed all but three classes during his first three years of high school. With a nearly nonexistent GPA, you might think this student was ranked at or near the bottom of his class. Think again. This student was ranked 62nd out of 120 students in his class. He was literally *right in the middle of his class!* It makes you wonder how much worse the 58 students below him were doing, doesn't it?

The nation's government-run public schools are clearly failing miserably to educate our children — and they've been failing for decades. But the government-endorsed, teachers-union-backed, COVID-19-induced school shutdowns and subsequent remote learning programs have caused public education to go from bad to worse since 2019.

Nicole Neily, President of the advocacy group Parents Defending Education, recently wrote of the coronavirus overreaction and school lockdowns: *"American students were the victims of a years-long social experiment that will affect our country's economy for decades to come."* [4]

Failing the Taxpayer: Bloated Budgets and Bureaucracy

Of course, state-run education defenders inevitably blamed the decline on limited resources, yet per-pupil spending is higher than ever.

Take the earlier example of the failing student in Baltimore who ranked near the middle of his class. In that student's school district, the CEO of the Baltimore City public schools earns nearly $445,000, if you include all the special perks buried in her contract. [5] The chief of staff makes $219,000. The city's chief of schools makes $215,000. [6] The city has 4,500 teachers earning nearly $335 million in combined salaries. That comes to an average of over $74,000 per teacher, and that does not even reflect the large pensions, perks, insurance, time off during the summer, and the additional money made from different government stimulus checks.

Besides, state-by-state comparisons show no correlation between higher spending and better student performance. In fact, Texas spends about 25 percent less per student than California, but Texas eighth graders still outperformed California students on the NAEP exam. [7]

As with anything run by the government, America's education system is marked by bloated budgets and inefficient bureaucracies. Billions of dollars flow from the government to school districts every year, but most of that money never reaches students and seldom reaches teachers in any meaningful way. Instead, the bulk of the money goes toward staff and outrageous bureaucratic bloat.

Despite the ever-increasing budgets, classrooms still experience supply shortages and teachers are often covering expenses out of their own pockets, far too many school facilities are often in horrible condition, and the student-to-teacher ratio far exceeds what any teacher could reasonably handle. It represents a top-down economic failure for the American taxpayer, and our students are paying the price for government's wasteful and gross mismanagement.

Failing Parents: Schools as Indoctrination Camps

I recently spoke with Meg Kilgannon of the Family Research Council for my podcast, *The Huey Alert.* She is an education specialist who's taking a stand against much of the indoctrination taking place in America's public-school systems.

Meg commented, *"I think most parents think their kids are getting basically the same education that they got when they were in school, except maybe with a little more technology information. And that is just very far from the truth."* [8]

In our short discussion, Meg brought up several examples of actual indoctrination happening in classrooms across the country every day. Racial politics, gender-identity issues, and outright socialism are being taught to our kids right under the noses of parents.

She even talked about how racial politics have impacted something as clear-cut, non-subjective, and universal as math! Did you know that believing a basic math problem can only have *one* correct answer is a form of white supremacy? I sure didn't! And yet this is the kind of nonsense that is regularly taught in the classroom today.

INDOCTRINATION, NOT EDUCATION

I am generally loath to quote someone as despicable as Adolf Hitler, but his 1933 comments on the state's role in education are particularly striking and relevant in light of the all-out indoctrination we're seeing in the public school system today: *"If the older generation cannot get accustomed to us, we shall take their children away from them and rear them as needful to the Fatherland."*

Today's teachers preach socialism and attack the free market. They reject capitalism, and they teach their students to embrace a command-and-control economy that makes the government larger and more centralized, while shrinking the power of the individual.

Teachers no longer focus on raising young people to be educated, but instead work to make them political activists who will support and fight for liberals' pet causes. In a sense, parents are sending their kids to school to become child soldiers, opposed to Western culture, free enterprise, and America itself. Schools are not providing education; they are providing ideological indoctrination and mobilization.

How is this happening, and how is it happening *out in the open?* The education system is controlled by radical pro-socialist bureaucrats, administrators, and teachers. Politicized and radical teachers' unions hold nearly absolute power over of the entire system, and socialist Democrat politicians and policies go in lockstep with the teachers unions' bosses, pouring money and influence into radical causes in the name of education. It is a grotesque, symbiotic relationship in which the last thing anyone is concerned about is the welfare and education of our children.

The public education industry is so connected to the Democrat Party that many K-12 schools and colleges even gave students the ability to skip mid-term exams after the 2016 election — so they could *grieve* Hillary Clinton's loss to Donald Trump! Do you think they offered the same post-election "bereavement benefit" to conservative students after Trump's loss in 2020? Of course not.

In this radical, pro-socialist and secular-dominated system, traditional values are not only dismissed as outdated, but they are openly mocked and often even treated as punishable offenses.

Christian students who maintain their faith when faced with social and administrative pressures to bend to new established norms of behavior or beliefs are often ridiculed by both peers and teachers alike.

If they dare speak out, they are mocked, shunned and censored.

In many cases, students whose work does not reflect the "accepted" beliefs are given failing grades. This is not because their work is poor; it's because their beliefs are deemed offensive by the sensitive Left. We can see this radical pro-socialist perspective in many areas these days, but perhaps none so clearly as the twin darlings of radical racialist and sex-obsessed ideology: Critical Race Theory and LGBTQI+ "tolerance."

Teaching Hate and Racism

When I was growing up, we were taught in school to love our freedom and the uniqueness of our country! We were taught to respect one another and that we had an obligation to American society to grow up and become productive members of this great country. And that, as Americans, we enjoyed an economy of great opportunity and possibilities.

Now, it's the complete opposite.

Today, students are taught that America is a dark, hateful, racist place whose laws and systems of government are fundamentally flawed. They are told that it's a country where there is little or no opportunity — a country where there is no freedom, and that statism is the sole goal.

We are being attacked by a cultural virus, and it is creating a societal rut that will destroy our country if we don't fight back.

I am talking specifically here about the so-called Critical Race Theory (CRT) and the indoctrination of children to hate one another in our classrooms.

To illustrate, allow me to tell you about a book sitting on the library bookshelf in a Middle-Tennessee elementary school near me that has caused quite a stir in recent years. Parents have complained multiple times to the local school board, arguing that the book presents nothing but vile, hateful and blatant racism — and yet the school board has taken no action.

The book jacket of *A Place Inside of Me: A Poem to Heal the Heart* describes the contents:

> *"Written in verse, it explores the emotions of a young Black boy after a girl in his community is killed by police."*

The book's imagery depicts a Black girl who is murdered by black-booted, Nazi-looking, racist police officers. There's one illustration that shows police officers with clubs threatening peaceful Black protesters. BLM — Black Lives Matter — branding is all over the book. This is what the school board has deemed perfectly appropriate for children ages 4 to 8. This is the twisted, distorted, and evil vision of the country the radical ideologues want to impress upon our children.

Critical Race Theory, or CRT, is nothing but a form of Marxist, race-baiting, White-hating brainwashing that rewrites American history and works to convince students that all White people are racists and all Black people are victims.

Children are taught that long-held, fundamental keys to individual success such as working hard, being on time, being polite, owning property, and even the scientific method are all examples of white supremacy.

Capitalism is especially targeted as inherently racist because it does not provide equal outcomes for people.

This is a message that is now reaching our children as early as kindergarten. For example, in the Beaverton School District just outside of Portland, Oregon, third-grade students were shown a video promoting CRT principles. At one point, the video told these young boys and girls that, if they were White, they should free themselves by admitting out loud, *"I am racist."*

To those who promote these sick lies, every White person is racist. It does not matter who they are, where they are from, how old they are or what they have actually said and done throughout their lives. All that matters is the color of their skin. And if that color is White, they are racist. This disgusting point of view is harming an entire generation of boys and girls.

These sub-literate concepts abound in a revisionist history curriculum that has been gaining steam over the last several years called *The 1619 Project.* This movement, based on a book by author Nikole Hannah-Jones, reframes American history as the story of Black oppression and systemic racism that permeates every facet of American society. It oozes errors and lies.

Mary Grabar, author of *Debunking the 1619 Project,* said:

> ***"The 1619 Project*** *is the perfect tool for making angry, anti-American student activists. It's history told through the lens of critical race theory ... substituting objectivity with narrative storytelling.*
>
> *The Project engages students, and it makes them activists, which is what a lot of teachers want to do. There are way too many woke teachers. They've been trained in colleges of respected education to produce not knowledgeable citizens, but Left-Wing social activists."* [9]

Despite the backlash from respected historians and concerned parents, the U.S. Department of Education and the teachers' unions are pushing for *The 1619 Project* to be taught in every school across the country. These students will be voting in a few years and many will support reparations pushed by radical socialists with an evil focus on Marxism — because that's all they'll have been taught in school.

Former U.S. Attorney General William Barr did not hold back when asked about the role of Critical Race Theory in our public school system, and his statement sums up what I believe as well. In an August 13, 2020 appearance on the Fox News show *Hannity,* Barr said: "

> *If you want to find systemic racism in America, then look no further than the public school system, which is maintained by the Democratic Party and the teachers' unions (which keeps) inner-city kids in failing schools, instead of putting the resources in the hands of the parents to choose the schools to send their kids to."*

Teaching Radical LGBTQI+ Ideology

In some schools, children as young as kindergarteners are being taught that there is a wide spectrum of genders, that anyone can choose their gender and change their gender, and that all "good" people respect each individual's right to identify as whatever gender they choose.

Very young children are being read to and shown books that are nothing short of propaganda and pornography supporting homosexuality at an age when they should be learning their ABCs and about zoo animals.

Kids are being taught in government schools and even some private schools that sex change operations are a viable option and should be considered by those who feel uncomfortable in their own body.

Can you imagine the impact this kind of radical normalization has on a pubescent child who is experiencing the perfectly normal questions, concerns, embarrassment, and discomfort that come with growing up?

People in positions of authority are telling vulnerable children who are uncomfortable with the changes happening in their bodies that transgenderism could very well be the solution to their (nonexistent) problems. And sadly, children are listening and falling for this lie — with horrific life-long consequences.

Abigail Shrier, author of *Irreversible Damage: The Transgender Craze Seducing Our Daughters,* calls transgenderism and sex changes the *"social contagion of teenage girls."* Our culture and many teachers proclaim that not only is it okay to want to change your gender, but it is a positive good. Changing your gender makes you brave and cool. It makes you praiseworthy. That is a powerful lure for a child who is already struggling with the normal identity issues that come with growing up.

Just this morning, as I was eating breakfast, I read an article discussing some rather questionable books that the nation's largest teachers' union has recommended teachers read over the Summer Break. One of the books is a sexually explicit and graphic novel titled, *Gender Queer.*

The Daily Wire reports that this book *"includes pornographic cartoon illustrations of sex between two males with a sex toy, as well as oral sex, masturbation, and other sexually explicit content."* [10]

Now, I personally can't understand why anyone would want to read such filth. And I absolutely don't agree that such a book helps teachers accomplish their primary mission: helping students learn valuable skills, knowledge and information that will help them lead productive and fulfilling lives. What exactly is the teachers' union trying to communicate to its teachers? Or, more importantly, what are the Big Union Bosses trying to inflict on little school children? And why?

It has been clear for a while now that the public education machine in this country is racing toward all-out acceptance and celebration of any and all alternative or deviant lifestyles.

For example, the Centers for Disease Control and Prevention — which did such a *phenomenal* job with its COVID-19 recommendations (sarcasm intended) — issued a "self-assessment tool" for teachers and school administrators to use to become an "awesome ally" to LGBTQI+ students and causes in school. The assessment measures a school's "LGBTQI+ inclusivity" to ensure the staff is doing everything possible to fully indoctrinate children.

The CDC document claims:

> *"Schools play a critical role in supporting the health and academic development of all youth, including the success of lesbian, gay, bisexual, transgender, and queer/questioning (LGBTQ) youth. Creating and sustaining inclusive school environments, policies, programs, and*

> *practices that include LGBTQ youth is one strategy for improving the health and academic success of all youth."*[11]

Teachers are also encouraged to decorate their classrooms with LGBTQI+ imagery, such as rainbow flags, pink triangles, and unisex bathroom signs to create "safe spaces" for LGBTQI+ children.

Perhaps most distressing is the fact that numerous teacher workshops are educating teachers on how to facilitate a child's gender transition *without the parent finding out.* They are taught how to lie to and hide their obstinate and perverse actions from their students' parents, effectively painting the parents as "the enemy."

These are our children we're talking about! When did it become remotely acceptable for teachers or any other adult to talk to young students about who they are sexually attracted to and how they feel about their young bodies? When did Americans agree that teachers, not parents, should be ultimately responsible for an innocent child's well-being?

Portland, Oregon, public schools have adopted a new curriculum teaching K-5 students to subvert the sexuality of "white colonizers" and begin exploring "the infinite gender spectrum." The government-sponsored school curriculum begins in kindergarten with an anatomy lesson featuring graphic drawings of children's genitalia.

The lesson avoids the terms *boy* and *girl* in favor of the gender-neutral variants *person with a penis* and *person with a vulva,* because, according to the curriculum, some girls can have penises and some boys can have vulvas.

In first and second grade, Portland students are introduced to the key tenets of gender-identity theory: *"Gender is something adults came up with to sort people into groups. Many people think there are only two genders, girls and boys, but this is not true. There are many ways to be a boy, a girl, both or neither.*

Gender identity is about how you feel about yourself inside." [12]

Does this sound like the kinds of conversations you had in first grade? It certainly doesn't sound like mine! And it is a complete rejection of every science-based biology lesson I ever had from elementary school all the way up through college! But it's not the science that changed. It's the ideological motivations of the Marxist, anti-Christian ruling class.

But the transgender-agenda absurdity does not end there. In just the past year or two, as I write this, I have been shocked at the number of news articles I've seen that have put a spotlight on "drag shows" targeted at school children.

These are nothing but sexually explicit, modern-day burlesque shows designed to normalize homosexuality, transgenderism, pedophilic and debauchery in our society. Moreover, these are clear signals to children that these kinds of sexually alternative lifestyles should not only be *tolerated* but publicly *celebrated* in our society.

Making things even worse (if that were possible) is that public funds are being used to pay for these outrageous events. Because many of these events are hosted and funded by public school systems, your tax dollars are funding the transgender indoctrination of your children whether you approve of it or not. If you're reading this book, my guess is that you are outraged to know that these innocent little children are being preyed on by these potentially dangerous adults.

Teaching Political Activism

Government schools are brainwashing our children into thinking that humans cause the normal fluctuation of weather and temperature, and that it is more "extreme."

These are the same people who tell us that there are more than two genders, that masks work to stop viruses, and that we cannot identify what a woman is.

They have made many innocent children neurotic, irrational, and panic-stricken; so much so that they are now ecowarriors who will do anything to support their "cause," even attack or destroy anyone who disagrees with them.

You may have seen on the news kids gluing themselves to walls and floors, destroying artwork, blocking roads, protesting for "Palestinians," and supporting sickening antisemitism.

The teachers and radical groups politicize the kids, turning them into activists.

And a lot of these climate warriors' activities are even being supported with our tax dollars.

For example, in California, the state is paying college students through its College Corps Program $22 per hour for 450 hours of work (that's $7 above the state's minimum wage) to hit the streets with their message: "The Earth is doomed."

Yes, kids become climate-change political activists, and California colleges will pay you close to $10,000! Not a bad haul for the summer.

The College Corps Program has more than 3,200 "low-income" students who are on the public dime already, including illegal immigrants.

According to The College Corps Program, 30 percent of the students focus on "food insecurity," and 22 percent focus on "climate action," (which includes wildfire mitigation, energy conservation, urban greening, waste diversion, food rescue, and environmental education), and 80 percent of the participants in this program are "students of color."

Washington State's ClimeTime is a state education program that *"helps high school teachers introduce climate change and environmental justice into their classrooms by focusing on how the issues are playing out in their backyards. Through seminars and in-person sessions, teachers (who participate voluntarily) become the students — soaking up knowledge from climate scientists, activists, and science education professors."*

Currently, there are at least 11 states that have pending bills related to climate change education, including Rhode Island, Connecticut, Iowa, Wisconsin, New York, Maine, Minnesota, Massachusetts, Virginia, Hawaii, and California.

Serving Unions and Political Interests, Not Students

The education system has long been ruled by the Big Teachers Unions' Bosses. We have known this for decades, but it became very clear during the COVID-19 pandemic. Following the often-quoted advice of Rahm Emanuel, President Obama's chief of staff, the unions were careful not to *"let a serious crisis go to waste."*

After refusing to return to school for months in the waning days of the pandemic, the United Teachers Los Angeles (UTLA) union released a document titled, *The Same Storm, but Different Boats: The Safe and Equitable Conditions for Starting The Unified Los Angeles School District in 2020-2021*.

If you think this document was meant to simply outline working conditions that would make teachers feel safe from COVID-19, you'd be quite wrong. As I noted in my book *The Christian Voter,* the list of non-educational demands in this so-called education document was as striking as it was revealing.

Among the health precautions the union wanted for teachers, they also demanded:

- The defunding of police departments throughout the state of California.
- Single-payer, government-provided healthcare.
- Full funding to house California's homeless population.

- The closure of all publicly funded, privately operated charter schools.
- A new set of programs to address "systemic racism."

What do these things have to do with educating California's school children? Absolutely nothing. Again, the unions were showing their cards. They were making it clear to anyone paying attention that they were using education as a front for their radical activism.

College-Level Indoctrination

The indoctrination issue is not just a K-12 problem, either. It is just as bad (if not worse) in college and post-graduate institutions.

I sent my children to college at great expense and great personal sacrifice. They had a lot of fun and made a lot of friends, but they learned very little except for a pro-socialist, secular worldview and an anti-freedom ideology.

Throughout their years in college, it became painfully clear to me that Marxism and socialism have completely dominated every aspect of a college education today. Colleges and universities often become simple propaganda mills, and professors who do not toe the party line will either not get hired or find themselves out of a job very quickly.

As a result, college students are not exposed to a wide diversity of experiences, information, and perspectives, as you would expect. Instead, students get the same message, usually presented in the same way, from all their professors all the time. And sadly, brave students who disagree with or push back against the dominant slogans will pay a price in the form of lower grades, potential disciplinary action, and censorship.

For example, University of Cincinnati student Olivia Krolczyk received a 0 grade on her final project proposal. What was the problem? Her professor, while admitting the proposal was good, failed her for using terms she called "exclusionary" and that "reinforce heteronormativity." [13] The term at the heart of the issue is jaw-dropping: Olivia used the term *biological women* in her proposal, which was focused on the issue of transgender women (biological males) competing in women's sports.

Making the issue more absurd is the fact that the name of the course was "Gender in Popular Culture." That's right — references to *biological women* were deemed too offensive for a course focusing entirely on *gender.*

Many Americans were shocked and horrified on October 7th, 2023, when Hamas, in the most barbaric terms, slaughtered, burned, beheaded, raped, killed, and kidnapped innocent civilians in Israel. But what happened in our nation's high schools and college campuses is atrocious. Instead of the students protesting the slaughter of the innocents, they rejoiced at Hamas' barbaric attack and butchery.

Students and their teachers took to the streets, rallied, and spread lies and hate-filled propaganda about Jews, absurd historical and factual distortions.

But since they know almost nothing about history, they have been brainwashed by their teachers and professors. None of this should come as a surprise or shock. It is Marxist dogma and a strategic success for the radical pro-socialists.

Truly, the world's gone mad.

PUBLIC EDUCATION'S WAR ON PARENTS

Parents, not governments, bureaucracies, unions, or even teachers, are chiefly responsible for their children's education. This has long been the cultural ideal, going back thousands of years. In ancient Judaism, parents were commanded to teach the basic tenants of the Jewish faith to their children:

> *"Hear, O Israel: The LORD our God, the LORD is one. Love the LORD your God with all your heart and with all your soul and with all your strength. These commandments that I give you today are to be on your hearts.* ***Impress them on your children. Talk about them when you sit at home and when you walk along the road, when you lie down and when you get up."***
> (Deuteronomy 6:4-7, New International Version (NIV), emphasis added)

Similarly, Proverbs offers this wisdom:

> *"Train up a child in the way he should go [teaching him to seek God's wisdom and will for his abilities and talents], even when he is old he will not depart from it."*
> (Proverbs 22:6, Amplified Bible)

Many people have believed and taught that this proverb is talking only about teaching children spiritual things. However, the Amplified Bible translation makes it clear that this proverb is talking about a complete, well-rounded education customized specifically for each child's characteristics and blessings (giftings) or their particular abilities and talents.

Who better to customize a child's education than the parent who has literally known the child and spent every day with him or her since birth?

Of course, there are exceptions to this. Sadly, there are many parents who have neither the time nor interest in getting to know and care for their own children at this level. Many children have no relationship with their biological mother or father because of divorce and cohabitation.

The danger here, of course, is that if parents do not fill this role in a child's life, someone else will. And if that person represents ideologies and special interests that do not align with your family values, you will lose your children to the ideologies to which you are surrendering them.

In contrast to the biblical view, the attitude of many public school administrators and teachers — and of higher-level education bureaucrats, teachers, and politicians — is that the responsibility for how and what your children are learning falls exclusively on them as the so-called "experts."

Their self-focused, self-important attitude goes so far as to make them feel justified in "protecting" their students from their own parents!

And I'm not talking about protecting children from abusive parents. Clearly, all decent and reasonable people want to protect their children from actual harm. However, the "harm" that many in the education industry accuse parents of today includes such things as holding traditional values, loving our country, promoting capitalism, fostering biblical ideals, and of course the greatest sin of this liberal age: maintaining that there are only two genders and that gender is not a *decision* anyone can make for themselves.

And if a parent were to show up at a school board meeting and actually voice their concern for the rampant anti-Christian, anti-parental-rights, anti-Constitution indoctrination happening in their own children's schools? Well, those parents would be deemed "radicals" and "domestic terrorists" by the FBI and U.S. Department of Justice!

The DOJ actually issued a memo targeting everyday moms and dads who dared to question the education establishment and literally accused them of being *domestic terrorists* — the same designation given to the Unabomber, Oklahoma City bomber Timothy McVeigh, and the Boston Marathon bombers, brothers Oz Hokhar and Tamerian Tsarnaev.

The Department of Justice memorandum is chilling and bizarre. It's designed to scare those disagreeing with school policies from coming to school board meetings and vocally protesting school policies. But it fails to cite any crime, nor does it show any constitutional basis for the federal government to interfere with the operations or proceedings of a local school board.

The DOJ has inserted itself between parents and school board members simply because it thinks it can. This type of intimidation is wrong, and the power of the federal government should never be abused by either Democrats or Republicans to frighten and silence opposition. But it does begin to make at least a *little* sense when you understand how the radicals view your children.

In April 2023, President Biden made headlines for *"saying the quiet part out loud."* At a White House event honoring teachers, the President declared, *"There is no such thing as* ***someone else's*** *child. Our nation's children are* **all** *our children."* [14]

The radical pro-socialists have long assumed some false, inappropriate parental authority over America's youth, but it is rare to hear them make the claims so publicly. The fact that he made this claim at an event honoring *teachers* — and the fact that his comments were warmly received by that audience — tells you everything you need to know about how these "education experts" view your children and your role as parent.

I have no hope for the government-controlled, union-run schools.

But I do have great hope for superior education and a turnaround for parents and kids.

ALTERNATIVES TO GOVERNMENT-CONTROLLED PUBLIC EDUCATION

School board changes and legislation alone will not disrupt the union and ideological government-run schools. The best way to fix the broken system is by breaking the government's education monopoly. That means supporting, and using alternative educational options, such as private schools, Christian schools, charter schools, and homeschooling.

Private Schools

Perhaps not-so-surprisingly, it seems public school teachers themselves realize how poorly the public school system is preparing children — because public school teachers are increasingly sending their own children to private schools. *Education Next* reports that *"School teachers are much more likely to use a private school than are other parents. No less than 20 percent of teachers with school-age children ... have sent one or more of their children to private school."* [15]

The numbers are even more staggering in several Democrat-run cities:

- Chicago: 39 percent
- San Francisco: 34 percent
- New York City: 33 percent

Members of Congress themselves are perhaps the most "in the know" about how bad public education is, as a whopping 33 to 44 percent of them send their children to private school. That's three to four times the national average! [16]

Though the trend toward homeschooling and private schools has been growing in recent years, enrollments in those options rose sharply during the pandemic-related lockdowns of 2020 and beyond. For perhaps the first time, because teachers were having to teach students at home via Zoom, parents could hear firsthand what their children were learning — and a large majority of them were shocked and disgusted.

Moreover, parents became increasingly alarmed at the long, drawn out, and medically unnecessary lockdowns of the school systems across the country. In California, for example, most schools were closed for a year and a half. That is more than one-third of a typical student's four-year high school experience. As a result, more and more parents began exploring private school options — schools that were much less affected by the whims of government bureaucracy and the radical pro-socialists' wild ideological agenda.

Christian Schools

Christian schools, obviously, are much more likely to have Christian teachers, who educate children from a biblical world view. They will not undermine the faith-building efforts you are making at home as a parent.

Moreover, they are free to teach creationism, biblical history, math, science, and world history, while recognizing God's role in all of it. However, the media, education establishment, and progressives are saying that parents who do not send their kids to public schools are racist lunatics. They accuse you of being:

- Racist because you are being obedient to God's Word and direction, and because of their false and ridiculous assumption that anyone who takes their kids out of public schools only does so to avoid having their children learn alongside minority students.
- An enemy of democracy because you are not supporting the government-run school system.
- An anti-government rebel because you do not want absolute government-control over your child's education.

In fact, one editorial appearing in *The New York Times* claimed that parents who abstained from public schools engage in a subversive and anti-democratic behavior.

The editorial goes even further to assert that those who oppose *"government schools"* only do so because of their devotion to *"Confederate-era beliefs about a godless, encroaching, racist state."* [17] That is, they are equating private and Christian school families with modern-day slave owners!

It is all painfully revealing of what these socialist really want: for the government — not God-fearing parents — to raise your children.

Charter Schools

A charter school is a free public school that is operated independently of the government-run state and local school-district bureaucracies. Because they don't operate under government control, most charter schools aren't subject to many of the regulations and union controls that stifle educational innovation and hinder academic achievement.

Parents, teachers, community leaders, entrepreneurs, businesses, or any combination of these can submit a proposal for a charter school to the state's charter authorizing entity.

By charter — or contract — charter schools are given greater flexibility in their operation in return for greater accountability in performance. These schools have a proven track record in helping children achieve better outcomes and academic performance than most government-operated public schools.

That's why there are huge waiting lists of parents wanting their kids out of the failing government schools ... and why the government's school establishment and the unions hate charter schools.

One word of caution here, though. A charter school in your area may not necessarily be the best choice for your children *only* because it isn't run by the state. There is a wide variety of charter schools, and each can be, and often is, vastly different from another. And, because charter schools have more leeway in directing their academic programs, a particular charter school may be a *perfect* fit for one student and a *terrible* match for another.

The best advice when it comes to charter schools, then, is to do your research and learn everything you can about the charter school options in your area. Only then can you make an informed decision about the best option for each of your children.

Homeschooling

Finally, we have the alternative that is the least favorite and most hated option in the eyes of the government-run education system. That option, of course, is homeschooling.

Homeschooling experienced a massive boom as a result of the COVID-19 lockdowns, in 2020. Because students were sent home and parents had to make accommodations for being there and for helping with their children's education anyway, many parents simply decided to go all the way, remove their students from the public system, and manage their education themselves.

In fact, the number of children who are being homeschooled nearly *doubled* between 2019, before COVID-19, and May 2023. The U.S. Census Bureau reports that the percentage of children being homeschooled the year before the pandemic was 2.8 percent. Three years later, it had risen to 5.6 percent. [18]

One of the biggest advantages of homeschooling is the fact that the subject matter can be determined by parents, not by state or district education bureaucrats. Parents should be able to decide when their children are introduced to complex, sensitive, and controversial issues in politics, society, and sexuality. Furthermore, they should be the ones to make decisions about the particular value system or religious framework from which these concepts are taught from.

Homeschool parents are not left to their own devices when it comes to how and what to teach their children, either. There is a wide range of curriculum materials to choose from, all specifically tailored to homeschool settings.

And let us not fall for the union and educational establishment lies about the quality of these materials or about a homeschool education in general. Numerous studies have found that homeschooled children achieve higher standardized test scores than children attending a public school system. [19]

While it may be true that homeschooling does not offer as many socialization opportunities as traditional school, there is an ever-growing number of associations, conventions, and enrichment opportunities in practically every community across the country. Homeschool kids are gaining access to all kinds of social opportunities, including group activities, sports programs, music camps, and even traditional social events like prom.

THE OPPOSITION TO ALTERNATIVE OPTIONS

Unsurprisingly, all the options mentioned above have been attacked at all levels of government and by the education bureaucracy. The power brokers in charge of the public school sector do not like it when viable alternatives appear that threaten their hold on America's schoolchildren.

One of the most blatantly disturbing objections I have seen to these alternative education methods and homeschool in particular comes from Harvard Law professor Elizabeth Bartholet, whom I also quoted in my book, *The Christian Voter.*

Bartholet argues, *"Many homeschooling parents are extreme ideologues, committed to raising their children in evangelical Christian 'belief systems.' This is a problem,"* she says, *"Because society may not have the chance to teach them values important to the larger community, such as tolerance of other people's views and values."* [20]

The arrogance and dismissive attitude towards people of faith is shocking here. She's literally saying we need public schools to *correct* the foolish, faith-based, and apparently harmful views of America's extremist and (no doubt) stupid parents.

I wonder what this professor would define as "extreme ideologue" behavior. Is it simply believing the truth of the Bible? Is it following Jesus? And would she feel as comfortable making these exact claims against people of other faiths, such as Muslims or Jewish parents or is it only Christians that she feels so comfortable ridiculing?

Bartholet is certainly not alone in her objection to homeschooling, however. Many states, such as Maryland and (of course) California, have had socialist, anti-Christian politicians attempt to regulate — and eventually destroy — homeschooling.

Proposed legislation in these and other districts would assume parents are guilty until proven innocent:

- Guilty of not being qualified to teach their children.
- Guilty of right-wing extremism.
- Even guilty of *child abuse.*

Why? On what grounds would the state assume a homeschooling parent is abusive? In the case of California's proposed legislation several years ago, the potential of abuse was brought up because David and Louise Turpin — the horrible Riverside County, California, couple who police say tortured their 13 children by chaining them to their beds, abusing, and starving them — were registered with the state as homeschoolers.

California lawmakers would not be caught missing their opportunity to use a manufactured crisis to expand their bureaucratic power, attack people of faith, and destroy homeschooling as an educational option all in one fell swoop.

The bills in California and Maryland were thankfully defeated. But the politicians keep fighting for restricting and banning homeschooling. However, the remedies to the "crisis" they sought should frighten any parent, homeschooling or not. Through these bills, the states would have introduced an unnecessary and near-impenetrable wall of government review, oversight, intrusion, and control over a parent's right to homeschool their child.

Parental privacy rights would also have been gravely threatened, as both bills would have allowed government officials — for the first time ever — to enter a private home *without having any reason to suspect there's a situation in that home that required their attention and intervention.*

Parents would have been assumed to be abusing their children simply because they had removed them from or kept them out of the public school system. Never mind the statistical evidence to the contrary: rates of abuse are much higher for children who attend public schools.

However, opposition remains tough, fierce, and growing. Parents who want to take responsibility for educating their children themselves or in a private, Christian, or charter school must be prepared to fight for that right. And the other side fights dirty.

Many politicians, bureaucrats, education administrators, and teachers' unions believe that all children should be required to attend government-run public schools and that there should be no competing options available.

Why? Because all alternative options to the public school system represent a loss of control by the government bureaucracy.

And bureaucrats are all about power, money, and control. And whoever controls the education system literally controls the future of our country. Today's students are tomorrow's leaders and lawmakers. In their minds, the best way for the radicals to achieve its unachievable fantasy of a future socialist utopia is to indoctrinate today's students with their twisted ideas.

WHAT CAN WE DO?

Why haven't our public schools improved?

Because most schools are controlled by the government, and

the government is a monopoly. Monopolies resist change. They don't want to give up the way they've always done things. But when there is competition, they are forced to change or get left behind. If they don't adopt better ways of doing things, they go out of business. It makes freedom and choice the answer.

But government-run schools never go out of business. That means principals, school bureaucrats, and teachers — especially teachers unions — have little incentive to try anything new or do something different.

Take the case of teacher Jaime Escalante, who taught many disadvantaged students at Garfield High School, in Los Angeles. His successful teaching model was the basis for the movie *Stand and Deliver.*

More Garfield High students passed advanced placement calculus tests than did students from Beverly Hills High School. Why? Because Escalante was a better teacher with better ideas, teaching his students that with enough drive and hard work, the sky is the limit.

Why wasn't Escalante's successful teaching model duplicated across the country? It would have been in any other field, but unionized teachers resented his fame. Before long, the teachers' union used its organizing power to oust Escalante as the math department chairman. It's just one more example of how without choice and innovation, the student is the loser.

It is time for taxpayers and every state's political leaders to defund the government-run, public school system. It is time for parental choice. It is time for parents to retake the responsibility for their children's education. It is time for parents to exercise their right to choose where and how their children will be educated, be it through a public, charter, private, Christian or homeschooling option.

It is time for all of us, as American voters, to throw the bad actors out of office and out of our schools! From school board members to county bureaucrats to U.S. Senators and Presidents, it is time — well past time, in fact — for us to take a stand against the radical political, social, and economic indoctrination of our precious children in America's schools!

It is time for us to act as though the future depends on the education we provide our children.

Because it does.

Chapter 10

Danger #9: The War on Christianity

Throughout this book, we have examined many critical dangers to your prosperity, freedom, and future. These are attacks that the federal government, unelected bureaucrat activists, and our Big Tech overlords are waging against Americans who do not fall in line with their radical socialist and divisive agenda.

We've seen how they want to pick apart our economy, judicial system, Electoral College, and the U.S. Constitution.

We explored socialism's reach into education and the weaponized "diversity, equity, and inclusion" strategy in our places of work.

We've even examined how Artificial Intelligence (AI) is being used to deceive us into believing the lies the radical socialist ideologues are constantly spreading.

The bureaucratic reach of the federal government is something we should all fear.

But ... do you know what the socialist radicals fear the most?

The church.

Faith in God stands in stark opposition to the goals of socialism, Marxism, Communism, and statism. That's why religion has always been Public Enemy No. 1 any time a communist or socialist regime has taken over a country.

Communists and socialists cannot allow any challenges to

their power. The government's rules and policies flow from its authority, and that authority tolerates no challengers.

But Christians recognize a power that is higher than the state. They recognize the higher authority of the Almighty, living, active God who reigns over all.

The government bureaucrats, by contrast, believe that the *state* is their god. The state is responsible for everything. The state will supply all you could ever need.

Policies are their religion and the path to their utopia.

Christians, however, believe that governments are ordained by God. For example, the American Revolution was a challenge to the state — specifically, to the king of England. One of our most celebrated founding documents, the Declaration of Independence, states:

> *"We hold these truths to be self-evident: that all men are created equal, that they are endowed by their Creator with certain unalienable rights, and that among these are life, liberty, and the pursuit of happiness."*

The government bureaucrats do not accept or believe this.

This is a challenge to their coercive power.

This is a challenge to their coercive policies.

This is a challenge to their determination that the state knows what's right and best for the individual and is the final authority.

As a result, a war has been brewing in America for many years — a war against Christianity. For the socialist agenda to proceed, faith must be squashed and God must be erased. They would never admit this outright, of course. But they will — and have — come after the church with a "death by a thousand cuts" approach. And if we don't wake up and face what is happening head on, this danger could overtake us all — Christians or not.

INDOCTRINATION OF OUR MILITARY

Let's begin by examining the anti-Christian indoctrination of one of our nation's most important and respected sectors: the military. Our men and women in uniform have long held the line against and defeated the world's most despicable tyrannies: The National Socialists, Marxists, Fascists, Communists, and many other atheists and Totalitarian regimes. But now, sadly, a new breed of socialist aggressors are reshaping and destroying the U.S. military *from the inside.*

Marxist political indoctrination by the politicized military leaders is one of the biggest threats to American freedoms, our Republic, and your safety.

To be blunt, the U.S. military leadership is deceiving and deliberately indoctrinating the troops, cadets, and new recruits.

This politicization of the military started under the Obama Administration, and it continued — although covertly — under President Trump's Administration, despite Trump's strong actions and specific orders to put a stop to the cancerous doctrines that Marxism and socialism comprise. Once Biden took office, the Obama-era racists and socialist brainwashing efforts came back in full force.

I've seen this play out in at least three key areas:

First, the military is being actively trained with an overemphasis on politicized Critical Race Theory (CRT), DEI, ESG, LGBTQI+ initiatives, and other political propaganda.

West Point cadets are being taught that "whiteness" connotes "race privilege" and confers a "structural advantage."

That garbage is pure, racist Marxism.

Yet this teaching is being pushed in all the military ranks, coming all the way from the top — Commander-in-Chief Biden and the recently retired Chairman of the Joint Chiefs of Staff, General Mark Milley.

For example, our troops used to be trained in military history, strategy, doctrine, tactics, combat, military discipline, and war-winning principles. Now, they are being trained on using the right "pronouns" and making "safe spaces" for transgender recruits.

In a recent Navy training video, Undersea Warfare Center Engineer Jony Rozon opens the video wearing a rainbow sweater and says, *"Hi. My name is Jony, and I use he/him pronouns."* [1] He then continues to describe other pronouns and the proper etiquette on how to use them.

As Russia continues to decimate Ukraine, as China stands on the verge of invading Taiwan, as Iran-backed Hamas launches unprovoked terror attacks on Israel, and as North Korea lobs missiles over Japan, our commander-in-chief and top brass in the military are worried about our soldiers not using the right pronouns and LGBTQI+ etiquette, so as not to hurt our soldiers' feelings.

The official naval training video was produced and posted online to show our troops the importance of *"using the correct pronouns and polite etiquette when you come across someone you don't know, and you're not sure how they identify."*

Does that make you feel safer from our nation's most dangerous enemies? Is that the kind of strength Russia, Iran, and China will respect?

No.

Second, the military is recruiting new members by promoting America's perceived shortcomings rather than its strengths.

New recruits are being politicized through new, shocking video promotional commercials that embrace LGBTQI+ and other woke issues — while taking not-too subtle jabs at America in the process.

In one commercial, a female corporal talks about being *"raised by two mothers"* as she sits behind the controls of our missile defense system. She continues to describe how, at a young age, *"she marched for equality"* and that she's still *"defending freedom."* The animation in the segment flashes an image of an LGBTQI+ pride parade. [2]

There's no pride in America. No waiving of the American flag. No celebration of traditional American values or American exceptionalism. It's all racism, division, and loathing for everything America stands for.

How do they expect to win any wars by softening our military soldiers and making them hate our country and the principles it was founded on?

Third, the military is actively targeting Conservatives, Libertarians, and Christians in its woke, LGBTQI+-driven indoctrination sessions.

Again, a socialist state has no room for dissent or challenges to its authority — especially in its military. So, military members who are least likely to embrace these radical ideological beliefs are being put through what could best be described as *re-education.* Those who still won't bend to the new Left-Wing, anti-American, Marxist ideology are purged.

This should not be too surprising. After all, this is the same government that isn't timid about labeling everyday conservative American moms and dads "domestic terrorists" simply for pushing back on school boards or holding faith-based beliefs. *Of course,* they'd react even more strongly against soldiers and sailors who resist these pernicious new policies.

This toxic brainwashing is not only costing our valuable service members their careers; it's deliberately weakening our country. When we look back on this in 20 years, I think we will realize that our leaders were actively engaged in getting rid of the strongest, most motivated, most pro-America soldiers, sailors, Air Force, and Marines from the military at a time when we needed them the most.

MEDIA AND BIG TECH CENSORSHIP

We've discussed how the"mainstream" legacy media and Big Tech act together to censor conservative voices and stories — often at the request or direction of the government. Sadly, that includes censorship of faith-based speech and beliefs, and practices.

Big Tech Censorship

Media and Big Tech moguls seem to put Christians in the same ostracized and "cancelled" bucket as Republicans, Conservatives, and Libertarians — never mind the fact that Christianity is not a political philosophy or anti-government movement. Christians can disagree on political issues but still be united in their faith in Jesus Christ.

I won't question someone's faith based only on how they vote; that's between them and God. As I explained in my book *The Christian Voter: How to Vote for, Not Against, Your Values to Transform Culture and Politics,* Christians have non-negotiable issues that transcend politics. God is neither a Democrat nor Republican.

What I will question, however, is how the government, media, and Big Tech justify state-imposed censorship of Christians, Judeo-Christian values, and religious beliefs.

For example, Facebook openly censors Christian, Jewish, and other religious bloggers for quoting the Bible and citing passages related to a biblical view of homosexuality, marriage, abortion, child abuse, transgenderism, pedophilia, and other important social issues. They usually do so not by deleting the post entirely but instead by limiting its "reach" — meaning the algorithm prevents the post from appearing in most people's feeds.

Facebook and other platforms take sneaky actions like this to limit the distribution of dissenting voices while still giving the pretense of free speech. They're saying, in effect, "Sure, you are free to *say* that. But we're going to restrict who gets to *see* it."

Because our Big Tech oligarchs have the power to control which voices are amplified and which voices are silenced, they get to decide what is and is not "hate speech." To no one's surprise, basically anything that does not affirm — and certainly anything that contradicts — their secular, socialist ideology is censored.

Social media companies are especially quick to label foundational Christian beliefs going back two millennia as "hate speech." In doing so, they equate someone quoting Scripture with someone quoting Hitler.

It's disgusting — and evil.

And it's happening to Christians online every day.

For example, nationally popular radio host Dennis Prager regularly puts well-produced, well-researched teaching videos on YouTube under his PragerU brand. Many of those videos, however, have faced bans and restrictions that have limited their reach and made them ineligible for monetization. What were the offensive videos that required decisive action by YouTube?

- "The Most Important Question About Abortion"
- "Where are the Moderate Muslims?"
- "Is Islam a Religion of Peace?"
- "The World's Most-Persecuted Minority: Christians"
- "Why America Must Lead"
- "The Ten Commandments: Do Not Murder"

These topics were deemed too sensitive for YouTube viewers to see. Heaven forbid that anyone should actually be invited to *think* about any of these issues while they're scrolling through their YouTube feed.

I believe Prager's true offense is that he takes his Jewish

faith very seriously, and he dares to view American life and government through a lens of that faith. Apparently, that's not allowed on YouTube — and it's increasingly not allowed anywhere else.

I listed a handful of similar examples in my previous book, *The Deep State: 15 Surprising Dangers You Should Know.* I think they're worth repeating here:

- Apple has taken down some Christian applications from its App Store, making them almost impossible to access or download. The reason? The Christian apps provide biblical views on marriage and homosexuality.

- YouTube has censored Catholic Online's videos with Scripture readings, even though these videos contain only content with Bible readings.

- Google for Nonprofits does not list churches and other religious organizations that apply biblical views on sexuality when hiring people. They also use algorithms in search results that intentionally exclude Christian viewpoints and organizations.

- Facebook censored an ad by Gov. Mike Huckabee in support of Chick-fil-A's prior stance on same-sex marriage.

- Twitter removed an ad posted by Tennessee's U.S. Senator Marsha Blackburn, who stands for biblical morality in her politics. The ad was falsely labeled "inflammatory" because it opposed Planned Parenthood, an organization involved in killing millions of defenseless unborn babies throughout America. [3]

The bottom line with Big Tech censorship of Christianity is that socialists want to keep religious thought hidden away and locked inside churches, synagogues, and mosques — at least until they can shut those down too.

Media Censorship

Most people have no idea how much censorship is going on in the mainstream media. No matter where you get your news — whether it's from ABC, NBC, CBS, CNN, MSNBC, Apple News, Google News, Facebook, X (formerly Twitter), or anywhere else — you are not getting the full story. You're getting some of the facts, purposely arranged by agenda-driven producers to build their greater narrative.

Many times, the villain of that narrative is Christianity and those who dare to believe and follow it.

The public is being misled and/or outright lied to about Christians every day. And in most cases, the media seems to bend the facts over backward to slander Christians in an unbalanced and unfair way.

For example, the nation was shocked on March 27, 2023, when a gunman walked through the halls of a private Christian school in Nashville, shooting and killing young schoolchildren and teachers before being shot and killed by police. The killer was a female, 28-year-old former student who identified as transgender (a biological female living as a man).

In the aftermath of the shooting, I was disgusted — though not surprised — to find much of the news coverage focused not on her horrific actions or history of mental illness but instead on how transgender people and others in the LGBTQI+ community have been abused by the church. I have never seen the media work so hard to sympathize with a child-killing, school-stalking mass murderer.

But, of course, they had to. If the two parties in a story are a Christian school and a transgender person, the real villain *has* to be the Christians. It's as though the media aren't *allowed* to vilify any member of the radical favored and protected class.

What should have been labeled a hate crime became an

attack on Christianity and a rallying cry to protect the radical transgender ideology.

Christians in America have been a powerfully positive influence on the direction of culture and politics from the very beginning of our nation. And yes, every one of those Christians has made mistakes. We are all sinners saved by God's grace, and sometimes we should be called out when we make a mistake or sin against others. I have no problem with that.

But what normally happens instead is that any mistakes (or perceived mistakes) are blown wildly out of proportion and applied across all of Christendom. The media implies that every Christian needs to be feared, mocked, or marginalized.

Take the January 6th, 2021, incident at the U.S. capital, for instance. Several people charged with insurrection were Christians. Many had signs, jewelry, or shirts that clearly identified them as Christ-followers. After one arrest, I saw a headline that read, "Bible study insurrection: Latest FBI Arrest."

Of course, the video that went along with the story never explained what the "Bible study" was. The news agency just thought that would make a good headline, I suppose. It was a broad stroke to associate "Bible study" with "insurrection."

The story also included plenty of pictures and video of January 6th protesters holding faith-based signs, such as "Jesus Saves." Again, the chance to connect Christians with what was breathlessly being described as "an attack on democracy" was too good to pass up.

Stories like these make it clear to me that there is a concerted effort in the media to paint Christians as domestic terrorists and to present Christianity as an equal or worse threat to America than ISIS or Al Qaeda. It is especially apparent when you consider that groups like Antifa — who dress in all black, cover their faces, and routinely commit acts of violence (on video) against peaceful conservative and Christian protesters

— are brushed off by the radical pro-socialists and its media partners as "no big deal" and "not a real threat."

This is part of a political campaign specifically designed to undermine, discredit, and smear Christianity and to associate Christians with the worst, most dangerous members of society.

The key to targeting Christians is having the ability and desire to label any dissenter from liberal ideology as a hate group. The media looks to organizations like the radical, widely-discredited Southern Poverty Law Center (SPLC) to label and smear such Christian or Conservative organizations as "hate groups," which gives news outlets like CNN and MSNBC pseudo-permission to ignore, insult, and demean them.

The SPLC's so-called "hate map" includes organizations like Alliance Defending Freedom, a conservative and Christian organization that defends religious freedom; the Pacific Justice Institute, a legal-defense organization that provides civil-liberties representation at no charge; and Family Research Council, a nonprofit research organization dedicated to advancing faith in public policy. They've even attacked individuals like Franklin Graham, founder of the faith-based, global humanitarian aid organization Samaritan's Purse.

The SPLC's influence has grown rapidly over the years, guiding not only media bias but also public policy. In fact, the SPLC "hate map" was even used by the U.S. military, Justice Department, and FBI for years until President Trump put a stop to it.

Sadly, Biden's Deep State bureaucracy brought it back, never pausing to question whether the Southern Poverty Law Center is itself a dangerous "hate group."

Putting good, moral, godly, faith-based organizations in the same ideological bucket as the Ku Klux Klan is utter madness. It's deliberate attacks and smears against Christians and other groups, and it must stop. It's pure evil.

Its deliberate attacks and smears against highly respected

Christian leaders and other religious organizations are pure evil and a shocking example of hateful, anti-Christian bigotry.

ATTACKING CHRISTIAN BUSINESS OWNERS AND EMPLOYEES

I discussed the issue of judicial activists targeting Christian businesses at length in Chapter 7. The most famous example is probably the case of Colorado cake baker Jack Phillips, which I've already explored.

While Jack took the brunt of the biased smears and media and public backlash, there have been several other cases that have been just as important for religious liberty. Two examples include lawsuits filed against:

- Emilee Carpenter, a photographer who declined a request to photograph a same-sex wedding due to her deeply-held religious beliefs. She was sued and lost the case presided over by an activist judge. She now faces penalties for violating a New York State law, which includes fines of up to $100,000, a revoked business license, and up to a year in jail.
- Lorie Smith, a web designer who creates customized art and websites for clients. Although she has done plenty of work for clients from all walks of life, including LGBTQI+ clients, she declined to create a custom wedding site for a same-sex couple for religious reasons. This resulted in a prolonged legal battle spanning more than seven years that resulted in a 2023 Supreme Court victory for religious liberty.

Of course, media bias ran rampant in the way they covered these important cases. The first line of an Associated Press article about the Supreme Court ruling read, *"In a defeat for gay rights, the Supreme Court'sConservative majority ruled on Friday that a Christian graphic artist who wants to design wedding websites can refuse to work with same-sex couples."* [4]

That opening phrase — *"in a defeat for gay rights"* — shows how mainstream media views the case. Changing that one phrase changes the whole tone of the article. For example, it would be *more* accurate to replace the opening phrase with, *"In a victory for religious liberty ..."*

Furthermore, the end of the AP's opening line is a flat-out lie that misrepresents Lorie's case. She never "refuse(d) to work with same-sex couples." By her own admission, she has had many LGBTQI+ clients who never complained about her or how they were treated. It was only when she was asked to apply her God-given creative talents to the specific issue of gay marriage that she had a crisis of conscience.

These cases demonstrate how important it is to prevent the U.S. Supreme Court from being packed with judicial, activist judges. The only way to prevent that is to support Conservative presidential candidates. Elections have consequences — and a major consequence has been and will continue to be the rights of business owners to operate their businesses in line with their religious faith.

While Christian business owners tend to take the most public pressure and criticism, many Christian employees have just as much difficulty practicing their faith at work.

For example, Kroger Supermarket recently lost a discrimination case brought against the company by several employees who said they were fired for their religious beliefs. Their "fireable offense," according to Kroger, was their faith-based refusal to wear aprons emblazoned with gay pride messaging at work.

The employees sued and later won in court.

When later called into a Senate Committee hearing to discuss an unrelated matter — a potential merger between Kroger and another grocery chain — Kroger CEO Rodney McMullen faced the ire of Conservative senators whose constituents are tired of having their rights trampled on by big, powerful corporations.

McMullen was hoping to gain Republican support against the Democrats' move to block the merger. He was surprised by what he got instead.

Sen. Tom Cotton addressed McMullen:

> *"I've cautioned [corporations] for years that if they silence conservatives and center-right voters ... if they discriminate against them in their company, they probably shouldn't come and ask Republican senators to carry the water for them whenever our Democratic friends want to regulate them or block their mergers."* [5]

Signaling no support for Kroger, Cotton ended his time saying, *"I'll say this: I'm sorry that's happening to you. Best of luck."* [6]

THE HISTORIC 2020 CHURCH CLOSURES

"You never want a serious crisis to go to waste ... It's an opportunity to do things that you think you could not do before." [7]

Those are the often-quoted words of President Obama's Chief of Staff Rahm Emanuel before the then-president-elect was sworn in. I am not sure those words have ever been more relevant than they were in 2020, when the government formally forced the closure of churches across the country.

Church was outlawed, right here in the United States of America — just as it has been in socialist, communist, and dictatorial regimes around the world.

At this point, I need to admit something to you:

I'm a lawbreaker.

I willingly broke the law, and I even traveled across the country to do it.

During the COVID-19 church lockdowns in the spring of 2020, my wife and I traveled from our home in Nashville, Tenn. — where we had recently moved — back to California to attend church at Calvary Chapel Chino Hills. We were there to show support for Calvary Chapel Pastor Jack Hibbs who "illegally" opened the church doors for worship.

Pastor Jack and other bold Christian leaders in other "disobedient" churches stood firm for the gospel and for truth — not backing down in the fear of man — and risked their freedom by practicing their religious faith and welcoming anyone who wanted to worship God during the outrageous church lockdowns.

These powerful church leaders faithfully followed Peter's admonition, *"We must obey God rather than human beings!"* (Acts 5:29, NIV) And their congregations stood with them.

In fact, some congregations practically *dared* the police to arrest them.

For example, I also visited Godspeak Calvary Chapel in Newbury Park, Calif., during the lockdowns. This church had faced direct legal pressure from the state when a judicial activist judge ordered them not to hold church services. If they did, the pastor would likely be arrested and fined for contempt of court, the church could have its water and electricity shut off, and those attending services would have risked being jailed or fined.

Pastor Rob McCoy held services anyway.

And people came. A *lot* of people came.

The church, which normally has crowds of up to 500 people on a typical Sunday, welcomed 2,500 worshipers that week. Dozens of other churches across Southern California bussed people in to worship at Godspeak Calvary Chapel — and that large group didn't even go inside the worship center.

They stayed in the parking lot.

Why?

Because they were willing to be arrested and fined *en masse* outside, keeping police too busy to bother the people worshiping inside the church.

These kinds of protests sprung up all over the country. It was a glorious sight to behold — but not for the government agents who couldn't believe what they were seeing. And in this case, they backed down and did nothing despite the county and court orders.

The state and federal government was taken aback by the intense pushback they received from otherwise calm, quiet, law-abiding men and women who simply wanted to exercise their constitutionally protected freedom of religion. Churches across the country were packed with hundreds and some thousands of worshipers in every church, some risking $1,000 fines just for being there.

This earned these daring churchgoers cheers from fellow Christians and jeers from the bureaucrats, pro-socialist, anti-Christian politicians, and stunned journalists who could not believe the audacity of these lawbreakers who dared to worship.

Here is just a taste of what I heard and read across the media landscape that spring:

- "A virus is not religious … it won't respond to prayer."
- "It's religion vs. science and data. These people are insane."
- "Church must adjust to new normal — no more than 10 people at a time for years to come."
- "Pastors are killing people."

- "Singing in church must stop. Praying with people in church can never happen again."
- "The church should congregate online only and not meet as a group — maybe from now on."
- "Churches, for the safety of its people, should not meet until next year ... maybe longer."

By June of 2020, most states had allowed churches to return to normal services, but about 20 states continued to impose their anti-church, pro-fear, and anti-First-Amendment restrictions against live, in-person worship services.

Many churches were issued exorbitant fines for staying open, and several of these cases went to court. I discussed a few of these in Chapter 7, including Pastor John MacArthur of Los Angeles' Grace Community Church and Pastor Mike McClure of Calvary Chapel San Jose.

Again, none of this should have been surprising. The church is the No. 1 target of secular, anti-Christian politicians and media pundits who despise our values — and the fact that we vote according to those values.

Fortunately, there have been major victories for churches who fought for their right to stay open. A milestone case involved California's Harvest Rock Church and its pastor, Che Ahn, who won a decisive legal battle with the state over the lockdowns in May 2021.

The United States District Court for the Central District of California approved a settlement that compels California to pay $1.35 million in restitution for the legal fees the church incurred fighting for the right to remain open.

But the real victory was much bigger.

Under the settlement, California may no longer impose discriminatory restrictions upon houses of worship. It covers all in-person services, singing, prayer meetings, and other church activities that California Gov. Gavin Newsom actually criminalized and outlawed.

This was the first permanent injunction in the United States that affected all states.

Sadly (but not surprisingly), the media and Big Tech were silent on this historic victory. CNN, MSNBC, ABC, CBS, NBC, *The New York Times,* the *Los Angeles Times,* and Apple News all ignored or downplayed the decision.

Pastor Ahn, however, could not contain his enthusiasm after the ruling:

> *"This is a momentous day for churches in America! After nearly a yearlong battle defending our religious freedoms, our lawsuit has reached a permanent settlement in our favor. I am thrilled to see a complete reversal of the last discriminatory restrictions against churches in California, knowing this case will act as a precedent, not only in our state but also in our nation."* [8]

Amen!

FIGHTING FOR RELIGIOUS LIBERTY

Most people on the Left don't seem to understand what "separation of church and state" means — and yet they never tire of saying it when they see or hear someone expressing their sincerely held religious beliefs.

For nearly all of American history, it was common to see and hear people pray in public. Sometimes, it was organized; other times, it was individual and spontaneous. No one batted an eye.

Today, the sight of private citizens praying in public seems to enrage many on the Left. Or, using their language, you could say it "triggers" them.

And what do the radical pro-socialists do when they're triggered?

They try to take away more of every citizen's Constitutional rights and to force all Americans to conform to the values and behaviors they — and only they — deem acceptable.

Make no mistake: the First Amendment gives every American the right to pray and worship without any infringement from the government. This applies to praying in public wherever you are and whenever you want. However, because the radical socialists like to pervert the clear language in the U.S. Constitution and twist what the words mean, they have used the "separation of church and state" language to ban religion in public spaces and in government buildings and institutions.

They've tried to turn one of our greatest protections into a blunt instrument to wield against people of faith.

Fortunately, the Supreme Court has stopped them in their tracks in two recent cases.

Protecting Public Prayer

Religious liberty scored a major victory, in 2022 with the U.S. Supreme Court's ruling that a Washington school district could not fire a high school football coach for praying on the field.

Coach Joe Kennedy faced backlash from a small but vocal group who objected to his public expression of his religious faith. He was eventually fired from his job at Bremerton High School in 2015 after a few onlookers complained to the school district about him praying on the football field and being voluntarily joined by students, before a game. His 2022 U.S. Supreme Court victory saw him reinstated to his position after several years of legal battles.

Coach Kennedy was represented by First Liberty Institute, which describes itself as *"the largest legal organization in the nation dedicated* ***exclusively*** *to defending religious liberty for all Americans."*[9] First Liberty President, CEO, and Chief Counsel Kelly Shackelford celebrated the Court's decision:

"Our Constitution protects the right of every American to engage in private religious expression, including praying in public, without fear of getting fired. We are grateful that the Supreme Court recognized what the Constitution and law have always said — Americans are free to live out their faith in public." [10]

Writing for the Court majority, Justice Neil Gorsuch came down hard on the school district and on its misuse and misapplication of the U.S. Constitution, while also giving an important history lesson to anti-Christian activists. Writing in the Court's opinion, he argued:

"Here, a government entity sought to punish an individual for engaging in a personal religious observance, based on a mistaken view that it has a duty to ferret out and suppress religious observances even as it allows comparable secular speech. The Constitution neither mandates nor tolerates that kind of discrimination ... That the First Amendment doubly protects religious speech is no accident. It is a natural outgrowth of the framers' distrust of government attempts to regulate religion and suppress dissent." [11]

The First Amendment states that *"Congress shall make no law respecting an establishment of religion or prohibiting the free exercise thereof."* [12] This means the government cannot create a government-run religion or take over an existing religion. It also implies that a religious body can't have the power and control to govern.

It has nothing to do with praying in school or displaying the Ten Commandments in a courthouse — both of which are permissible under the First Amendment. It has everything to do with the radical pro-socialists' obsession to erase God and replace Him with the government.

Having gone through years of abuse and legal fights with radical pro-socialists, Coach Kennedy voluntarily left his coaching position in 2023 to focus his time and efforts on advocating for religious liberty full-time. On his departure, Coach Kennedy declared:

> *"As I have demonstrated, we must make a stand for what we believe in. In my case, I made a stand to take a knee. I encourage all Americans to make their own stand for freedom and our right to express our faith as we see fit."* [13]

We need more battle-tested champions for religious liberty like Coach Kennedy to take on the radical tireless campaign against our religious freedoms.

Protecting Christian Schools (and Parents)

Religious freedom was also at the heart of *Carson v. Makin,* a case disputing a Maine state law that prohibited parents from using state-funded tuition vouchers to send their children to religious private schools.

In its 2022 decision, the Supreme Court ruled that this prohibition was unconstitutional. In the opinion written by Chief Justice John Roberts, the Court found that Maine had violated the Free Exercise Clause of the First Amendment by excluding religious schools and parents from participating in otherwise available public benefits.

In short, it said the state can't discriminate against a private school because it is religious or run by a religious organization.

The ruling opens the doors to all Americans of faith to be able to choose the best schools for their children without fear of government punishment or reprisal for their faith.

Of course, the Court's three liberal justices dissented. Justice Sonia Sotomayor wrote that the majority had "upended constitutional doctrine" and expressed her concern for "where this Court will lead us next." [14]

Where will it lead, indeed?

Hopefully, this amazing victory opens the door for Christian schools and homeschooling parents to become eligible for tax credits or vouchers — a major step towards school choice, which, as I argued in the previous chapter, is an essential step toward righting the sinking ship of our country's education system.

A NEW THREAT TO RELIGIOUS LIBERTY: ARTIFICIAL INTELLIGENCE

I have already dedicated an entire chapter to the enormous threat the misuse of AI has on our privacy, security, electoral integrity, and fundamental perceptions of "truth." But AI will also have major ramifications for the church — some good, some bad.

For example, I recently came across a new AI app that lets users have a one-on-one text message chat with Jesus.

Yes, you can text back and forth with Jesus. Sort of.

Some don't like the concept and feel uneasy with it. They may even call it blasphemy. But this relatively elementary AI app is based on sound biblical doctrine — so far, anyway — and Jesus' answers exhibit a true biblical worldview.

Someone took this concept in a different direction by creating a "chat with Satan" app. But again, the answers are all based on what we know about the demonic ... so far.

Tools like this can be helpful in spreading the gospel, making Jesus more approachable and relevant to younger generations who have grown up looking at phone screens instead of old, leather-bound books.

AI will also be a tremendous aid to pastors doing research and preparing sermons. As I said in Chapter 8, I use AI apps regularly in my personal research and writing. Worship pastors can also use AI to pick the perfect songs to go with that week's sermon. In these and other uses, AI will make a positive impact on all Christians' worship experience.

But, of course, AI can also work against us.

The terrifying reality is that AI can be used to silence, marginalize, or persecute Christians around the world and right here in America.

Dr. David Curry is the President and CEO of Global Christian Relief (GCR), an organization that advocates on behalf of those who are persecuted for their Christian faith throughout the world. When I had dinner with him recently, he told me the potential misuse of AI is one of his primary concerns for Christians worldwide. We discussed his four biggest concerns:

1. **Programmed Biases:** As we discussed in Chapter 8, AI is largely in the hands of radical-socialist, Big Tech companies. That means their products, even independent "thinking machines," will take on the biases of their programmers.

2. **Targeting Christians:** Communist China is already using AI to monitor Chinese citizens' physical and online activity, including their religious practices. This makes it much easier to identify "underground churches" and those who attend, which results in penalties to citizens' valuable social credit scores.

3. **Using Deepfakes to Frame Innocent People:** In many areas worldwide, Christians face persecution based on baseless accusations. Deepfakes could be the smoking gun that gets a Christian killed or a church burned to the ground.

4. **Assisting Terror Groups:** Islamic terrorist groups in Africa, the Middle East, and other places worldwide that already persecute Christians will be able to do so more effectively. They can use technology to target Christians, cut them off from cellphones and technology, and then attack.

David argued, *"We have to be clear that the basic biblical story is a challenge to the culture now. I think it's going to be banned on public platforms in the not-too-distant future ... We're not looking at a far horizon. I think in the next five to 10 years, you're going to see this escalate and possibly become* ***the*** *issue of our time."*

For this reason, David and others, including myself, support Christians creating their own platforms that are not beholden to Google and Facebook's rules and therefore cannot be banned. This would require more than just one company setting up a website, though. The entire online infrastructure, including web hosting and domain registry, would need to be separate from the standardized options most sites use today. It will require a lot of moving parts and a lot of expensive development, but I think it's the only way to ensure Christianity has any kind of future online.

As with any new technology — the printing press, the radio, television, the Internet, virtual reality, and now AI — Christians need to be at the forefront to leverage the benefits and protect against the dangers of artificial intelligence.

FREEDOM OF WORSHIP VS. FREEDOM OF RELIGION

Throughout this chapter and, in part, throughout this entire book, I have shown all the different ways the media, Big Tech, politicians, and bureaucrats have tried to silence Christians from speaking out, and offering their faith-based perspective on political and moral issues, and even the truth about Jesus Christ.

They want Christians utterly and completely silenced in the public square.

They want *freedom of worship.*

This is what President Biden wants. This is what Big Tech and mainstream media want. This is what all the other anti-Christian, socialist-minded politicians, bureaucrats, teachers, and activists want.

Freedom of worship.

Now, that might seem like a good thing at first glance. After all, we like *freedom.* We like to *worship.* You might ask, "Isn't *freedom of worship* a good thing?"

No.

No, it's not. And I'll tell you why.

There is a world of difference between *freedom of worship* and *freedom of religion.* The latter is what is enshrined in the Constitution. Freedom of religion is our fundamental right as Americans to *choose* which (if any) religion we follow, to *change* which religion we follow, and — and this is the fundamental difference — to *practice* whatever religion we follow *in public or in private.*

Freedom of religion means I can not only worship alongside like-minded people within the confines of my church but also talk about my faith publicly. I can view and interpret the world through a religious lens — in my case, a Christian worldview. It means I can talk about my beliefs in the public square, bringing biblical truth to bear on modern issues.

Freedom of worship, by contrast, means I can believe whatever I want — but I cannot share it. I have to keep it to myself. I can't burden someone else with my own "religious opinions."

Freedom of worship is what you find in many socialist and communist countries. In China, for example, you can *believe* in Jesus Christ, but you better keep those beliefs to yourself. If you don't, you could be arrested and thrown in a communist prison or labor camp for the rest of your life.

In modern America, we aren't quite that extreme — yet. COVID-19 lockdowns notwithstanding, you won't get arrested for praising Jesus out loud. But you could be "canceled." You could be kicked off social media platforms. You could lose your job because your employer gets bullied by an online mob of thugs decrying your "hate speech." You could be widely and publicly shamed for daring to offer a dissenting view to whatever social fad or radical political ideology is in vogue at the time.

Freedom of worship says:

> *"Don't disagree with the culture. Don't question our political or bureaucratic leaders. Don't suggest that the world's standards are misaligned with reality. Don't imply that what's 'true for you' is true for everyone. Above all else, don't offend anyone."*

And if you *do* break one of these rules?

You're labeled a hatemonger, ridiculed, and effectively removed from society.

This, sadly, is nothing new in the history of the world.

In fact, this is exactly what happened to the earliest Christians in ancient Rome. They, too, were called *haters.* They were mocked, blamed for heinous crimes, thrown in prison, run out of town, and even killed.

Why?

It wasn't because they actually *hated* anything; it was because they boldly professed a different way of living. A better way. The government and the easily offended called them haters because they wouldn't go with the flow. They were different ... and bureaucracies don't like different — at least when *different* means *different from what we tell you to do.*

These early "hateful" Christians were known for — and punished for — their love. Christians found and adopted newborn babies left on the side of the road — the ancient world's way of dealing with an "unwanted pregnancy." Christians opened hospitals, took care of the sick and elderly, and provided education. Christians lived in community, helping, loving, and serving each other and their neighbors.

But the culture still thought of them as hateful and despicable people.

We can see this throughout the New Testament. For example, Acts 16 recounts just a few of the apostle Paul's many hardships at the hands of a godless culture. At one point, he literally saves a young slave woman from a lifetime of demon possession. That may sound strange to you, but no one questioned it at the time. In fact, it was so accepted as demonstrably true that the slave girl's owners had Paul arrested for it!

I find these men's complaint to the authorities both fascinating and remarkably similar to today's "cancel culture." The Bible recounts:

> *"They seized Paul and Silas and dragged them into the marketplace to face the authorities. They brought them before the magistrates and said, 'These men are Jews, and are* ***throwing our city into an uproar'*** *by advocating customs unlawful for us Romans to accept or practice."* (Acts 16:19-21, NIV, emphasis added)

They weren't mad that Paul and Silas *believed* in Jesus; they were mad that they *lived out their belief* in Jesus. The apostle's boldness and tenacity did then what it would do today: it throws our culture into an uproar by confronting us with something different from the accepted norms of today's society.

Rather than dragging us to jail, though, they are "canceling" us. They are trying to de-platform us online. They are trying to close our private Christian schools. They are trying to prevent Christians from adopting children who need a home. They are trying to use our tax dollars to fund controversial or depraved medical procedures that violate our conscience. They are trying to prevent us from homeschooling our children rather than placing them under the state's tutelage.

They are telling us (sometimes quite literally):

> *"Believe whatever you want. But say what we tell you to say, affirm what we tell you to affirm, and do what we tell you to do — whether it violates your 'religious principles' or not."*

It's interesting that this is exactly what we see in Scripture. Over and over throughout the Bible, we find calls to *stand firm.* Don't give in. Don't compromise. Don't turn your back on what you know is right. Don't sacrifice your faith on the altar of the prevailing culture.

Thankfully, the Founding Fathers made sure we don't have to.

The First Amendment reads:

> *"Congress shall make no law respecting an establishment of religion, or prohibiting the free exercise thereof; or abridging the freedom of speech, or of the press; or the right of the people peaceably to assemble, and to petition the Government for a redress of grievances."*

It is no coincidence that the constitutional restriction against the government "prohibiting the free exercise" of religion is *immediately* followed by the prohibition of the government to "[abridge] the freedom of speech."

We have a God-given right to believe and to speak about our faith.

We should not, we will not, and we cannot be silenced.

If you are a Christian, you have not been called to choke down anti-Christian cultural ideologies that are wholly foreign to the Word of God. You have been called to:

> *"Live as children of light ... and find out what pleases the Lord. Have nothing to do with the fruitless deeds of darkness, but rather expose them. It is shameful even to mention what the disobedient do in secret. But everything exposed by the light becomes visible — and everything that is illuminated becomes a light."* (Ephesians 5:8, 11-13, NIV)

The answer to today's war on Christianity has been right there in Scripture for 2,000 years.

Live as children of light.

Have nothing to do with the fruitless deeds of darkness.

Instead, *expose* their dark deeds.

Fight the darkness with truth and with light. Uncover their lies. Stand firm when they try to push you into a corner. Exercise your constitutional right to freely exercise your religious beliefs. *Speak* up when they tell you to *shut* up.

Yes, there is a war against Christianity, and it's being fought in the media, online, in school board meetings, behind the closed doors of Deep State bureaucracies, and in the halls of Congress. But we are not helpless. Both God and the U.S. Constitution have equipped us for this fight.

This is a war we can win.

This is a war we *must* win

Chapter 11

Danger #10: The Age of Deception's Three Ms: Messaging, Misinformation, And Mobilization

Have you ever found yourself "stuck" in front of the TV watching an infomercial?

Of course, you have. We *all* have.

We've all had that moment when we're channel surfing and land on an energetic presenter showing someone how to slice and dice onions in seconds (no tears!); how to vacuum gravel, wine, and pet hair out of carpet; how to get six-pack abs in seven minutes a day; or how to squeeze the vitamin-rich juices out of anything from oranges to coconuts. And we just sit there watching, captivated by the solution to a problem we have never cared about but suddenly can't ignore any longer.

Sometimes, we even pick up the phone or go online to place an order.

Don't beat yourself up. That's why infomercials exist — and that's why they are so effective at driving direct-to-consumer sales for even the most niche product.

That is the power of good messaging.

Guess what? This also explains how so many radical socialist Democrats, with insane policies that most Americans don't want, keep getting elected — they're winning at messaging. In fact, I'd argue that the Democrats are 15 to 20 years ahead of Republicans when it comes to writing effective, results-driven copy that mobilizes volunteers, donors, and voters.

This is an area where my two professional passions — politics and marketing — intersect. I've been in the messaging business for 50 years. Way back in college, I started writing copy and opened an advertising agency that has grown to serve clients around the world and win more than a hundred advertising awards for creative breakthroughs and excellence in marketing.

I have written copy for radio and TV, infomercials, Google ads, Facebook ads, YouTube pre-roll ads, geofencing, and pretty much every other format from the past half-century. I've also given speeches on writing great copy to persuade people to buy a product or service, to make a donation, or to vote for a candidate. Plus, I have written two marketing books, each with a chapter on how to write copy for sales and marketing.

All that to say ... I know a thing or two about the power of messaging — and I have several old scars that represent *bad* messaging.

So, when I look at what the radical, socialist Democrats have been doing ever since Barack Obama's first presidential campaign in 2008, I can see and even respect it for what it is: a new, effective, and powerful form of messaging that most Republicans, Cconservatives, Libertarians, and Christians can't match.

Obama helped revolutionize political messaging by breaking with tradition, not using the traditional Democratic Party consultants, and hiring his own digital marketing and copywriting geniuses. Since then, the radical pro-socialists have learned how to craft their messages to drive the cultural and political changes they're after.

Today's messaging, mobilization, and misinformation are the underpinnings of a powerful, invisible political force. And if we leave it only in the hands of the radicals, it could very well lead to the end of the Republic.

MASTERING EMOTIONAL TRIGGERS

When marketing and advertising professionals create a video, commercial, direct mail piece, or digital ad, we will use certain keywords or phrases I call *emotional triggers.* These triggers are customized per product and per market segment to motivate the largest number of people toward a desired purchasing decision.

In commercial marketing, we often use what I call the *triple emotion triggers:*

1. Fear.
2. Anger.
3. Moral Self-Righteousness.

These three elements work together to trigger an emotional response, thereby motivating people to move toward a decision and take action.

The radical pro-socialists have caught on to these age-old marketing tactics. They've discovered that using fear, anger, and moral self-righteousness in their speeches, ads, commercials, and videos motivates a person to volunteer for a cause or campaign, to make a donation, and ultimately to vote.

This approach has been so effective for the past 15 years or so that the radical pro-socialists have ramped up their use of triple emotion triggers exponentially, testing and tweaking their messaging several times until it is *perfect* — that is, until it is most likely to achieve the results they want for that specific message to a specific target market.

Whatever the issue is, it's tested on focus groups. It's tested with AI. Then, it's tested in digital ads to see its reaction among a broader (but still relatively small) audience. The messaging is never meant for anyone else to respond to except the specially chosen target/test audience. That test audience could be reliable Democrats, young people, people concerned about an issue like abortion, the Black community, the Hispanic community, Gen Z, and Millennials.

It's microtargeting small, niche audiences for maximum results.

People and groups with a history of supporting Democratic candidates and initiatives will get one message, while *persuadables* — those who have been identified as being likely to become supporters with a little nudge — will get an entirely different message. They'll even target Republicans who have demonstrated some chance, however slim, of voting Democrat on some issues.

The big point here is that ads — especially in this new digital world — are entirely customized based on who is seeing them right down to the individual level. In fact, two people living in the same house can look at the same webpage on two different computers and get an entirely different piece of ad copy customized for each one based on advanced data profiling on each individual, even your past transactions. This is called Transactional Data Modeling (TDM).

Social media, Big Tech, your search history, the websites you visit, the YouTube videos you watch, your purchase history on Amazon or MasterCard or American Express … it all comes together to create a shockingly accurate profile of who you are, your values, your voting preferences, your stance on key issues, and everything else about you. That online profile is used to serve ads that are most appealing to and effective for you.

With all that information, the radical socialists can ratchet up the intensity of each of the triple emotional triggers:

- **Fear** becomes *intense* fear — of climate change, MAGA Republicans, taking away a woman's "freedom of choice," or a "growing fascist threat to our nation."

- **Anger** becomes *intense* anger — directed towards Trump, "climate deniers," or parents challenging what teachers can do and say in the classroom.

- **Self-righteousness** becomes *intense* self-righteousness — devolving into moral superiority and rage toward anyone who dares to disagree about "women's health," "transgender rights," or "Black Lives Matter."

It's all based on data, targeted only to that specific group — microtargeting *only* to that specific group.

If you are not in the group and somehow see the messaging, you would be confused, react against it, maybe even mock it.

But it's not for you. It triggers its target audience.

When you know what to look for, you start to see it plain as day all over the radicals marketing messages. They're mobilizing their voters and potential voters using misinformation driven by fear, anger, and self-righteousness.

And ... it's working.

DECEPTION THROUGH DOUBLESPEAK

Language is powerful.

The words we use to explain the world around us.

The words *others* use to define who *we* are.

These labels stick. They stick in the hearts and minds of people. They change how others perceive us. Though they may be baseless, even if they are factually and demonstrably untrue, the terms people use to describe their "enemies" have massive cultural power.

In today's world of instant, global communication — a world in which everyone has a megaphone through Facebook, X (formerly Twitter), Instagram, TikTok, and whatever other social platforms may come — anyone has the power to label anyone else whatever they want. And those labels can ruin someone's life.

We are heading for a world even George Orwell could not have predicted. Well, Orwell did predict one glaring problem of modern life in his 1949 novel, *1984:* he coined the term *doublespeak* — something that now permeates most of the social media posts *and* established, mainstream media news reports we see every day.

Doublespeak is the uses of euphemistic or ambiguous language to deliberately obscure, distort, and disguise what someone actually means by what he is saying. Doublespeak can also involve reversing the meaning of words or using buzzwords as labels to attack someone's character without bothering to give specific examples of the implied bad behavior.

Some of the most commonly used doublespeak terms we see "in the wild" today are:

- Racist.
- Woke.
- Radical.
- White Supremacist.
- Christian Nationalist.
- Fascist.
- MAGA.
- Extremist.

If you follow politics at all, you've no doubt heard some or all of these terms, probably in the past day or two. They are *everywhere* — and that's no accident. Most of the doublespeak terms we hear today are carefully crafted, researched, tested, and even focus-grouped to ensure they are eliciting the desired negative reaction.

Did you think it was a coincidence when every mainstream news outlet started using terms like *radical MAGA extremists* practically in unison?

It wasn't. It was part of a plan to demonize Conservatives, Libertarians, and Christians and paint every Republican with the same vile strokes.

Knowing the terms the radical socialists use against us are intentional, let's break them down just a bit to see what the radical messaging means by word (and what the terms *really* mean).

Racist

An actual *racist* is historically someone who believes that race is the fundamental determinant of human traits and capabilities and that racial differences therefore cause one race to be inherently superior to another race or to all other races.

As someone who grew up in the 1950s and 1960s, I've seen racism — *real* racism. It was then and is today absolutely disgusting and immoral. For my entire adult life, calling someone a *racist* was just about the worst thing you could say about them. It had real weight and meaning. People knew exactly what it meant.

Not anymore.

In recent years, the term *racist* has been used to attack anyone who disagrees with a particularly vocal social or political group. It isn't an insult of last resort; it's the first line of attack. Every issue that can be racialized by the radical pro-socialists *will be* racialized by the radical pro-socialists. It has become their shortcut to win any argument.

For example:

- Conservatives and Libertarians have been called "racists" for favoring free-market capitalism over government-controlled socialism.
- Christians have been called "racist" for believing in biblical truth and the need for everyone to accept

Christ as their personal savior.

- Former President Donald Trump was called a "racist" because he didn't want to allow terrorists, criminals, drug dealers, and members of the MS-13 gang to come into the United States from Mexico.
- Anyone who questions the legitimacy of the Black Lives Matter movement or organization for any reason has been cast as "racist."

If there is any ethnic or racial diversity involved in an issue, you can be sure one of the first accusations the radicals will hurl at the Conservatives, Libertarians, and Christians is racism.

And if you demand evidence for their accusations of racism?

Well, that also makes you a "racist."

Woke

The terms *woke* and *wokeness* are probably the most popular examples of doublespeak so far in the 21st century. The term is so wrapped in doublespeak, in fact, that no one seems to agree on what *woke* actually means.

The dictionary defines *woke* as "aware of and actively attentive to important societal facts and issues." [1] But which facts? Which issues? And what does "actively attentive" mean? Every political identity group and every corporate board of directors has their own ideas.

For some, you cannot be "actively attentive" regarding gender identity and transgenderism unless you support and celebrate transgender medication, surgery, and preferred pronouns for children in elementary school.

If you don't agree with the social agenda of the radical socialists regarding Critical Race Theory, celebrating Pride Month for the LGBTQI+ community, multiple gender identity, and transgenderism, you are not woke enough — and therefore, you are to be shunned and ostracized.

Can you be woke if you support environmental activism but question transgender surgeries for children? Can you be woke if you march in a Pride parade but have questions about what BLM did with the millions of dollars it collected in 2020? Is *woke* an all-or-nothing proposition, or can you be woke on one issue and un-woke on another?

Again, this may well be the term of the century, but it is utterly meaningless if no one — including those who proudly wear the woke label — can even agree on what it means.

Radical

The word *radical* used to describe those with extreme views outside of the traditional views that most Americans have. Now, the word means just the opposite.

The new concept of a *radical* is a conservative Christian with traditional values — as opposed to someone on the extreme Left who wants to destroy freedom of speech by censoring all Conservative or Christian content from the public square. That person is fine. Today, it's the quiet, middle-America, churchgoing family man that's considered radical.

For example, parents who complain to their local school boards about their children being subjected to Critical Race Theory and transgender ideology in school are not only labeled as radicals but have been called domestic terrorists by the Biden Administration and the U.S. Department of Justice!

Sensible, respectful people who peacefully protest against radical pro-socialist initiatives are called radicals and haters — even though it's those persecuting them who are yelling vile obscenities, physically attacking them, bullying and "canceling" them online, and exhibiting obvious hateful behavior.

The modern use of *radical* isn't just doublespeak; it's a double standard of moral right and wrong.

White Supremacist

White supremacist is another doublespeak term that is bandied about almost as much as *racist* these days. And as is the case with many of these terms, *white supremacist* is never clearly defined by those who use it.

The dictionary definition of white supremacist is *"a person who believes that the white race is inherently superior to other races and that the white race should have control over people of other races."* [2] This absolutely does not describe the views of the vast majority of white people in America. But the radical pro-socialists don't care.

Instead, the term *white supremacist* has come to mean "white conservative" in many circles and media outlets. They assume the only reason a white person could possibly object the radical pro-socialists' cultural agenda of socialism and government censorship is because that person hates all other races and believes he is superior to everyone else. In doing so, the radical pro-socialists try to frame any objection to their ideology as, *"You're just trying to hold onto your power and privilege as a white person."*

This isn't just nonsensical; it's a diversion. This is an example of the radical pro-socialists accusing us of doing the very thing *they* are doing. They're trying to divert attention away from the fact that the self-proclaimed experts, elite radical pro-socialist politicians, and socialist government leaders are the ones who are trying to categorize and control people according to their race.

Christian Nationalist

Another term radical pro-socialists use to attack both Conservatives and Christians is Christian nationalist. Again, those who use it to negatively describe political opponents never bother to define it. They just imply that a *Christian nationalist* is someone who wants the federal government to be a theocracy ruled by intolerant, wide-eyed, Bible-thumping fanatics — and by implication, a lover of Nazi Germany.

A nationalist is simply someone who opposes having open borders and who believes in preserving the sovereignty of individual nations throughout the world.

The globalists — those who advocate for no national boundaries and a one-world government — characterize their opponents in the worst way possible to squash debate and persuade the masses to follow their agenda without thinking for themselves.

Fascist

Fascist has become quite the common insult in recent years. As with the other doublespeak terms, it's generally hurled at conservatives to cast them as narcissistic, power-hungry bigots and warmongers.

And again, the radical pro-socialists don't stop to actually define the term or give specific examples of how someone's behavior qualifies as *fascistic.* Instead, they ignorantly throw this historically significant term around like little children calling each other names on the schoolyard.

It seems impossible to count the number of times Donald Trump specifically has been labeled a fascist, but let's look at the record and see if this insult makes any sense whatsoever. Fascism is a political philosophy that emphasizes:

- Exalting the nation/state above the individual.
- Centralized autocratic government.
- Dictatorship.
- Socialism and economic extreme regulation.

- Forcible suppression of opposition and censorship.

Donald Trump stands for exactly the opposite:

- Individual freedom for all — including Blacks, Latinos, and other ethnic minorities.
- Decentralized government.
- Representative government.
- Social and economic deregulation.
- Freedom of speech and open debate of opposing views.

This isn't just my perspective; his presidential record reflects every one of these principles and demonstrates how Trump was one of the most *un-fascistic* Presidents in American history.

But again, the radical pro-socialists don't care.

In fact, this is yet another example of the radical pro-socialists accusing conservatives of the very things they are doing. If you look at the characteristics of fascism I listed above, it's not hard to see parallels with the radical pro-socialist agenda of the modern Democratic party.

MAGA

Donald Trump's campaign slogan in 2016 was Make America Great Again, which everyone came to know as *MAGA.* It was a rallying cry depicting Conservatives, Libertarians, Republicans, and the Right as the most despicable — or, in Hillary Clinton's words, *deplorable* — type of person imaginable for the radical pro-socialists.

For Trump, his supporters, and many Conservatives and Republicans in general, MAGA referred to an intentional effort to restore America to its former leadership socially and economically, while also restoring America's stellar reputation on the world stage.

This stood in stark contrast to President Obama's "Apology Tour" during his first few years in office. Liberals cheered and Conservatives were stunned and horrified as the President traveled around the globe, apologizing to different world leaders for America's past mistakes. Ever since then, our leadership position has sharply declined among other countries and world leaders. President Obama effectively invited the world to lose respect for America as a moral, economic, social, and military superpower.

Trump took the opposite approach. He was bold in expressing his pride in America and support for the concept of American exceptionalism. He spent his term working to increase our power, prestige, and stature as a world leader — and he succeeded, much to the dismay of those who support open borders and a one-world government.

Today, the radical pro-socialists and many in the media use MAGA with all the hate and vitriol you'd expect of someone describing Nazis or Adolf Hitler himself — and they use it against proud Americans who only want to preserve our country as a strong and sovereign nation.

Extremist

Finally, we have the doublespeak term that is probably used most often second only to *racist,* and that is *extremist.* Pretty much anyone who doesn't fall in lockstep with any part of the radical pro-socialist agenda is quickly labeled an *extremist* and disregarded as a quack.

This includes those who:

- Are pro-life.
- Support free speech and oppose censorship.
- Think we should secure our national borders and require immigrants to enter the country legally.

- Believe capitalism is the best, most opportunity-rich economic system in the world.
- Recognize the biological reality of two distinct human genders.

Whatever the subject, those who disagree with the radical pro-socialist agenda are accused of being extremists.

Of course, the word elicits an immediate negative response, so it never needs to be defined. It's yet another convenient and effective attack word.

I've covered here the eight key doublespeak terms that I've most often seen thrown around in public discourse over recent years — and been called myself — but there are many more. Once you know what doublespeak is and how it is used, it's not hard to identify it when you hear it.

Whatever the term and context, doublespeak is used to infer a negative connotation upon someone or something — usually with no burden of proof. In political campaign advertising, these terms are used to:

- Persuade undecided voters to support a candidate or cause.
- Alienate voters who don't support a particular candidate or cause.
- Rally voters, volunteers, and donors to make contributions of time and money by vilifying their opponent.

As you listen to news reports and hear public or campaign statements from politicians, keep a watchful ear on the use of doublespeak. Don't take it for granted, don't be blindly persuaded by it, and whenever possible, demand clarification of what the person is saying and ask for specific examples to justify their claims.

And don't be shocked if, most of the time, whoever you're discussing it with won't be able to provide it.

RELATIVISM: AN ASSAULT ON MEANING

If the growing prevalence of doublespeak in our national discourse weren't bad enough, we're facing an even greater threat in the messaging we encounter every day. That danger is *relativism.*

Relativism itself is not a term we hear often, but we do indeed hear the *influence* of relativism hundreds, if not thousands, of times per day.

In short, relativism is the belief that there is no absolute truth; rather, "truth" is in the eye of the beholder. So, different people can have different views about what is or is not true or moral. This is why you may hear someone say something like, *"That may be true for you, but it's not true for me."*

That may sound like a quick and easy way to get along with each other, but there is a major problem with relativism that few are taking seriously: If there is no such thing as *absolute truth,* then *nothing has any meaning whatsoever.*

If there is no firm, concrete basis for what is true (and therefore what is false), then all you are left with are lies and misinformation contrived to fit certain narratives. For example, it is nonsense for one country to say capitalism is the greatest economic system in the world and for another country to say socialism is the greatest economic system in the world. The relativist can say, *"Well, it depends on who's saying it and where they live."*

No.

Those are two *objective* statements. Two systems that stand in complete opposition with each other cannot *both* be "the greatest economic system in the world." At least one of them has to be wrong — but the modern world says we are not allowed to tell *anyone* they're wrong about *anything.* That is the influence of relativism.

This is a dangerous road to take.

When society doesn't have absolute truth — a universal and real standard that guides us all — then what's left is anarchy and the destruction of society.

We all know that stealing is wrong. Jews and Christians see this in the Bible's Ten Commandments. Muslims see this in the Koran. Even atheists intuitively know stealing is wrong. No one in any country or culture in the world would be okay with someone stealing their stuff. The understanding that stealing is immoral is an absolute truth.

But consider the recent nationwide phenomenon of snatch-and-grab thievery plaguing America's major cities. Individuals or entire groups descend on a store, clear the shelves, and walk out without paying. The store employees are told not to intervene. These people are never arrested. As a result, businesses like Walmart, Target, Best Buy, and Macy's have permanently closed their stores in many cities. [3] They simply cannot afford to operate while their merchandise continues to be stolen and walked out the door.

A relativist can rationalize and even condone this rampant crime as "reparations for the underserved or repressed." To the relativist, this isn't *stealing;* it's *justice.* And those committing the act are not *criminals;* they're the *victims* — victims of "systemic racism" and "white privilege."

It has taken less than a decade for activists and socialist politicians to erase centuries of cultural norms and absolute truths — truths that have been the basis of civilized society throughout human history.

Wisdom, reason, and truth are now the enemy, replaced by propaganda, lies, and misinformation. Relativism is replacing absolute truth, even though relativism often contradicts itself. For example:

- A man can now declare he is a woman, and a woman can declare she is a man — and we are all expected to accept it 100 percent, no questions asked.
- There is no such thing as gender — and yet there are simultaneously *dozens* of genders.
- The radicals celebrate Kamala Harris as the first woman Vice President. However, they can't define what a woman is. (In fact, a U.S. Supreme Court Justice refused to even attempt to define the term *"woman,"* in her Senate confirmation hearing.)
- We must "believe all women" and protect women's private spaces, but we must also allow trans-identifying biological males to walk around naked in women's locker rooms. And if a woman complains that one of these transgender women (a biological male) is "peeping" at her, we *shouldn't* "believe" her and should instead cast her out as a "transphobic hatemonger."
- The country is systemically racist, yet we have twice elected a Black man to the presidency, we have elected a black woman to the vice presidency, we have installed three Black Supreme Court justices, and there are more Black millionaires and billionaires than ever before. If you point that out, though, the relativists call you a racist.

The sick, twisted reality that is relativism has even infected our schools and colleges. Math itself — the fixed, concrete language of the universe — has become subjective, and students are often not required to get the *correct* answers. For example, many educators would argue that 2 + 2 no longer equals 4. It equals whatever you feel the answer should be; there are no wrong answers. *"What is **four?**"* they say. ***"Four** is just a word someone* *made up. We can make up any word to answer what 2 + 2 is."*

It's no wonder kids today can't read or perform math calculations at their grade level.

But when parents or critics point out that their kids can't pass basic math tests, relativist school officials claim that "math is a racist construct." (If you think I'm exaggerating, just Google "math is racist" and have fun reading all the articles from major outlets like *The Washington Post, Scientific American,* and yes, even the National Institutes of Health that have popped up since 2020.)

This dumbing down of the population through relativism only makes the radical, socialist, secularists in government more powerful and makes the population more susceptible to government control and propaganda. In short, the government becomes stronger, and the individual becomes weaker.

If you can convince little Johnny or Janie that men can have babies, you can convince them of anything. We're creating an ignorant, gullible, and totally captive audience that has total trust in the propaganda they've been force-fed from kindergarten all the way through college — whole generations without the capacity or the ability to engage in critical thinking.

This is exactly what every socialist/Marxist/communist society has done to their populace in Eastern Europe, China, and Cuba. During World War II, we rightly called it brainwashing. This is the same pattern of forced-fed propaganda that made the Hitler Youth turn in their own parents to the Nazi SS for not thinking the "right" way or criticizing Hitler's government.

Even here in the land of the free and home of the brave, relativism has created a fear of speaking one's mind in the last few years. We've all seen how easy it can be to lose your job because you said something your company's DEI leadership doesn't agree with. Every word we say online and even in a private conversation has to be "politically correct," because the social justice gatekeepers are always listening and watching.

Today, social media has accelerated the problem with the help of the federal government and has been taken over by radical, socialist Marxists who use relativism to weaponize the government to de-platform, cancel, and destroy not only political opponents but anyone who disagrees with them or criticizes the government's propaganda and narratives.

Without a broadly understood, obvious foundation of absolute truth, everything boils down to forced agreement with those in power, no matter how bizarre, illogical, or strange their positions are. Truth becomes, in effect, whatever they say it is. Until they change it to something else, of course. And if you don't agree, you'll be punished.

Relativism destroys the truth.

Relativism destroys free speech.

Relativism destroys a free society.

Relativism is the serpent, and Marxism is the apple.

Only truth and the Word of God can prevent us from taking a bite.

PRIVATIZING MISINFORMATION: FUNDING THE RADICAL PRO-SOCIALISTS' CAMPAIGN OF LIES

How did all this misinformation and the widespread growth of relativism happen so quickly? And, perhaps more importantly, *who is paying for it?*

After all, the radical pro-socialists' new, twisted reality is being accepted as truth by Big Tech, Hollywood, mainstream media, and the education bureaucracy. Anyone who questions the established narratives — especially anyone who is a Christian, a conservative, or a libertarian — is quickly and viciously dispatched in a smear campaign and/or "canceled" for public discourse.

Disagreement is not allowed.

Questions are not allowed.

The establishment will accept *only* your complete and unwavering acceptance. Anything less, and you'll be castigated as a radical, an extremist, or a fascist.

Of course, you certainly cannot debate anything the radical pro-socialists are presenting as "facts." In their view, the *facts* are only whatever information supports the narrative that the radical politicians and biased media want you to believe. There's no room for any facts that don't "fit." And any *actual* statistics or research that opposes the narrative is disregarded as "misinformation."

These misinformation and discrediting efforts have grown much more sophisticated (and expensive) in recent years. In fact, to outright silence public debate, the creators and leaders of the radical pro-socialist narratives in the United States have developed a new "misinformation research" industry funded by a network of dark-money nonprofit organizations. Misinformation is whatever claims are made by the radical's enemies. Disinformation is the radicals active and deliberate communication of lies and false narratives.

Dark money is political spending meant to influence the decision of a voter — and thereby election results — in which the donor is not disclosed and the original source of the money is unknown. Basically, *dark money* represents a hidden figure in the backroom who's secretly paying the bills and wants to remain anonymous. Dark money is also used to support political candidates and/or to influence public policy.

Arabella Advisors, run by former Bill Clinton official Eric Kessler, manages certain administrative, legal, and philanthropic functions of several nonprofit funds. These funds, in turn, sponsor research that looks at the online presence of conservatives, libertarians, and Christians and recommends strategies to mitigate the spread of what they call "misinformation."

Here are just a few examples of how some of these funds are

being used: [4]

- **The New Venture Fund**
  - Sponsored a research project at the Harvard Kennedy School's Shorenstein Center on Media, Politics, and Public Policy. The study, called "The True Costs of Misinformation," sought to determine the effects of online misinformation on "vulnerable communities."
  - Presented a workshop at the Carnegie Council titled, "What is Driving Conservatism's Post-Democratic Turn in America?" that examined the effects of misinformation on the perceived "anti-democratic" attitudes of conservatives in the United States. The description of the presentation asked the question, *"How did American Conservatism reach a point where the main political messages are either blatantly anti-democratic or outright falsehoods?"* The presentation description further alleged that "political partisanship" in the United States was "largely stoked by Conservative propaganda and misinformation."
- **The Hopewell Fund**
  - Sponsored a research project that examined how misinformation spreads on Facebook via "superusers." A research paper citing the results of the study appeared in *The Atlantic* and suggested censorship as the most effective way to curb misinformation. *"If each of Facebook's 15,000 U.S. monitors,"* the paper stated, *"aggressively reviewed several dozen of the most active users and permanently removed those guilty of repeated violations, abuse on Facebook would drop drastically within days."*
- **The Media Democracy Fund**
  - Partially funds the Disinfo Defense League, which

describes itself as *"a distributed national network of organizers, researchers and disinformation experts."* The purpose of the Disinfo Defense League is to disrupt online disinformation campaigns that target Black, Latino, Asian American/Pacific Islander, and other minority groups.

- **The North Fund**
  - Operates a group called Accountable Tech, which organized a campaign to pressure advertisers to boycott Twitter after Elon Musk took over the platform, citing the threat of the spread of misinformation as a concern.
- **The Sixteen Thirty Fund**
  - Explicitly donates its funds to Democratic Political Action Committees (PACs) and Democrat candidates.

These and other funds within the Arabella Advisors network also support socialist and Democrat-affiliated groups that engage in issue-based advocacy activities and electoral activism. Overall, Arabella Advisors and its network of funds use charitable giving and tax exemption laws to aid Democratic electoral victories, performing an end run around the IRS prohibition against electioneering.

Hayden Ludwig, senior investigative researcher at Capital Research Center (CRC), a conservative watchdog group that tracks liberal financial influence, summarizes Arabella's activities:

> *"Nonprofits pour hundreds of millions of dollars into voter registration and get-out-the-vote (GOTV) campaigns which micro-target likely Democratic voters. The Arabella nonprofits are a massive funnel to shift those millions from foundations and mega-donors to these professional activists."* [5]

Bring the Money Out of the Dark

Most people — including our elected officials — are not even aware of how much dark money is being used to create such a large volume of misinformation, messaging, and mobilization. That is largely by design; most of these dark money donors hide their giving in tax shelters and IRS red tape by taking advantage of lax *nonprofit organization* rules and 501(c)(3) entities.

This type of giving should not be allowed under nonprofit and charitable giving tax status. It should be taxable and transparent, because it is being used to deceive American voters and as a political tool to transform our culture and politics.

THREE EFFECTS OF THIS NEW FORM OF MESSAGING

To explore the different ways messaging, misinformation, and mobilization are reshaping American life, I want to look at three key areas and give real-world examples of what doublespeak and relativism look like in action. My hope is that, once you know what the radical pro-socialists are doing with their messaging, you'll be able to spot it when you see it — and, hopefully, dismiss it as the misinformation and misdirection it usually is.

Effect on Political Speech

President Biden gave an address in 2022 that left many observers scratching their heads. Viewers on the political Right and Center almost universally declared it the most divisive presidential speech in history. Even the liberal media seemed taken aback by the angry tone of the president's remarks — not to mention the dark, red, foreboding background behind him. He was even flanked by Marines posted over each shoulder, giving the entire scene a distinctly dictatorial atmosphere.

It was, in a word, weird.

No one seemed to understand why Biden came on so strong, sounded so angry, and dressed the background so ominously.

Marketers like me, however, knew exactly what he was doing. He wasn't addressing the nation; he was addressing a specific target audience of hardcore, radical pro-socialists, dedicated, and loyal supporters. His goal was to fire up his base and get them to volunteer, donate, and show up to vote in the 2022 midterm elections — which, incidentally, were just two months away at the time. And, while he focused on Trump and MAGA, it's worth noting that Trump was not even on the ballot in that election.

His secondary audience was the small number of *persuadables* — voters who hadn't decided on a candidate and were still "up for grabs." If they were even slightly uncomfortable with Donald Trump, Biden tried to push them over to the Democrat agenda.

And he pushed *hard.*

The President openly and angrily attacked not only Donald Trump but any American who dared to agree with any of Trump's policies. He cast a wide net, framing anyone who didn't vehemently oppose Trump as "extremists" and "a threat to our democracy." He accused them of fanning *"the flames of political violence."* He claimed many Republicans "promote authoritarian leaders" and *"do not respect the Constitution."* He snarled as he repeated the terms *"MAGA"* and *"MAGA Republicans"* more than a dozen times, while raising two clinched fists in the air. [6]

This hateful, spite-driven rhetoric is the result of the radical pro-socialists' new style of messaging. They resort to name-calling, doublespeak, and self-righteous anger.

They bandy about terms like *extremist, threat to democracy, do not respect the Constitution,* and *promote authoritarian leaders* in their attempt to redefine reality. They are literally accusing Conservatives and Republicans of doing *exactly* what they are actively doing themselves. And they're using this style of messaging specifically to both mobilize their base and villainize anyone who does not share their twisted, distorted vision for America.

Sadly, this is the state of political speech in America today, and we're all supposed to accept it as the new normal. Unless, of course, you happen to disagree with the radical pro-socialists and/or use these same messaging tactics against them.

Then, you're a hateful, phobic, racist, extremist, pro-authoritarian, anti-Constitution, threat to democracy.

Obviously.

Impact on Elections

Every election cycle from now on will be forever stained by the radical pro-socialists' new messaging, mobilization, and misinformation machine. To be clear, this will affect every election, every candidate, and every voter — regardless of political party lines.

Why?

Because elections are no longer about issues that actually matter. Instead, they're targeted smear campaigns against whoever the radical pro-socialists deem "Public Enemy No. 1." Everyone knows who that is these days: Donald Trump.

Practically every Democrat candidate in every race, from school boards to U.S. Senate seats since 2020, has campaigned against Trump rather than their actual Republican challengers. They almost ignore the other name(s) on the ballot and instead focus all their time, money, and vitriol on Trump. They go out of their way to connect their opponent to Trump, personally and policy-wise.

If their opponent has ever said anything remotely positive about Trump, they splash it across TV screens. If there's a picture of Trump standing with their opponent, it becomes front-page news in the relevant markets. If there is not, they will use AI to create one.

To further support these efforts to politically demonize Trump and therefore poison anyone connected to him, local prosecutors have filed charges against him — indicting a former U.S. President no fewer than four times.

Funny how all four of these indictments went nowhere for three years after he left office and only became "urgent" 18 months before Election Day 2024.

The radical pro-socialists and their bureaucratic stormtroopers aren't even trying to hide their political bias and motivations. They're changing the electoral process right out in the open.

To be clear, though, the broader issue is not about Trump; he's just the issue *today.* Ten years from now, the radical pro-socialists will still be playing by these rules, only they'll have identified a new "threat to democracy" as a rallying cry for tomorrow's radical candidates.

By focusing their messaging on a single individual, the radical pro-socialists have chosen not to address the wide spectrum of issues Americans care about — immigration, inflation, gender identity, parents' rights, rising crime, pushback against DEI and ESG efforts, and more. There's a good reason for that: they know that once they start talking about specific issues, they lose. They know the majority of Americans do not share their radical values, so they don't talk about them. They *can't* talk about them. They instead distract voters with a stand-in for a modern-day Hitler while they make their devastating policy changes in the background.

The Americans who *are* paying attention and object to radical pro-socialist policies and candidates are easily castigated as "domestic terrorists" and "election deniers," who have been "radicalized" and "mobilized" to "overturn democracy" by their "treasonous" leader.

Today, that's Trump. Tomorrow, it could be anyone.

Literally anyone.

For goodness sakes, Biden once even threatened that Mitt Romney — the weakest, most milquetoast, barely-a-Republican presidential candidate in modern history — would put Black Americans "back in chains." [7] If they'll say that about Mitt Romney, of all people, they'll say much worse about anyone else.

Effect on Big Government

The radical pro-socialists' new messaging techniques will also have a tremendous effect on the size and scope of government — most notably through their "sales pitches" for ever-expanding entitlement programs.

These programs, lumped together, represent the single biggest expenditure of the federal budget. More than half of every dollar the government spends goes toward Social Security, Medicare, Medicaid, unemployment benefits, and other types of federal handouts. [8] It's clear these programs are out of control ... and the problem is only getting worse.

Most people are disgusted when they see the actual numbers, so again, the socialist Democrats driving most of these programs (and fighting for new ones) avoid that part of the discussion. Instead, they target their messaging directly at the voters who do and/or would benefit from existing, proposed, and expanded entitlements.

On the surface, these programs look good. They are sold to us as programs that help the poor, fight poverty, provide for our nation's seniors, and give all citizens a chance to win.

Who doesn't want that?

But that's just the sales pitch. That's the messaging. That's the misinformation.

The reality is much darker and much, much more dangerous.

I believe this short-term help is just a side effect, not the intent behind our government's massive entitlement spending.

These programs are deliberately designed to destroy the free market, take away our freedoms, and create a socialist society built on government dependency. This, in effect, not only grows the size and reach of our federal government but also expands its power and influence over all our lives.

The result is what I believe the government *wants* — which is what any socialist government wants: dependency, in which the populace *depends* on the government for their necessities and livelihood.

Welfare, food stamps, and other transfer payments have created a dependent class that is increasingly more content being trapped in poverty. And future tax-funded programs the radical pro-socialists are fighting for, such as free childcare, free college, free healthcare, and free paid leave are all designed to take dependency to the next level, which is ensnaring the middle class as well.

You can be sure of one thing: once more Americans get used to this next wave of bigger, bolder initiatives — more *free stuff* — they will never allow these government payouts to go away.

Even programs deemed temporary would be here forever. Once the weed takes root, it will never stop growing unless someone pulls it out of the ground. But that never happens in government.

As Ronald Reagan famously said, *"No government ever voluntarily reduces itself in size. Government programs, once launched, never disappear. Actually, a government bureau is the nearest thing to eternal life we'll ever see on this earth!"*

The radical pro-socialists' game plan — and the truth they'll never admit in their messaging — is to create an entitlement state to eliminate our individual freedoms, destroy free enterprise, and create a collectivist, socialist society.

TRUTH: THE MOST POWERFUL WEAPON WE HAVE

I love marketing and messaging. Crafting the perfect message for a target audience has been a huge piece of my life's work. I have the utmost respect for the craft. And that's why it bothers me so much to see the art of messaging twisted into disinformation and outright deception by radical forces intent on redefining reality and destroying the America we have known for generations.

The words we use to explain and describe something matter. They are powerful. As Dr. Jordan Peterson explains, *"If you can think and speak and write, you are absolutely deadly. Nothing can get in your way. That is why you learn to write ... It is the most powerful weapon you could possibly provide someone with."* [9]

Today and moving into the future, the radical pro-socialists are wielding the weapon of messaging against Christians, Conservatives, and Libertarians. And frankly, they are wielding it far, far better than we are on the Right. They have a massive head start on us, but I believe we can catch up.

We *have* to.

If we do not engage the radical pro-socialists in their messaging, disinformation, and mobilization war, they'll get so far ahead that we'll never be able to catch up. The good news is that all we need to do is bring *truth* and *facts* into their web of disinformation. Their arguments are built on doublespeak and emotion. They sell what people want to hear but deliver what nobody wants to get.

To defeat their message, we only need to push back with reality.

Arm yourself with information. Press on through their smoke and mirrors, and never stop shining the spotlight of truth on their lies and deceit.

Never stop asking the key questions:

> *Why? How? Who benefits? Who is penalized? Who pays for it? What is the financial cost? What is the cost in personal freedoms? Is this a short-term band-aid or a long-term solution? Does this give me more liberty, or does this make the government more powerful? Does this work toward a culture of personal responsibility, or does this lead us further into dependency?*

Keep digging for the truth, and when you find it, shout it from the rooftops for all to hear! And, though some will certainly try, don't let anyone silence you.

Chapter 12

Understanding Modern Democrat Campaign Strategies

Politics and the art of winning an election are radically different today than at any time in the past — and most people are oblivious to the changes.

The 2024 presidential campaign is unlike any in history.

And it should concern every American.

You do not have to be a Republican, Democrat, Libertarian, or Independent to be concerned.

Why?

Because this isn't an election about policies or even personalities.

In the past, it was about who had the best policies and who could attract more supporters *because* of those policies. Or it was about who had the best personality. Who was the better speaker? Who looked better? Who came across as more energetic, youthful, and smart?

They would win, and the other candidate would lose.

In the past, the election was about who had the best newspaper ads, direct-mail, radio ads, direct mail ads, and TV commercials. But those days are gone. Each of those things is now either insignificant or only a minor part of a successful campaign. Each one is obsolete compared to today's political influences.

Indeed, politics is evolving right now, even as you read this. It never stays the same. Each election cycle brings new technology, data and media strategy, and campaign tactics, steadily improving on past performance.

Many were shocked when President Biden basically stayed in his basement throughout his entire 2020 campaign and yet still managed to win the election.

The same thing happened, in 2022, when John Fetterman was unable to speak intelligibly due to a recent stroke — leading to a cringe-inducing debate performance against his Republican opponent — and yet he still won the Pennsylvania U.S. Senate race.

We've seen other Democrat candidates buck tradition and win elections using new, seemingly radical campaign tactics that look nothing like what's been done in the past. And we've seen those unconventional tactics *work.*

The disturbing truth is that Republicans have not embraced the new strategies and tactics that work today. They have so far relied on the old approaches to winning elections.

And — *big surprise* — they keep losing.

Not understanding the real causes, they blame minor problems and turn a blind eye to any effective solutions.

For example, some blamed Biden's presidential win on voter fraud, and yes, fraud *did* happen. Some blamed it on voting machines and software, but this has not yet been proven. Some blamed it on the Deep State and Big Tech censorship: and while this certainly had a big effect, it can't explain the full outcome. Some blamed it on Trump's "weakness" ... or on Biden's "strength."

As I said in the earlier chapter on voter fraud, voter-integrity laws have been passed in dozens of states, and there is still much more to be done. But now is the time to focus on winning — not on ignoring the realities of politics today.

Modern Republicans are still blind to how much the strategies and tactics behind winning an election have radically changed since

2008. As I've said, it is clear that Republicans are 10 to 15 years behind the Democrats' advanced strategies and tactics on how to win an election. That was the case in 2018, 2020, and 2022.

We saw it play out yet again in elections across select states in 2023. Despite the terrible economy, widespread cultural backlash to "woke" policies, a literal invasion of illegal migrants at our southern border, a disastrous and humiliating defeat and withdrawal of the U.S. military forces from Afghanistan, two massive foreign conflicts, runaway inflation, and the bottomless pit of national debt, Election Day 2023 was a wipeout for Republicans and a big win for Democrats.

It left the Republicans scratching their heads in disbelief.

Again.

But why were they surprised? What happened in 2023 also happened in 2022 — a year that was *supposed* to be a "Red Tsunami" of Republican victories.

It happened in 2020.

It happened in 2018.

Why are Republican consultants and Conservative commentators still so shocked that we keep getting the same results when we're still using the same tired, outdated methods?

The 2023 losses weren't a surprise to those of us who realize the hapless Republican National Committee, leadership, the consultants, and the Republican establishment don't really understand how President Obama and his ideologically driven staff and bureaucrats transformed politics.

I warned about this on TV, on radio, online, in podcasts, and at Republican, conservative, and Christian leadership meetings. Nobody listened then. Maybe they will now.

Let's look at how it all began.

Back in 2008, Obama fired all the traditional Democratic consultants and instead ran a campaign that utilized three new strategies:

1. Mobilizing get-out-the-vote (GOTV) strategies and techniques he had developed as a community organizer.
2. Data-collection profiling that identified supporters by interest and race and organized them into voting blocs.
3. Digital marketing using the most advanced and up-to-date strategies and tactics.

This relatively unknown "community organizer" and two-term junior U.S. Senator won the election and shocked Republicans. And he dramatically outdid John McCain's feeble marketing efforts.

Two years into his administration, President Obama's campaign had a major setback as people were revolting against his policies. He lost Congress in the 2010 mid-terms, and his re-election in 2012 looked doubtful.

He then secretly did something brilliant by assembling a group of high-tech geniuses from Microsoft, Google, Facebook, and other Big Tech companies, who helped create for him the most advanced and transformational marketing program to Get Out the Vote (GOTV) than any that had been used at any other time in American political history.

It wiped Romney out in 2012.

How did he do it?

I know because, under the radar, I was his test case in proving a new high-tech strategy never used before.

I ran for Congress in a special election in 2011 as a Republican in a Democratic district.

It was an impossible task.

I had zero name recognition.

No one knew who I was.

And I was running against well-known candidates, including the most powerful politician in Los Angeles, the Secretary of State of California, a local city councilman, and a mayor of a city in the district.

And me, the nobody.

Using my marketing skills and energizing the Christian vote, I shocked everyone, attracted national headlines, ended up on national talk shows, and created pure panic on the part of the entire Democratic establishment. Why? Because I came in at a very close second in a district where Democrats enjoyed a 20 percent advantage. A safe Democrat district that I should have lost, I was winning.

Then, the Obama marketing machine came in.

As a marketing and advertising professional (I've won 111 marketing awards), I relied on Republican consultants, traditional campaign strategies, and Obama's 2008 strategies.

I was not aware that President Obama had unleashed a new, amazing high-tech campaign. No one knew about it. I was his test case.

Voters, consultants, the media — everyone, including the Democrats in my district, were confused because our campaign had more lawn signs. We had more support than was traditionally generated for Republicans by volunteers from all over the state, who helped me out in this special election.

However, we lost. Not by much. But we lost.

And why did my opponent win, especially after keeping a fairly low profile? Why weren't they running a traditional marketing campaign? I didn't know why until the *LA Times* revealed that my race for the U.S. House seat in California's 36th District was used by Obama's campaign as a test run for their new GOTV strategies. [1]

Obama's Organizing for America took over the campaign for my Democratic opponent, Janice Hahn. The *Times* reported:

> *"According to a Democratic official, Organizing for America's California operation organized 41 phone banks during the get-out-the-vote phase, 33 of which were run by volunteers. All told, the official estimates, volunteers worked 1,509 hours making calls on Hahn's behalf. On election day, 394 people signed up through the group to work on phone bank and canvass events ... The Democratic Congressional Campaign Committee and the California Democratic Party also assisted Hahn's campaign, making nearly 410,000 live voter calls along with the organizing groups in the last 20 days of the campaign."* [2]

I had no idea I was on the receiving end of such a massive, well-organized, hyper-motivated political machine.

The Democrats seemed invincible.

From that moment on, I studied what the Obama marketing machine did in transforming politics and elections. I've carefully followed, tracked, and written about what they have been doing ever since.

I won't sugarcoat it, either: What they're doing in marketing and advertising is brilliant. As for what the Republicans are doing? The Democrat marketing professionals I know just laugh at it.

Here is an example:

According to Sam Cornale, Executive Director of the DNC, here is a breakdown of the Democrats' four steps to winning in 2024:

1. **Money for advanced high-tech marketing and organizing to Get Out the Vote.**

They describe the plan as paying special attention to what Sam calls *"voter protection, organizing, and getting communication embeds on the ground in key states."* In other words, having paid activists organize and mobilize to GOTV, including by early voting and ballot harvesting.

This is a trained, disciplined army using advanced data to identify only their voters and a systematic strategy to make sure they vote.

It's the only way they can win — to identify and then make sure their supporters vote, while the Republicans use the same old-fashioned techniques they used more than a decade ago.

The Republicans are behind in AI messaging and data technology to identify microtargeted voters, advanced tested training, organization, and GOTV.

2. **Flip red (Republican) states, just like they did in Arizona and Georgia in 2022.**
   According to Sam:

   "Millions are being spent in Republican states as part of our strategy, creating a first-of-its-kind program called the Red State Fund."

   Just like the elections of 2018, 2020, 2022, and 2023, they are targeting GOTV efforts in Democrat areas and — using highly targeted data on voter preferences and issues — they are applying these strategies to turn red states like they did Arizona and Georgia.

   Local city council, school board, county, and judicial races are also being targeted. They look at vulnerable statewide candidates.

And in the red states, the Republican leadership is oblivious to the assault.

3. **Advanced marketing technology and voter education.** The socialist Democrats have a big advantage in using advanced marketing strategies to win in this upcoming election cycle. This includes AI, advanced messaging, microtargeted data collection, GOTV, and more.

   They are committed to out-marketing the Republicans — who are still using grossly outdated techniques anyway.

4. **Voter registration by race, age, and targeted groups.** Sadly, the socialists are attacking The American Dream in America by dividing us by race and age.

   It's wrong.

   But they are having success in creating hatred and fear in minority groups and dividing us by age.

   It's a political and electoral extension of the Marxist Critical Race Theory (CRT).

   According to Sam:

   "Prioritizing outreach to communities of color — it's the DNC's largest commitment to voter registration and will focus specifically on battleground states."

   This is their outreach to community-organizing groups targeting Hispanic, Black, Native American, and Asian communities.

Sadly, this is not the only organization; there are dozens of other organizations in every state doing similar things.

The minority community should be friendly to Conservatives, Libertarians, and Christian policies, but the Republicans are inexplicably ignoring the possibilities with these groups.

The Democrats have Spanish websites, digital ads, and radio commercials.

The Republicans don't.

The Democrats believe this is one of their keys to election success.

The Republicans don't, even though the Hispanic community is not growing exponentially but are friendly to conservatives, free-market principles, and anti-Communist values.

Using these four strategies that Sam laid out for me, the Democrats have managed to do several key things that Republicans have failed miserably at doing. I'll spend the rest of this chapter unpacking what I think are the seven most important areas in which the Democrats are currently trouncing Republican candidates and strategists.

Democrat Win #1: Getting Out the Vote

Getting Out the Vote is an art and skill.

Republicans treat it as a way to knock on doors, particularly targeting high-propensity Republican voters, or those who have voted many times as a Republican. These are safe votes.

But the Democrats do it better. They can increase voter turnout for their candidates 10 to 18 percent better than the Republicans — a percentage that allows them to win when they should not.

The Democrats look at GOTV based on data, as I will explain. They train people how to engage in GOTV through personal contacts and through a voter data list based on political preferences and propensities for voting the "right way."

Democrats utilize microtargeted messaging to speak to the precise needs of a very specific segment, targeting potential voters by demographic categories like age, race, gender, and education, and by other key factors, such as whether they have student loans or if they have signed a petition stating their position on key issues like education, gun control or abortion.

Their GOTV efforts include intense training based on messaging — that is, what to say and how to say it. It's based on test-group research that reveals what they will and won't respond to and includes new data and instruction based on AI research. And of course, they train people how to do ballot harvesting where it's legal.

These strategies are so effective because it's an intelligent way of addressing the needs of the *individual,* not a big group en masse.

The Democrats also ask their targeted voter for a genuine commitment to vote, unlike the Republicans, who seem more interested in simply *asking* people to vote. The Democrats will use much more committed language, such as:

- *"Can you promise — make a contract or a pledge — to vote?"*
- *"Do you need someone to watch your kids so you can go vote?"*
- *"Do you need a ride to the polling locations?"*
- *"Can I take your ballot to the poll for you?"*
- *"Can I help you fill out the ballot based on the voter guide I have?"*

They will engage in a one-on-one conversation and conclude it by sealing the deal, saying something like:

> *"It was great talking to you. I'm going to keep in touch. I feel like I made a new friend! Would you mind if I called you later to make sure that you vote? We can chat about how it all worked out a few days after the election."*

Can you see how that level of communication goes far beyond simply knocking on a door and asking the person to vote? The Democrats have made an art out of making meaningful personal connections with potential voters, getting their commitment, and holding them accountable for following through.

Plus, they excel at driving early voting, mail-in voting, ballot harvesting (both legal and illegal), increasing Election Day turnout, and delivering a strong final push all the way up until the polls close on Election Day.

And it works. All of it works exceptionally well, increasing voter turnout far more than the ancient Republican strategies.

Democrat Win #2: Microtargeted Voter Data

Advanced microtargeted voter data is knowing how to segment voters into different buckets, which allows us to send special, uniquely relevant messaging only to them.

We can collect this data through petitions, polls, door-to-door canvassing, telephone, and other ways to directly identify key interests.

For example:

- Who is interested in the plights of the Palestinians?
- Who is interested in defending Israel?
- Who is interested in lowering taxes, and who's interested in raising taxes?
- Who is interested in school choice?
- Who is interested in increasing taxpayers' spending for government-run schools?

This type of information gives you what the person's hottest topic is and the thing that's most on their mind that would drive them to vote, volunteer, or donate.

Microtargeted voter data can be based on age, race, or gender. It can be based on status, such as students versus seniors. It could be based on the type of media someone uses, like Instagram and TikTok versus TV. It can be based on what networks they watch, such as MSNBC versus Fox News. It can be based on the products and services they use, such as Apple, Facebook, Google or YouTube.

It's simply breaking your audience down into very small, targeted segments and then tying that specific segment to the preferred messaging content and format that best fits their preferences.

The Democrats and Republicans both know they need to identify their loyal voters as well as the *persuadables* who could go either way. They also know they need to identify their opposition and suppress or emphasize the negatives in *their* messaging. Microtargeted data helps both sides do this ... but Democrats are far better at it.

The voter data Democrats use is robust, dynamic, and far superior to that of the Republicans. Candidates who are running for a Democratic seat utilize databases that use AI to create the data as well as other sources. Importantly, they're able to access this without starting over every election, compared to Republican candidates who usually start from scratch every campaign and thereby launch with an immediate disadvantage.

When it comes to winning elections, "He with the best data wins."

And sadly, the Republicans don't get the best data ... which leads to painfully predictable results.

Democrat Win #3: Training and Organization

One of the keys to the Democrat's election success is advanced training integrated with their mobilization.

They train an army of people nationwide for the election every year, even in non-election years.

You could be in Alaska calling somebody for a candidate in Des Moines, Iowa.

You could be in New York City texting someone in Tennessee to GOTV.

You could be in Illinois but fly down to use your skills in Georgia for a candidate.

The Democrats excel at training their base and then mobilizing them, injecting each operative in whatever campaign across the country their skills are most needed.

How do they train their people? They have different extensive events and training sessions.

For example, Netroot Nation is a radical mobilization and training organization that teaches young people in their teens and 20s how to mobilize for radical causes and candidates using modern strategies for winning elections. They train them via classroom instruction online and by onsite instruction, as the students work alongside actual candidates in a campaign.

The Democrat National Committee also has a wide selection of education sessions for phoning, texting, community organization, GOTV, ballot harvesting, and engaging in community activism.

For example, here is how they describe a training event for someone who has never been involved in politics before:

> ***About this event***
> *Learn how to make calls to voters in priority states* ***on your schedule*** *with the DNC National Call Crew! The DNC National Call Crew brings volunteer power where it's needed most! And we need you to help us power up!*
>
> ***What will you learn?***

In this Zoom-based training we'll teach you how to make calls, have you try making some calls with us, and show you how to get your questions answered through our amazing online community. After training, during our calling hours, you'll be able to schedule shifts on the hour or stop by to call when it's most convenient for you.

What's the training schedule?
The first half of the session we'll be getting you set up to make calls into battleground states. In the second half we'll help you join our online community.

We're excited to have you join our community!

The bottom line is the Democrat socialists can recruit, train, and send out an army of volunteers ... while the Republicans struggle with a handful of dedicated but untrained volunteers.

For the Democrats, their god is the government. Politics and winning an election is their religion, bordering on a zealous passion for the more radical activists.

For Republicans, by contrast, it's a short-term patriotic duty ... if and when they have the time to serve.

Democrat Win #4: College Radicals Mobilize Voters to Transform Cities

American college towns are turning their cities and communities into radical election victories ... and pro-socialist communities.

The American Communities Project cataloged the voting patterns of 171 college towns, where major colleges or universities are located.

Since the 2000 presidential election, when the purposeful organization and mobilization of students spread from California across America:

- 79 Left-leaning communities started to support

Democrats even more, resulting in changing city councils and school boards, plus county and legislative elections.

- 38 communities flipped from being predominantly Republican to Democratic in election outcomes ... but are in danger of falling into this trend.
- 47 Right-leaning towns became more Republican.

In the 2000 presidential election, 48 percent of all college towns in the country voted for Democratic Vice President Al Gore. In 2020, that number had increased to 54 percent for Joe Biden.

That percentage gives radical candidates a favorable chance to win every election, changing the election outcome in the cities with colleges.

And it's worse for a Republican presidential candidate in swing states, where a few thousand voters often decide presidential elections.

For example, Dane County, where the University of Wisconsin-Madison is located, had a higher Democrat margin of victory in the recent Wisconsin state Supreme Court election than any other county in the state.

Or in Washtenaw County, the home of the University of Michigan, swing state Michigan voters chose Biden over Donald Trump in the 2020 election by a margin of more than 50 percent, or approximately 101,000 votes. If Hillary Clinton obtained such a margin in 2016, she would have won the state of Michigan, which Trump won that year.

In swing-state Colorado, Larimer County, the home of Colorado State University, the Democratic margin of victory was increased by 169,000 votes over the 2000 election, while the Republican margin increased by only by 21,000 votes. This type of voter shift makes it impossible for Republicans to win even in a statewide race.

The only way to change this megatrend is to mobilize and organize activist Republican Conservative and allied groups and make smart outreaches to the colleges to show the students a different side.

Democrat Win #5: Digital Marketing

Digital Marketing was perfected by the Obama marketing machine in 2012. However, Hillary Clinton made a major mistake in 2016 by falling back on old digital techniques when she ran against Donald Trump for President. Trump had learned from the previous elections and used the newest, most-advanced digital strategies to completely overtake the much-favored Hillary Clinton.

Unfortunately, Trump didn't do as good a job in 2020, and Democrats caught up, winning elections in 2020, 2022, and 2023. And it looks like they'll be ahead in 2024.

Big Tech has made it harder for the Republicans to be able to successfully use digital marketing, but they still can ... and they can do it better than the Democrats. But they must use the latest and best strategies.

Democrat Win #6: The Invisible Army of Influencers

Biden is using a successful political strategy to gain votes, volunteers, and donors through *influencers,* people who have built and maintained a large social media following.

For example, Biden's digital strategy team will connect with influencers across the nation, targeting those who may not follow the White House or Democratic Party on social media — or "cord cutters" who have tuned out mainstream media altogether.

Biden has a team of digital staffers who are focused on influencers and independent content creators. The staffers officially work for the White House, not Biden's campaign — but reaching young and suburban voters is clearly a priority.

Influencers are valuable because they typically have thousands or millions of followers and therefore have sway over a specific target audience. Their dominance on social media or entertainment makes them a useful voice for brands or political candidates in search of instant credibility.

For example, one of Biden's influencers is NYU student Harry Sisson, whose TikTok account has more than 700,000 followers.

Vivian Tu, another influencer, gives financial advice on TikTok to over 2 million followers.

According to Pew Research Center, young voters under age of 30 who follow and listen to influencers voted for Biden over Trump by a 26-point margin in 2020, and Democrats voted over Republicans by 28 points in the 2022 midterms.

Influencers helped shape the election results, becoming Biden's "invisible army."

So influencers are a smart strategy for reaching young people, mobilizing activists from a voting segment whose main way of getting information is through social media like TikTok.

Who do the radical groups and candidates want to reach?

Young woman about abortion ... Hispanics on immigration ... Climate activists who believe the end of the world is coming. Radical Palestinian Dogma believers with anti-Jewish/Israel hate. Young people who want student-loan relief — another government giveaway.

Right now, hundreds of (unpaid and like-minded) content creators are working with Biden's White House, making it a briefing space for influencers to meet in person or remotely with Biden campaign officials and staff. The administration has even given influencers opportunities for access to Biden — something the press doesn't have!

In 2020, the Biden campaign used the pandemic to move more of its strategy to marketing online. The boost from influencers on Instagram, TikTok, and YouTube was an increasingly important campaign tactic.

"We were forced to do everything virtual," Adrienne Elrod, the director of surrogate strategy for Biden's campaign, said in an interview with Recode, according to Vox, *"We're forced to do more [Instagram] Lives. We're forced to do more Twitter conversations. We're forced to go to Occupy Democrats."*

How powerful are influencers?

The 2022 Detroit Auto Show, for example, invited Daniel "Daniel Mac" MacDonald to the event, a social-media influencer with 13.8 million followers. He asked drivers if they had any questions for Biden. The video got 38 million views!

Elle Walker's YouTube channel called WhatsUpMoms has more than 3 million subscribers. Dulce Candy, a beauty vlogger, has more than 2 million subscribers on YouTube. Both women interviewed Biden, who talked to them about his Build Back Better campaign.

Comedian Ilana Glazar, who has over 1 million followers on Instagram, is helping Biden with swing-state voters. Her job is to do video chat interviews with celebrities like Eric Andre and Zoë Kravitz to encourage people who may not be so excited about Biden to vote for him anyway.

Lifestyle influencer Chloe Homan has more than 50,000 Instagram followers. She's urged her followers to register for an absentee ballot.

When Biden signed the same-sex marriage bill, his staff invited LGBTQI+ influencers who created a massive viral campaign for the administration.

Some of the best support comes from influencers who speak to comparatively smaller but targeted audiences, like persuadables, voters by race, and those engaged in emotional hot-button issues like abortion.

The key is whether the influencer actually *influences* their followers to follow through.

So, if you see Biden doing a live Facebook or YouTube chat with an influencer you have never heard of, it's because the influencer reaches an audience that cares about one of those targeted hot-button issues.

The goal is to engage with as many influencers as possible, interviewing people who have credibility with certain targeted audiences and getting those influencers' audiences interested and excited about Biden.

Biden's influencer outreach is intentionally engaging. For example, the popular social-video game, Animal Crossing, included Biden/Harris campaign signs within the video game environment.

The Biden campaign is also using celebrities like Andy Cohen and Dulé Hill to fundraise on Cameo, a video app that allows influencers to post fan-requested video messages in exchange for donations.

Singer Cardi B's posts bashing Trump have garnered more than 20 million viewers.

San Francisco billionaire activist Tom Steyer has an email list of 7.6 million, which he uses to bash Trump and build up interest in Biden. He also tours the country, holding town halls to support Democrats. He's also looking to recruit influencers, including those who focus on beauty, fitness, lifestyle, and even comedy, to reach young people online and urge them to vote for Biden and other Democrat candidates.

Wielding the power of influence and influencers is another key area where the Republicans are forced to play catchup or risk losing every election from now on.

Democrat Win #7: Peer to Peer Marketing

The Republicans laughed when they heard about peer-to-peer marketing. It sounded so small and insignificant.

Until it wasn't.

Peer-to-peer marketing concentrates efforts on one's family, friends, and neighbors. It uses local organizations, chats over coffee, potlucks, get-togethers, wine parties, and various events to build a powerful relationship as a foundation for influencing people and identifying who would likely vote for their candidates on the local to the national level.

Republicans used peer-to-peer marketing 45 years ago to help Ronald Reagan win the White House in 1980, but Conservatives have since dropped the ball. And the Democrats picked it up.

Peer-to-peer interaction can dramatically increase voter turnout. This is even more effective when you combine peer-to-peer networks with data for a digital marketing campaign and proper social media messaging to boost the party's GOTV efforts and to make sure those in the network have done early voting, ballot harvesters have picked up the ballots, voter guides have been shared, and so on.

Peer-to-peer efforts have become so important to the Democratic election machine that the Democratic National Committee holds weekly virtual workshops to train engaged voters how to activate their friends and family for Joe Biden. Pay close attention to the language they use in promoting their virtual event, "Organize Your Community: Sharebank":

> *"We're building an organizing program around a simple principle: that our supporters are the best advocates with the closest people in their lives.*
>
> *Every single member of this team will play a role in ensuring the people closest to us know what's at stake for our families and for our country. That means having*

conversations directly with our friends, our families, and sharing key campaign messaging and content within our communities online.

This event is a volunteer shift to share content and organize for President Joe Biden and Democrats up and down the ballot using our new tool, Reach. So come ready with your phone and laptop!

Sign up today!" [3]

Note the energy, enthusiasm, and personal engagement in the description. The Democrats have learned the power of getting each individual voter excited and willing to share that excitement with everyone in their lives.

These techniques are so much more effective today than the political strategies of the past, and they're not impossible for the Republicans to do. But it isn't coming from the Republican consultants, and it's not coming from the Republican Party or its establishment.

So, it has to come from *us,* the grassroots movement. We have to say enough is enough. We're going to win elections, and we're going to do this right.

You personally may have the talent to be involved in some of these technical areas. If not, you at least have a personal network you can activate through peer-to-peer efforts. Whatever resources and gifts you have to offer, *please* do your part.

We *all* must do our part if we want any chance of turning America around from this downward socialist spiral and reclaiming The American Dream.

Chapter 13

How to Defeat the Dangers and Turn America Around

As we begin to bring these warnings and dangers to you and your family to a close, I want to leave you with 12 things you can do to fight back against these growing dangers.

I'm optimistic we can restore The American Dream.

I'm sure you can be part of this. And I am sure we can overcome each danger ... but it requires each of us to get involved.

More importantly, though, I want to leave you with an encouragement. Don't allow the radical forces in our country to steal your voice.

No matter who you are, how old you are, what race or ethnicity you are, what you do for a living, where you live, or how much you know (or don't know) about politics, you have just as much right and authority to act as anyone else.

You have a voice. All that is required for you to be able to use it is *courage.*

Speaking out against a large, well-funded, carefully crafted socialist narrative may seem risky ... and scary. We've all seen people who were "canceled" for speaking the truth with boldness. Such men and women are heroes. They refused to buckle under the social and political pressure of our age, and their boldness stands as an encouragement for the rest of us.

You may have been "canceled" by a family member, friend or business associate. It hurts. But we must have the courage to speak the truth in love.

These are good people who stood up, spoke out, took action, and created change. That's how the Founders declared America's independence from Britain. That's how the despicable practice of slavery was brought to an end in America. That's how American women gained the right to vote. That's how African Americans won the battle for civil rights. And that's how our country moves forward today against all the pressures, hurdles, and obstacles the radical pro-socialists put in our way.

12 ACTIONS YOU CAN TAKE TO TURN THE TIDE

I've discussed at length the 10 greatest dangers to our prosperity, freedom, and future. Now, allow me to present my list of 12 action steps you can take to turn the tide and ensure our prosperity, freedom, and a better future. Each one of these things is incredibly important, and it will take all of us doing what we can to truly ensure the best outcome for America and Americans.

Action #1: Vote For, Not Against, Your Values

I've said this several times already, but the single most important thing any American can do to ensure a government that is truly *"of the people, by the people, [and] for the people,"* to quote Abraham Lincoln, is to vote in our elections.

And sadly, the stats show us that most Americans don't or won't.

This is true for Conservatives, Libertarians, Republicans, and Christians.

This is something I watch closely. After one recent election, I looked at the list of who did not vote. Many targeted, friendly potential voters had said in the door-to-door and phone canvassing that they would vote for the conservative candidate on the ballot.

But they didn't.

Some of the non-voters were what is called "high-propensity" voters. These are the most likely to vote because they had voted in the last several elections. Yet they didn't vote in this one despite saying they would. I even knew some of the people on the list.

Why didn't they vote?

Perhaps they forgot. They got too busy. They weren't feeling well. Their car broke down and they couldn't get to the polls. Maybe they sat down, filled out a mail-in ballot, signed it, and sealed it, and simply forgot to mail it in or misplaced it. Or maybe:

- *"Oh, I gave my ballot to my son, and he must've forgot to drop it off."*
- *"I had both ballots in my coat pocket and forgot to drop them in a ballot-collection box."*
- *"I didn't know about all the initiatives or judges on the ballot, so I didn't complete my ballot and get it in."*

This is why conservative candidates need to have far more effective approaches to identifying our voters and votes (data) in advance, maintaining and updating that list so it doesn't get old, and helping people get their ballots in before election day.

The Democrats do this exceptionally well. Republicans? Not so much.

These are called Get-Out-the-Vote (GOTV) initiatives. The Democrat machine is at least 15 years ahead of the Republicans in training, data, identifying voter interests and top targets, and early-voting strategies; and Dems have practically perfected the art of ballot harvesting.

It's time for the Republicans to wake up. Because Conservatives have long resisted many of these practices, the Democrats have overtaken us by several miles.

To be clear, I am not suggesting Conservatives engage in any illegal GOTV efforts. And I am not saying that Republican lawmakers and politicians should stop fighting against many of the GOTV efforts that skew election results, such as widespread early voting, ballot harvesting, and mail-in voting. However, as long as each of these avenues is available and being legally used by the radicals, we *must* use all of these methods as well — and even better — while still fighting against them in Congress and at the state and local level.

I understand that might sound ... "icky"... to some, but it is a necessity. If we do not use every legal GOTV effort, we may never have enough lawmakers to enact important changes to our electoral process. In fact, if we don't use the same tools the Democrats use so effectively, we may never win another election at all.

In fact, we will simply repeat the election losses of 2018, 2020, 2022, and 2023.

Action #2: Encourage Your Own Circle to Vote

I don't want to seem negative, and I certainly do not want to insult your loved ones, but I want to make a suggestion: Assume that everyone you know — your parents, your adult children, your friends, your siblings, your church members, your coworkers, your neighbors — is *not* going to vote.

Double, then triple check. Do they need help with a voter guide? Do they need help with a sitter?

It's a great motivation for each of us to do whatever we can to encourage everyone in our personal circles to vote.

If you have early voting in your area, find out where the polling place is and encourage people to go early, when the lines are much shorter or non-existent.

If you have elderly friends and family members, offer to drive them to the polls and wait in line with them.

If ballot harvesting is allowed in your state, offer to collect your friends' and family members' ballots and deliver them to the polling place or drop box.

If mail-in voting is allowed in your area, mail in the ballot as early as possible.

If every person who reads this book would commit to getting at least three people in their circle to vote — not just *say* they're *going* to vote but actually turn in a ballot — I believe we could make a dramatic impact on the next election, whether it's local, state or national.

Every vote counts and matters, so make sure you're doing your part to help ensure your family and friends' voices are heard!

Action #3: Use a Voter Guide

Voter guides are incredibly helpful tools that educate voters on the candidates in an election and what their stance is on different key issues, and they almost always have a particular bias toward one political party's candidates and policy positions.

Know your source. Sometimes, an ill-intentioned organization will attempt to fool voters into thinking they are consulting a fair, impartial, unbiased resource when, in reality, they're looking at highly partisan material. So, be careful if someone hands you a voter guide and suggests you follow it. If you don't know where it came from and what the intentions were behind it, you could be tricked into voting for candidates who do not represent your values.

I take voter guides very seriously and for years have created guides to help Conservatives, Libertarians, Republicans, and Christian voters select candidates in local, state, and national elections in California and Tennessee, the two states I've lived in and have thoroughly researched. You can find my voter guides at ElectionForum.org for California or at TennVoterGuide.com for Tennessee.

I also recommend the voter guides you can find on iVoterGuide.com, which is a great resource for most of the country.

You can also consult JudgeVoterGuide.com for information on judicial elections in all 50 states.

The radical pro-socialists have long used voter guides to influence elections, and this is another area where we have dragged our feet. Guides can be powerful educational and motivational tools, and it is high time we used them on our side to gain an advantage ourselves.

Action #4: Volunteer for a Political Action or Education Group

Political action and political education groups are persuasive forces at the local level. There are always groups meeting in most communities across the country, and you can find groups that are based on political party affiliation and groups that are not.

Political action groups meet to discuss policy issues and upcoming local, state, and national elections. They can help organize GOTV activities, produce or distribute voter guides, and serve as watchdogs in the community and its voting sites to ensure election integrity. These groups, though they can sometimes appear small or even quaint in some communities, can become a powerful, influential force in politics at all levels.

Action #5: Bring Back Potluck Suppers and/or Community Coffee Groups

Back in the '60s and '70s, political talk was quite different than it is today. Sure, people were passionate about their beliefs, but we also seemed to have more patience and understanding for the beliefs of others — especially other people whose views were vastly different from our own. It was possible for conservatives and liberals to live next door to each other, go to church together, and even socialize together without all the partisan hate and vitriol we see today.

One of the most powerful political forces back then was neighborhood potluck suppers and community coffee groups. These were informal social gatherings that focused on actual *communication* with other people, even if those people had different backgrounds, political views, religious experiences and beliefs, etc.

We'd have a big potluck supper and invite the whole neighborhood. There was usually a main topic of discussion too. Maybe we'd all read a book beforehand to discuss, or we'd watch a movie together and discuss it. For example people across America have used my book *The Christian Voter: How To Vote For, Not Against Your Values to Transform Culture and Politics* by reading and discussing one chapter each week.

These potlucks gave us such wonderful opportunities to get to know other people, to see others as warm, kind, caring, and intelligent regardless of which way they voted. Someone wasn't *defined* by their preferred candidate in a given election back then.

Things are so different today. In modern-day America, it is rare for a liberal and a conservative, for example, to have a lively, intelligent political discussion without it ending in — or, in many cases, *starting with* — accusations of hate, racism, fascism, or any of the many other -ism and -phobic terms you see all over social media.

It is a tragic irony. People have infinitely more communication options today than we could even dream of in the '60s. We are truly a connected world. You can talk to someone across the globe just as clearly and easily as you can talk to someone next door. It's a miracle.

And yet, despite all this, we aren't really talking to each other.

Instead, we're talking *at* each other. We're isolating into partisan tribes, and we don't talk to members of other tribes. Instead, we go to war.

To save America's prosperity, freedom, and future, I want to make a radical suggestion: go talk to people. Hang out together. Invite people — whole *groups* of people — over for an old-fashioned potluck dinner or conversation over a pot of coffee. Engage with people. Find like-minded families who can encourage and support you. Find people with differing views to challenge and stimulate you. Find understanding and common ground. Learn how to see the *person* behind the *politics.*

These gatherings not only give you the chance to learn from each other; they also give you the opportunity to have a positive effect on the *persuadables* in your area. You can be the spark that lights a fire under an undecided voter. Your knowledge and insight might be the missing piece that will lead them to the polls.

The potluck supper has become a lost art for Republicans, Conservatives, Libertarians, and even Christians. But again, it's something the Democrats have leveraged to advance their many radical causes. It's such a shame. The undecided voters in your community represent low-hanging fruit. It should be easy to interact with them and educate them on the issues that matter to you, but most conservatives simply aren't doing it.

The radicals, however, are.

We've got to get back in the potluck-supper game.

Action #6: Use Your Own Networks to Get Out the Vote

Everyone has a massive network.

You've got a contact list. You email people. You send text messages. You might have accounts with Facebook, Instagram, X (formerly Twitter), TikTok, Snap Chat, or whatever other social network has hit the scene in the past five minutes. You might send messages through Apple Messages, Signal, Telegram, WhatsApp, or Google.

Whatever platforms you use, you can leverage those networks to communicate with and inform people about important issues. You can connect with individuals and offer to drive them to the polls, deliver their mail-in ballot, share a voter guide, and do any of the other things I've discussed.

You can also share articles, information, and voter guides on your social media feeds. You can share your excitement for a particular candidate or share your passion for a certain issue.

My newsletter articles, podcasts, and videos are spread across America by amazing subscribers to my newsletter *The Huey Report,* my podcast *The Huey Alert,* or my newsletter *Reality Alert for Christians.*

Again, we have communication abilities today that our parents could never have dreamed about. Let's use them to get out the vote!

Action #7: Volunteer for a Candidate

No candidate can win any election without a team of paid staff and motivated volunteers doing a lot of hard work over many months. The bigger the election, the more volunteers are needed. A local school board or mayor's race may only need to staff one small community, while candidates in a national election need volunteers in literally every community across the country.

These volunteers are always in short supply. Having spent several decades working in many elections, I can honestly say I've never known a single candidate for office who said, *"Boy, I sure do have too many volunteers! What am I going to do with all these people?"*

If you really want to make a difference in the direction of our nation, I strongly encourage you to get off the sidelines and volunteer to help a campaign with whatever they need. There are always a lot of opportunities to serve, such as:

- Manning a phone bank to call voters and ask for their support. These callers usually have a script to follow, so it's not difficult. It's just a matter of being comfortable talking to people and making a real, personal, one-on-one connection over the phone.

- You can make calls to a provided list at home or better yet with others at a campaign headquarters.

- Most campaigns now use texting as well as phone calls. Texting is a wonderful addition to the campaign scene, because studies show most people check their incoming texts right away, while they may ignore a phone call. Volunteers can work a text database of supporters and undecided voters and engage in real back-and-forth dialogue with people via text. Again, it can be done at home or at campaign office.

- The old standard in campaigning is going door-to-door, meeting residents, and asking for their support. Again, this is all about relationship-building, having conversations with people on their own front porch — just like we all did "in the good ol' days." This high-touch personal contact is still the most powerful way to spread the campaign message and win votes. You are trained in what to say, given a list of where to go, and two people always go together.

These three methods are incredibly effective, and Democrats train volunteers to use each one. In fact, this is yet another area in which the Democrats have a huge advantage on Republicans, because they've all but perfected their volunteer intense-training programs. Once again, we have fallen behind in a critical area of campaigning, and we need to catch up. You can help by volunteering for a candidate today.

Action #8: Help Register People to Vote

Every community has an influx of new voters every election cycle. New neighbors move in from other states or districts. Young adults turn 18 and become eligible to vote. Immigrants gain citizenship. Your candidates need your help in registering these people to vote in your district well before election day.

Oftentimes, people are eligible to vote in your area, but they have not voted in so long that they've been dropped from the voter rolls. You can help reach out to these people and get them re-registered.

The voter registration forms are freely available, and anyone can help someone register to vote. It's a great way to make a big difference.

Action #9: Be a Poll Watcher

Poll watchers play a vital role on election day and during early voting. These people are members of the community who serve by showing up at the polls and simply *watching.* You're watching to see who comes in and out, watching for any irregularities in how people are acting, watching how the poll workers are interacting with voters, watching what the poll watchers are saying to people, and so on. This is all done to ensure no bad actors are misbehaving at the polling place by trying to mishandle the ballots or voting machines or improperly influence voters' decisions.

You can be sure the radical pro-socialists have poll watchers standing around in every polling place in the country. We need to be just as vigilant.

Action #10: Send Postcards and Letters

The idea of sending postcards may sound quaint nowadays, but it remains an effective campaign strategy of the radical pro-socialists. Similar to having coffee with someone or chatting on their doorstep, a simple postcard can make a personal connection with a voter and get them to notice your candidate and vote.

Action #11: Multicultural Outreach

Members of multicultural communities, especially those in which English is not the primary language, may be new citizens or first-generation Americans who have stronger ties to their ethnic country of origin than they have to America.

Many of these people may have come from communist and socialist countries and therefore simply expect the government to strong arm and bully them in exchange for meager dependency programs. They may not fully understand their full rights and liberties as Americans.

I love working in these communities, because it gives me the chance to talk about how wonderful America is and how life-giving our freedoms as Americans are for every citizen at all social, political, and economic levels.

You can make a huge and positive difference by engaging these communities, promoting the American ideals of freedom and self-direction, and even translating voter guides and other election materials into that community's native language.

By making the election personal and relevant to them, you can bring voters into the process and make a big difference for your candidate.

Action #12: Encourage Someone to Run for Office (or Run Yourself)

Finally, if you see a need in your community or if you believe people who share your values are unrepresented or underrepresented, you should consider encouraging someone to run for office to meet that need. You might even realize that the best person for the job ... is you!

Even if you've never even considered getting involved in politics, you might find that no one else in your area is willing or able to represent people with values similar to your own. You might feel as though you could be doing more to serve. You might just be fed up with how the current local leaders are serving (or harming) your community.

I've been in that position myself. I even ran for Congress a few years ago. I'd never thought about it, but some political activists approached me and made a good case, so I ran. I didn't win, but I have no regrets about the experience. I learned a tremendous amount about the inner workings of a campaign, and I felt great satisfaction by raising my hand and being willing to serve my community.

Whether it's your local school board or alderman race, the state Senate, or a U.S. Congress position, don't immediately discount yourself when considering potential candidates for an open seat or a potential challenge to seats held by the radical pro-socialists. If you are smart, passionate, and committed, you just might be the perfect person to help change the nation — one campaign at a time!

As you read this, you may have physical limitations. You may be struggling with a mobility issue. You may be in a long-term care facility. You may be dealing with a serious illness that has confined you to your bed. Whatever physical challenges you are experiencing, please hear me loud and clear: *there is still plenty you can do, and you still can and should participate in each election by casting your vote.*

This was made powerfully clear to me by a note I recently received from a reader who follows my blog and subscribes to my *Huey Report* newsletter:

> *"I am a 98-year-old World War II veteran [who is] very concerned about what is happening in our country. Life at ninety-eight is still worthwhile but very difficult, especially being nearly blind. I just finished completing my ballot just in case I can't make it to vote at the vote center. I'm grateful for your voter guide, which reduced the time and energy to complete the ballot. My ability to read your emails is failing much too quickly. Stay healthy, happy, and safe, and have a great future." — Bill*

Thank you, Bill, for your service and for continuing to fight for this country at 98. You are an inspiration to us all!

CHRISTIANS: AMERICA'S SECRET WEAPON FOR TURNING THINGS AROUND

Beyond the 12 actions I outlined above, I believe there are things that American Christians can do to turn things around. Our nation and system of government were built by people of religious faith. Whether you follow Jesus or not, faith and the freedom to worship without government oppression are built into the very foundations of our country.

Those Judeo-Christian ideals and the importance of Christ-following politicians, leaders, and voters are just as relevant and crucial today as they were when the Founding Fathers declared that the United States is a nation founded on the belief that all people "are *endowed by their Creator* with certain unalienable Rights." The Constitution, America's founding document, testifies to the will and work of God in our lives and in our nation.

Put simply, our rights do not come from the government, the state, the President, the Senate, or the House of Representatives. Our rights do not come from the Declaration of Independence, the Constitution or its Bill of Rights.

Our rights come from God. Period.

Chief among those God-given rights is the freedom to worship our Creator and to exercise obedience to Him in both our private *and public* lives.

I believe that is not only our right; it is our calling. Our job. Our obligation as people of faith.

When Americans take this responsibility seriously, and when we marry that responsibility with our right as free people to exercise our religion, miracles happen. Lives change. Events and outcomes once thought "certain" suddenly change course. Ungodly and unconstitutional practices are suddenly struck down. "Can't lose" establishment candidates are defeated by grassroots, out-of-nowhere campaigns riding a wave of unprecedented populist momentum. We have seen this time and time again, and we will continue to see God move in these ways in the future.

So, how can we as Christians make a bigger, bolder difference in American politics and strengthen and improve our prosperity, our freedom, and our future? I can think of four specific tools and resources we should be leveraging for America.

Pastors

Pastors have a difficult job — probably one of the most challenging jobs on earth. They are always on call, never get a "day off," are dedicated to being available to everyone any time, and are expected to be equal parts teacher, speaker, scholar, counselor, and CEO. There are few other roles in which so much is expected of one person.

So, to pastors, I say a sincere, *"Thank you."*

In light of all those responsibilities and understanding the impossibility of pleasing *all the people all the time,* I certainly "get" why many pastors are hesitant to take a political or social-issue stand from the pulpit. It is, in many ways, a losing game. Regardless of what you say or which side of an issue you come down on, you are almost certainly going to anger at least a few people in the church.

For this reason, many pastors avoid these disagreements altogether, choosing instead to "just preach the Bible and let God guide the peoples' consciences on this issue."

But even that is no safeguard against conflict. In fact, the Bible is perhaps the *most* disruptive thing you can preach in church! The Bible even describes *itself* as divisive, saying:

> *"For the word of God is alive and active. Sharper than any double-edged sword, it penetrates even to dividing soul and spirit, joints and marrow; it judges the thoughts and attitudes of the heart."*
> (Hebrews 4:12, NIV)

There isn't a lot of gray area in Scripture. It boldly proclaims truth — even on issues where the *truth* is not the popular political opinion. And we do not help our congregations when we water down the Word to make it more palatable or outright avoid potentially "controversial" subjects altogether.

Pastors are called to proclaim sound doctrine, and sound doctrine separates the wheat from the chaff, the truly committed believers from the nominal believers who are more concerned with political correctness and politeness than truth and righteousness.

The major issues of our day — socialism vs. freedom, free speech vs. censorship, life vs. abortion, biology vs. ideology — have definitive answers in Scripture. These are not *political* issues and opinions; they are *biblical* issues and opinions. And pastors should teach them as such.

Will preaching the Word unapologetically cause you to lose some church members?

Maybe.

Probably, in fact.

But what is the alternative? A watered-down gospel that reflects neither the truth of God nor the whims of a culture? A weak, ineffective, and on-the-fence group of half-hearted Christians whose beliefs and values look like a slightly more polished version of everyone else's?

That's not the church Jesus died for. And it's not the church the apostles preached to their contemporaries before losing their own lives for it.

Preaching truth requires sacrifice; there *will be* a cost. But the costs of remaining silent while the world goes off a moral and spiritual cliff are far, far greater.

We need pastors who are committed to boldly proclaiming the Word of God, who are unashamed of preaching the Bible as it is for all to hear. We need pastors who dare to spark change in our school boards, cities, counties, states, offices, and congressional representation by the preaching of the Word.

That kind of preaching can change the course of our nation. It has done it many times before, from the American Revolution, to the abolition of slavery, and the Civil Rights Movement, and it can do it again.

The Church

Churches represent several unique opportunities for Christians seeking to make significant changes in America's political future. If you are active in a church, there are several things you can do:

- **Voter Registration:** A congregation is fertile ground for voter registration drives, as 30 to 40 percent of most church attendees are not registered to vote. However, these same people are likely to vote 84 percent conservative, which means we are desperately missing their votes! There is simply no better place for conservative voter registration than your local church.
- **Election Forums:** The church is also a great place to hold an election forum. This is an event in which a speaker like me comes in and makes a presentation to the congregation that identifies the key issues in a given election and a breakdown of where each candidate stands on the issues. This is a great way to educate people about the non-negotiables for Christians, such as the right to life, religious liberty, protecting the persecuted church, advocating for, and opposing antisemitism and supporting our brothers and sisters in Israel, Christian and homeschool education options.
- **Salt and Light Ministries:** These groups go by different names, but essentially, this is a ministry within the church that is specifically focused on engaging Christians in the political process. This could include any of the things we've already discussed, such as organizing registration drives, passing out voter guides, providing poll watchers, etc.

- **Church Ballot Harvesting:** Democrats have become masters at ballot harvesting — both in states where it is legal and in states where it is not. As I've said previously, if Republicans want to compete in modern elections, they must take advantage of every legal tool at their disposal, and that includes ballot harvesting (where it is legally allowed). This is such an important issue, and the church is so well-positioned to dominate legal ballot-harvesting efforts, that I devoted an entire chapter to church ballot harvesting in my previous book, *The Christian Voter.* I encourage you to grab a copy of that book to see how you and your church can help turn back the socialist tide in the United States through ballot harvesting and other church-specific tactics.

Now, what if you want to start one of these programs in your church but your pastor says no? You'll have a decision to make at that point. I certainly can't speak for you, but if I wanted to mobilize the Christians in my church to make their voices heard and my pastor refused, I'd have a hard time staying at that church.

The Power of Prayer

Obviously, prayer is of utmost importance as we seek to influence the direction of our country. Individual prayer should be a given for any believer. It is our opportunity to talk with the Creator of the universe just as we'd talk to a parent. There's nothing more powerful than that, and it is something anyone can do anywhere.

Church-wide prayers are also crucial. Many pastors resist "picking political sides" from the pulpit, but I think we can all agree that, at the very least, we should be praying for the protection of our religious liberties, praying for our leaders, praying for God to guide the right people into office, and praying for key issues the church should agree about, such as free speech and the right to life.

You can also organize what my wife, Shelly, calls *precinct prayers.* A *precinct* is a clearly defined geographical area where elections are held. You can put the precincts on a map and assign groups of prayer warriors in the church to walk those specific streets, praying for the residents' needs, their wisdom in the upcoming election, and for significant voter turnout.

Geofencing

Finally, Christians can use more-advanced strategies like *geofencing.* Geofencing is a powerful marketing strategy my marketing company uses for commercial clients. It targets prospects and gathers their mobile IDs based on their physical location. You can target your prospect by time and/or location — for example, anyone who went to a selected church in the last week, in the last month, or in the last six months. You can also select anyone who went just one time, two times in one month, four times in two months, and so on. It's a great way to get very specific contact lists that meet pretty much any criteria you can think of.

If a pastor simply won't talk about the election, geofencing their church is a good way to get directly to the church attendees.

For one campaign, my company "fenced" 74 different evangelical churches in a candidate's district and gathered 94,000 mobile IDs, thereby building a large database in a short amount of time. In the end, we collected the contact information of 10,000 highly motivated voters who were also considered "low propensity" voters for the clients' database.

We also generated potential voters by getting:

- 100,000+ landing page visitors.
- 942,000 ad impressions.
- 288,000 video views.

All these views and ad impressions led to increased voter awareness and turnout for our client.

Just think of the number of likely Christian, values-driven voters you could reach if you targeted people who bought tickets for recent Christian concerts and crusades, who is involved in homeschooling or Christian schools, church membership rolls, and so on. Then, you could specifically target those families and families who live near them with ads on Facebook, Instagram, X (formerly Twitter), YouTube, and other online platforms.

The ads we all see on these sites are not random; *someone* paid to put *that* ad in front of *our* eyes. We can and should use those same techniques to target likely pro-freedom voters.

These action steps and church strategies can and will turn America around.

It takes you and your friends and family to be part of turning America around.

It takes you and your friends and family to overcome these dangers we've discussed.

It takes you and your friends and family to restore The American Dream.

Chapter 14

Conclusion: You Can Save America

Well, here we are.

We have spent a lot of time together throughout this book exposing and picking apart what I've identified as the 10 greatest dangers to our prosperity, freedom, and future:

1. We've seen how the radical pro-socialists are intent on leading us down the **road to socialism,** often disguised as a new brand of *Democratic socialism,* even though socialism has failed every single time in every single country that's tried it.

2. We've examined how socialist-minded bureaucrats and politicians are guilty of **crippling economic mismanagement,** bankrupting America's future through inflation, debt, government waste, oppressive taxation, endless entitlements, and an impenetrable web of regulatory red tape.

3. I've revealed how the radical bureaucrats are trying to **force political, cultural, and moral change** through unfair, unconstitutional DEI, ESG, and LGBTQI+ initiatives.

4. We've explored how President Obama and others have **created and weaponized a *de facto* fourth branch of government** in the bureaucratic Deep State that targets political opponents, fails to uphold the law, colludes with media companies to

distort the truth, and bypasses Congress by creating *legislation through regulation.*

5. I've uncovered the dangerous realities of **voter fraud and its effect on America's election integrity.**

6. We've unpacked how the radical pro-socialists have advanced tactics in **messaging, misinformation, and mobilization,** and how they are playing on the public's emotional triggers and making people easily susceptible to a pro-socialist, anti-America redefining of reality.

7. I've warned that the **emergence and misuse of artificial intelligence** represents one of the greatest threats to our Republic in history, as bad actors can use AI to disrupt elections, falsify photo and video "evidence" of political opponents' alleged misdeeds, and inject partisan propaganda into allegedly unbiased search results.

8. We've explored the radical pro-socialists' highly successful **takeover of the American educational system,** bringing socialist indoctrination and government control into our classrooms and pushing controversial, age-inappropriate agendas on our children.

9. I've exposed the radical pro-socialists' **war on Christianity,** showing how a socialist, anti-religion atmosphere has permeated the military, infected the corporate world, attacked small business, corrupted our courtrooms, and biased the mainstream media against moral, upstanding people of faith whose only offense is believing and trying to live by the central tenants of their 2,000-year-old faith.

10. We've seen what happens to the American justice system when judges inject **judicial activism** into their interpretation and application of the law, legislating from the bench rather than viewing cases from a strict constitutionalist perspective.

Taken altogether, these 10 dangers are a lot to process.

It can feel like all bad news all the time.

It can feel like the radicals have too much momentum, that we're too late to change course as a nation.

It can feel ... hopeless.

My friend, let me assure you that it is *not* too late. We *can* change course. There *is* hope.

But it's going to take some effort to turn America around — and change starts with you.

Yes, *you.*

You can be the catalyst for restoring The American Dream.

You can turn the tide.

You can pull our Republic out of the same tragic death spiral that every socialist country in world history has experienced.

You can ensure American prosperity and freedom survive and thrive for all future generations.

You can save America.

A Personal Warning ... and Encouragement

The Cost of Pushing Back Against a Radical Culture

The way forward isn't easy. It will require tremendous faith and courage, and you can be sure the establishment will push back against you. If you speak up for the unborn, challenge DEI and ESG agendas, uphold traditional family values, or proclaim the name of Jesus, you will be targeted.

Many readers may already have experienced censorship, discrimination, or hatred from family members and friends. Some have lost relationships or jobs. But we must tell the truth in love. Courage requires love but not acceptance of evil or error. It requires standing firm.

In fact, the world may *hate* you — just as the Bible warned us thousands of years ago. Writing to his pastoral protégé, Timothy, the Apostle Paul flatly states that *"everyone who wants to live a godly life in Christ Jesus will be persecuted."* (2 Timothy 3:12, NIV)

Jesus Himself told His followers:

> *"If you belonged to the world, it would love you as its own. As it is, you do not belong to the world, but I have chosen you out of the world. That is why the world hates you."* (John 15:19, NIV)

Therefore, as you consider the following 12 things you can do to push back against the radical pro-socialists' radical modern agenda, I want to offer a prayer of power and authority over you. As Paul wrote to Timothy:

"For the Spirit God gave us does not make us timid, but gives us power, love and, self-discipline."
(2 Timothy 1:7, NIV)

Truth is on our side, and with truth comes power — the power we need to push back against radical ideology and rescue The American Dream!

Endnotes

Chapter 1:

[1] Ronald Reagan, "A Time for Choosing Speech, October 27, 1964," Ronald Reagan Presidential Library and Museum, https://www.reaganlibrary.gov/reagans/ronald-reagan/time-choosing-speech-october-27-1964#:~:text=You%20and%20I%20have%20a,Goldwater%20has%20faith%20in%20us.

Chapter 2:

[1] Jackson Elliott, "Nearly half of Gen Z Americans view socialism favorably: survey," The Christian Post, October 30, 2020, https://www.christianpost.com/news/nearly-half-of-gen-z-americans-view-socialism-favorably-survey.html.

[2] Jackson Elliott, "Nearly half of Gen Z Americans view socialism favorably: survey," The Christian Post, October 30, 2020, https://www.christianpost.com/news/nearly-half-of-gen-z-americans-view-socialism-favorably-survey.html.

[3] U.S. population by generation 2022 published by Statista Research Department, August 29, 2023.

[4] "About Us," Democratic Socialists of America, https://www.dsausa.org/about-us/.

[5] Colleen Johnston, "A DSA Where There are Millions: The Recommitment Drive and the Road to Building a Mass Organization," Socialist Forum, Fall 2022, https://socialistforum.dsausa.org/issues/fall-2022/a-dsa-where-there-are-millions-the-recommitment-drive-and-the-road-to-building-a-mass-organization/.

[6] John Stossel, "How socialism nearly killed the Pilgrims," *New York Post,* November 23, 2022, https://nypost.com/2022/11/23/how-socialism-nearly-killed-the-pilgrims/.

(Note: New Footnote: Khmer Rouge- by history.com editors, updated Aug. 21, 2018.

[7] Ludwig von Mises, "Planning for Freedom," *Planning for Freedom and twelve other essays and addresses,* Libertarian Press, 1974, page 1. *The essay reprints an address delivered before the American Academy of Political and Social Science, Philadelphia, PA, March 30, 1945.* https://cdn.mises.org/Planning%20for%20Freedom%20and%20Twelve%20other%20Essays%20and%20Addresses_2.pdf.

[8] Ludwig von Mises, "Laissez Faire or Dictatorship," *Planning for Freedom and twelve other essays and addresses,* Libertarian Press, 1974, page 38. *This essay reprints an article that appeared in the January 1949 issue of anti-Communist magazine Plain Talk, ed. By Isaac Don Levine.* https://cdn.mises.org/Planning%20for%20Freedom%20and%20Twelve%20other%20Essays%20and%20Addresses_2.pdf.

[9] Michael D. Tanner and Charles Hughs, "The Work Versus Welfare Trade-Off: 2013," Cato Institute, August 19, 2013, https://www.cato.org/white-paper/work-versus-welfare-trade-2013. (Note: New footnote: House Budget Committee march 15, 2023, Biden's Budget: A Future That's Built on Government Dependence.

[10] George Gilder, *Wealth and Poverty: A New Edition for the Twenty-First Century,* Regnery Publishing, 2012.

[11] Garry Kasparov Facebook post, March 1, 2016, https://www.facebook.com/GKKasparov/posts/10154026469573307.

Chapter 3:

[1] Johan Norberg, "Milton Friedman: No Free Lunch," PragerU, June 20, 2022, https://www.prageru.com/video/milton-friedman-no-free-lunch

[2] "'Shark Tank's Kevin O'Leary on why some states are 'univestable,'" Fox News, February 24, 2023, https://www.foxnews.com/video/6321172951112

Chapter 4:

[1] Aubrie Spady, "BlackRock CEO slammed for 'force behaviors' comment after 2017 interview re-emerges about DEI initiatives," *Fox Business,* June 5, 2023, https://www.foxbusiness.com/politics/blackrock-ceo-slammed-force-behaviors-dei-initiatives.

[2] Christian Watson for PragerU, "The DEI Disaster," YouTube, October 31, 2022, https://www.youtube.com/watch?v=1lPl80AqMDU.

[3] Christian Watson for PragerU, "The DEI Disaster," YouTube, October 31, 2022, https://www.youtube.com/watch?v=1lPl80AqMDU.

[4] John Stonestreet and Maria Baer, "Diversity of What, Exactly?" Breakpoint, June 9, 2023, https://www.breakpoint.org/diversity-of-what-exactly/.

[5] "Workplace diversity programmes often fail, or backfire," *The Economist,* August 15, 2022, https://www.economist.com/graphic-detail/2022/08/25/workplace-diversity-programmes-often-fail-or-backfire.

[6] John Stonestreet and Maria Baer, "Diversity of What, Exactly?" Breakpoint, June 9, 2023, https://www.breakpoint.org/diversity-of-what-exactly/.

[7] John Stonestreet and Maria Baer, "Diversity of What, Exactly?" Breakpoint, June 9, 2023, https://www.breakpoint.org/diversity-of-what-exactly/.

[8] Sonam Sheth, "Clarence Thomas says he's 'painfully aware the social and economic ravages which have befallen my race' as he rules against affirmative action," *Business Insider,* June 19, 2023, https://www.businessinsider.com/clarence-thomas-racism-opinion-supreme-court-affirmative-action-2023-6.

[9] Brianna Herlihy, "Tomas blasts Jackson's 'race-infused world view' in Supreme Court ruling outlawing affirmative action," Fox News, June 29, 2023, https://www.foxnews.com/politics/thomas-blasts-jacksons-race-infused-world-view.

[10] Ilya Shapiro, "The Way to Stop Discrimination on the Basis of Race Is to Stop Discriminating on the Basis of Race," Cato Institute, April 22, 2009.

[11] Justin Haskins, "How Biden Is Laying The Foundation For A 'Great Reset' Of America," *The Federalist,* November 10, 2021, https://thefederalist.com/2021/11/10/how-biden-is-laying-the-foundation-for-a-great-reset-of-america/.

[12] Lora Kolodny, "Why Tesla was kicked out of the S&P 500's ESG index," CNBC, May 18, 2022, https://www.cnbc.com/2022/05/18/why-tesla-was-kicked-out-of-the-sp-500s-esg-index.html#:~:text=In%20a%20blog%20post%20Wednesday,%2C%20California%2C%20affected%20the%20score.

[13] Aubrie Spady, "BlackRock CEO slammed for 'force behaviors' comment after 2017 interview re-emerges about DEI initiatives," *Fox Business,* June 5, 2023, https://www.foxbusiness.com/politics/blackrock-ceo-slammed-force-behaviors-dei-initiatives.

[14] "BlackRock C.E.O. Larry Fink on ESG Investing," YouTube video, November 30, 2022, https://www.youtube.com/watch?v=PSVpth7uqb4.

[15] Stephen Moore, "The Impact of ESG Policies on American Investors, Retirees, and Pension Plans," Testimony before the House Committee on Oversight and Accountability, June 6, 2023, https://oversight.house.gov/wp-content/uploads/2023/06/ESG-Hearing_Moore-Testimony_6.6.23.pdf.

[16] Steve Forbes and Stephen Moore, "Hey, Wall Street: Stop putting politics over my retirement savings," *New York Post,* May 16, 2023, https://nypost.com/2023/05/16/hey-wall-street-stop-putting-politics-over-my-retirement-savings/.

[17] "BlackRock C.E.O. Larry Fink on ESG Investing," YouTube video, November 30, 2022, https://www.youtube.com/watch?v=PSVpth7uqb4.

[18] Pranav Dixit, "186 US banks at risk of failure similar to Silicon Valley Bank, says research; here's why," *Business Today,* March 18, 2023, https://www.businesstoday.in/industry/banks/story/186-us-banks-at-risk-of-failure-similar-to-silicon-valley-bank-says-research-heres-why-373895-2023-03-18.

[19] Sanjai Bhagat, "An Inconvenient Truth About ESG Investing," *Harvard Business Review,* March 31, 2022, https://hbr.org/2022/03/an-inconvenient-truth-about-esg-investing.

[20] Kelly Laco, "19 states investigate major US banks for pushing ESG policies 'killing' American companies," *Fox Business,* October 19, 2022, https://www.foxbusiness.com/politics/19-states-investigate-major-us-banks-pushing-esg-policies-killing-american-companies.

[21] Alexandra Hutzler, "Trump Prayer Breakfast Speech Defends Faith-Based Adoption Agencies That Reject Same-Sex Couples," *Newsweek,* February 7, 2019, https://www.newsweek.com/donald-trump-prayer-breakfast-speech-defends-faith-based-adoption-same-sex-1322170.

[22] Steven Ertelt, "Congressman Jerry Nadler: 'God's Will is No Concern of This Congress,'" LifeNews, February 26, 2021, https://www.lifenews.com/2021/02/26/congressman-jerry-nadler-gods-will-is-no-concern-of-this-congress/.

[23] "The 14th Amendment and the Evolution of Title IX," United States Courts, https://www.uscourts.gov/educational-resources/educational-activities/14th-amendment-and-evolution-title-ix#:~:text=Congress%20enacted%20Title%20IX%20of,It%20authorizes%20any%20federal%20agenc.

[24] Lexi Lonas, "1 in 4 high school students identifies as LGBTQ," *The Hill,* April 27, 2023, https://thehill.com/homenews/education/3975959-one-in-four-high-school-students-identify-as-lgbtq/.

[25] It Gets Better Project homepage, https://itgetsbetter.org/

[26] Andrew Ross Sorkin, "BlackRock's Message: Contribute to Society, or Risk Losing Our Support," *New York Times,* January 15, 2018, www.nytimes.com/2018/01/15/business/dealbook/blackrock-laurence-fink-letter.html#:~:text=%E2%80%9CSociety%20is%20demanding%20that%20companies,a%20positive%20contribution%20to%20society.%E2%80%9D.

[27] Dana Kennedy, "Inside the CEI system pushing brands to endorse celebs like Dylan Mulvaney," *New York Post,* April 7, 2023, https://nypost.com/2023/04/07/inside-the-woke-scoring-system-guiding-american-companies/.

Chapter 5:

[1] George Will, "'Big Government' Is Ever Growing, on the Sly," National Review, February 25, 2017, https://www.nationalreview.com/2017/02/federal- government-growth-continues-while-federal-employee-numbers-hold/. April 2018.

[2] Zach Piaker, "Help Wanted: 4,000 Presidential Appointees," Partnership for Public Service Center for Presidential Transition, March 16, 2016. http://presidentialtransition.org/blog/posts/160316_help-wanted-4000-appointees. php. April 2018.

[3] Ali Meyer, "Porn-Watching EPA Employees Earning $120,000 A Year Put on Paid Administrative Leave," CNS News, April 30, 2015. https://www.cnsnews. com/news/article/ali-meyer/porn-watching-epa-employees-earning-120000- year-put-paid-administrative-leave. April 2018.

[4] "For Immediate Release: Stephen K. Bannon Sentenced to Four Months in Prison on Two Counts of Contempt of Congress," U.S. Attorney's Office, District of Columbia, October 21, 2022, https://www.justice.gov/usao-dc/pr/stephen-k-bannon-sentenced-four-months-prison-two-counts-contempt-congress.

[5] Alastair Talbot, "Moment crazed man, 31, smashes up door of Catholic church and sprays graffiti over the walls after Roe v. Wade was overturned," *Daily Mail,* July 1, 2022, https://www.dailymail.co.uk/news/article-10970171/Man-31-smashes-door-Catholic-church-sprays-graffiti-walls-Roe-v-Wade.html.

[6] Allum Bokhari, "Biden Admin's $40m 'Anti-Terrorism' Program Targets Breitbart News, Conservatives," Breitbart News, May 25, 2023, https://www.breitbart.com/tech/2023/05/25/biden-administrations-40m-anti-terrorism-program-targets-breitbart-news/.

[7] Allum Bokhari, "Biden Admin's $40m 'Anti-Terrorism' Program Targets Breitbart News, Conservatives," Breitbart News, May 25, 2023, https://www.breitbart.com/tech/2023/05/25/biden-administrations-40m-anti-terrorism-program-targets-breitbart-news/.

[8] Spencer Kimball, "Biden administration withdraws Covid vaccine mandate for businesses after losing Supreme Court case," CNBC, January 25, 2022, https://www.cnbc.com/2022/01/25/covid-vaccine-mandate-osha-withdraws-rule-for-businesses-after-losing-supreme-court-case.html.

[9] Emma-Jo Morris and Gabrielle Fonrouge, "Smoking-gun email reveals how Hunter Biden introduced Ukrainian businessman to VP dad," *The New York Post,* October 14, 2020, https://nypost.com/2020/10/14/email-reveals-how-hunter-biden-introduced-ukrainian-biz-man-to-dad/.

[10] Adi Robertson, "Fifteen important things to say about Facebook, Twitter, and the New York Post's Hunter Biden story," The Verge, October 15, 2020, https://www.theverge.com/2020/10/15/21516729/facebook-twitter-new-york-post-hunter-biden-emails-laptop-story-social-media-moderation-problems.

[11] Natasha Bertrand, "Hunter Biden story is Russian disinfo, dozens of former intel officials say," Politico, October 19, 2020, https://www.politico.com/news/2020/10/19/hunter-biden-story-russian-disinfo-430276.

[12] "Debate transcript: Trump, Biden final presidential debate moderated by Kristen Welker," *USA Today,* October 23, 2020, https://www.usatoday.com/story/news/

politics/elections/2020/10/23/debate-transcript-trump-biden-final-presidential-debate-nashville/3740152001/.

[13] Victor Nava, Miranda Devine, and Samuel Chamberlain, "Hunter Biden finally admits infamous laptop is his as he pleads for criminal probe," February 1, 2023, https://nypost.com/2023/02/01/hunter-biden-admits-infamous-laptop-is-his-in-plea-for-probe/.

[14] "The Hunter Biden Laptop Disinformation Is Exposed," *WSJ Opinion: Potomac Watch* podcast, April 24, 2023, https://www.wsj.com/podcasts/opinion-potomac-watch/the-hunter-biden-laptop-disinformation-is-exposed/4e8baf05-447c-419e-80d8-7424827c7b52.

[15] Geoffrey Dickens, "Nets Spend 527 Minutes on Trump Indictment, 0 Seconds on Biden Burisma Bribery," Newsbusters, July 18, 2023, https://www.newsbusters.org/blogs/nb/geoffrey-dickens/2023/07/18/nets-spend-527-minutes-trump-indictment-0-seconds-biden.

[16] Ari Blaff, F" Federal Judge Blocks Biden Officials from Coordinating Censorship with Social-Media Companies," *National Review,* July 5, 2023, https://www.nationalreview.com/news/federal-judge-blocks-biden-officials-from-coordinating-censorship-with-social-media-companies/.

[17] Ibid.

[18] Jack Goldsmith, "The Prosecution of Trump May Have Terrible Consequences," *The New York Times,* August 8, 2023, https://www.nytimes.com/2023/08/08/opinion/trump-indictment-cost-danger.html.

[19] Jack Goldsmith, "The Prosecution of Trump May Have Terrible Consequences," *The New York Times,* August 8, 2023, https://www.nytimes.com/2023/08/08/opinion/trump-indictment-cost-danger.html.

Chapter 6:

[1] "AG Paxton: San Antonio Election Fraudster Arrested for Widespread Vote Harvesting and Fraud," Texas Attorney General Press Release, January 13, 2021, https://www.texasattorneygeneral.gov/news/releases/ag-paxton-san-antonio-election-fraudster-arrested-widespread-vote-harvesting-and-fraud.

[2] Dinah Voyles Pulver, "US Postal Service blows court-ordered deadline to check for missing ballots. About 300,000 can't be traced," USA Today, November 3, 2020, https://www.usatoday.com/story/news/investigations/2020/11/03/postal-service-blows-deadline-check-missing-mail-ballots/6149643002/.

[3] Mallory Sofastali, "Mail-in ballots from 2020 discovered in Baltimore USPS facility," WMAR 2 News Baltimore, August 23, 2022, https://www.wmar2news.com/matterformallory/mail-in-ballots-from-2020-discovered-in-baltimore-usps-facility.

[4] Snead, Jason. "Why Dissolving the Election Fraud Commission Is a True Loss for the Nation." The Daily Signal, 5 January 2018. https://www.dailysignal.com/2018/01/05/379558/.

[5] Snead, Jason. "Why Dissolving the Election Fraud Commission Is a True Loss for the Nation." The Daily Signal, 5 January 2018. https://www.dailysignal.com/2018/01/05/379558/.

[6] Weston, Ethan. "11 California Counties Might Have More Registered Voters Than Eligible." ABC Channel 2 News, 6 August 2017. https://www.wmar2news. com/newsy/11-california-counties-might-have-more-registered-voters-than- eligible.

[7] Scarborough, Rowan. "Nearly 2 million non-citizen Hispanics illegally registered to vote." The Washington Times, 15 February 2017. https://www. washingtontimes.com/news/2017/feb/15/nearly-2-million-non-citizen- hispanics-illegally-r/.

[8] "Frank, Stephen. "Poll: 13% of Illegal Aliens ADMIT They Vote — 2015 Report." California Political Review, 26 January 2017. http://www.capoliticalreview. 252.com/capoliticalnewsandviews/poll-13-of-illegal-aliens-admit-they-vote-2015- report/.

[9] Snead, Jason. "Why Dissolving the Election Fraud Commission Is a True Loss for the Nation." The Daily Signal, 5 January 2018. https://www.dailysignal. com/2018/01/05/379558/.

[10] Lucas, Fred. "More Than 800,000 Noncitizens May Have Voted in 2016 Election, Expert Says." The Daily Signal, 28 November 2017. https://www. dailysignal. com/2016/11/28/more-than-800000-noncitizens-could-have- voted-in-2016-election-experts-say/.

[11] Craig Huey, *The Deep State: 15 Surprising Dangers You Should Know,* Election Forum, 2021, pg. 159–161.

Chapter 7:

[1] Craig Huey, *The Deep State: 15 Surprising Dangers You Should Know,* Election Forum, 2021, pg. 85.

[2] Craig Huey, *The Christian Voter: How to Vote For, Not Against, Your Values to Transform Culture and Politics,* Media Specialists, 2022, pg. 169-170.

[3] "DOBBS, STATE HEALTH OFFICER OF THE MISSISSIPPI DEPARTMENT OF HEALTH, ET AL. v. JACKSON WOMEN'S HEALTH ORGANIZATION ET AL," Supreme Court of the United States, Decided June 24, 2022, https://www.supremecourt.gov/opinions/21pdf/19-1392_6j37.pdf.

[4] Ibid.

[5] "Jack Phillips: Jack is Back in Court, Again. Enough is Enough." Alliance Defending Freedom, https://adflegal.org/client/jack-phillips.

[6] Ibid.

[7] Adam S. Minsky, "Pelosi: President Biden Does Not Have Power To Cancel Student Loan Debt — What It Means For Borrowers," Forbes, July 28, 2021, https://www.forbes. com/sites/adamminsky/2021/07/28/pelosi-president-biden-does-not-have-power-to-cancel-student-loan-debt/?sh=690de80e5504.

[8] Katelynn Richardson, "Left-Wing Activist Groups Seek To Make SCOTUS A Central 2024 Election Issue: 'Captured By Right-Wing Extremists,'" Daily Caller, June 12, 2023, https://dailycaller.com/2023/06/12/left-wing-activist-scotus-election-2024/.

[9] David Roos, "Why Do 9 Justices Serve on the Supreme Court?" September 24, 2020, History.com, https://www.history.com/news/supreme-court-justices-number-constitution.

Chapter 8:

[1] Emily Chang, "Microsoft CEO Says AI Is a Tidal Wave as Big as the Internet," *Bloomberg*, August 17, 2023, https://www.bloomberg.com/news/articles/2023-08-17/microsoft-ceo-says-ai-is-a-tidal-wave-as-big-as-the-internet?in_source=embedded-checkout-banner.

[2] "Generative AI could raise global GDP by 7%," Goldman Sachs, April 5, 2023, https://www.goldmansachs.com/intelligence/pages/generative-ai-could-raise-global-gdp-by-7-percent.html.

[3] Angela Watercutter, "Marvel's Secret Invasion AI Scandal Is Strangely Hopeful," *Wired*, June 23, 2023, https://www.wired.com/story/marvel-secret-invasion-artificial-intelligence/.

[4] Andrew Dalton, "AI is the wild card in Hollywood's strikes. Here's an explanation of its unsettling role," AP News, July 21, 2023, https://apnews.com/article/artificial-intelligence-hollywood-strikes-explained-writers-actors-e872bd63ab52c3ea9f7d6e825240a202.

[5] Audrey Decker, "Pentagon AI more ethical than adversaries' because of 'Judeo-Christian society,' USAF general says," *Defense One*, July 20, 2023, https://www.defenseone.com/technology/2023/07/pentagon-ai-more-ethical-adversaries-because-judeo-christian-society-usaf-general-says/388711/.

[6] Matt O'Brien, "Musk, scientists call for halt to AI race sparked by ChatGPT," AP News, March 29, 2023, https://apnews.com/article/artificial-intelligence-chatgpt-risks-petition-elon-musk-steve-wozniak-534f0298d6304687ed080a5119a69962#:~:text=WHAT%20DO%20THEY%20SAY%3F,the%20realms%20of%20science%20fiction

[7] Cade Metz, "'The Godfather of A.I.' Leaves Google and Warns of Danger Ahead," *The New York Times*, May 1, 2023, https://www.nytimes.com/2023/05/01/technology/ai-google-chatbot-engineer-quits-hinton.html

[8] Julia Mueller, "Musk: There's a chance AI 'goes wrong and destroys humanity,'" The Hill, May 17, 2023, https://thehill.com/policy/technology/4008144-musk-theres-a-chance-ai-goes-wrong-and-destroys-humanity/.

[9] Noam Hassenfeld, "Even the scientists who build AI can't tell you how it works," Vox, July 15, 2023, https://www.vox.com/unexplainable/2023/7/15/23793840/chat-gpt-ai-science-mystery-unexplainable-podcast#:~:text=He%20explains%20that%20ChatGPT%20runs,and%20predict%20patterns%20over%20time.

[10] Ibid.

[11] "Microsoft Confirms Its $10 Billion Investment Into ChatGPT, Changing How Microsoft Competes With Google, Apple And Other Tech Giants," *Forbes*, January 27, 2023, https://www.forbes.com/sites/qai/2023/01/27/microsoft-confirms-its-10-billion-investment-into-chatgpt-changing-how-microsoft-competes-with-google-apple-and-other-tech-giants/?sh=3a1374413624.

[12] Eric Spitznagel, "How woke ChatGPT's 'built-in ideological bias' could do more harm than good," *New York Post*, January 28, 2023, https://nypost.com/2023/01/28/inside-chatgpts-woke-ai-problem/.

[13] Nate Hochman, "ChatGPT Goes Woke," *National Review,* January 11, 2023, https://www.nationalreview.com/corner/chatgpt-goes-woke/.

[14] Scott Bomboy, "The drama behind President Kennedy's 1960 election win," National Constitution Center, November 7, 2017, https://constitutioncenter.org/blog/the-drama-behind-president-kennedys-1960-election-win.

[15] Reuters Fact Check, "Fact Check-Video of Hillary Clinton endorsing Ron DeSantis is AI-generated," Reuters, April 17, 2023, https://www.reuters.com/article/fact-check-video-of-hillary-clinton-endo/fact-check-video-of-hillary-clinton-endorsing-ron-desantis-is-ai-generated-idUSL1N36K1UJ.

[16] Nick Barney, "deepfake AI (deep fake)," TechTarget WhatIs.com, https://www.techtarget.com/whatis/definition/deepfake.

[17] Kelley M. Sayler and Laurie A Harris, "Deep Fakes and National Security," Congressional Research Service, April 17, 2023, https://crsreports.congress.gov/product/pdf/IF/IF11333. *Italics added for clarity.*

[18] Kelley M. Sayler and Laurie A Harris, "Deep Fakes and National Security," Congressional Research Service, April 17, 2023, https://crsreports.congress.gov/product/pdf/IF/IF113.

[19] Julia Mueller, "Musk: There's a chance AI 'goes wrong and destroys humanity,'" The Hill, May 17, 2023, https://thehill.com/policy/technology/4008144-musk-theres-a-chance-ai-goes-wrong-and-destroys-humanity/.

Chapter 9:

[1] "ason Song, "Teachers who don't teach," *Los Angeles Times,* May 6, 2009, https://www.latimes.com/archives/la-xpm-2009-may-06-me-teachers6-story.html.

[2] Larry Sand, "The Ongoing Deterioration Of U.S. Schools," The Heartland Institute, June 28, 2023, https://heartland.org/opinion/the-ongoing-deterioration-of-u-s-schools/..

[3] Chris Papst, "City student passes 3 classes in four years, ranks near top half of class with 0.13 GPA," Fox 45 Baltimore, March 1, 2021, https://foxbaltimore.com/news/project-baltimore/city-student-passes-3-classes-in-four-years-ranks-near-top-half-of-class-with-013-gpa.

[4] Samantha Kamman, "'Nation's Report Card' records significant decline in math, reading scores after pandemic closures," *The Christian Post,* October 25, 2022, https://www.christianpost.com/news/nations-report-card-records-decline-in-math-reading-scores.html.

[5] Chris Papst, "Baltimore City Schools CEO earns nearly $445,000 due to perks buried in contract," Fox 45 Baltimore, November 14, 2022, https://foxbaltimore.com/news/project-baltimore/city-schools-ceo-earns-nearly-445000-due-to-perks-buried-in-contract-dr-sonja-santelises-base-salary-car-allowance-deferred-compensation-retirement-state-pension-vacation-sick-personal-days-paid-time-off-holidays.

[6] Baltimore City Public Schools – Employee Salaries," https://erpextapps.bcps.k12.md.us/pls/sec5/f?p=184:2.

[7] Larry Sand, "The Ongoing Deterioration Of U.S. Schools," The Heartland Institute, June 28, 2023, https://heartland.org/opinion/the-ongoing-deterioration-of-u-s-schools/.

[8] Craig Huey, "The Shocking Truth About Your Local Schools: The Revealing Interview with One of America's #1 Education Experts [Podcast]," Election Forum, February 15,

2022, https://www.electionforum.org/events-2/the-shocking-truth-about-your-local-schools-the-revealing-interview-with-one-of-americas-1-education-experts-podcast-2/?highlight=meg%20kogan.

[9] Hannah Grossman, "Why schools adopted the 1619 Project as a curriculum when it was full of historical errors," Fox News, April 11, 2022, https://www.foxnews.com/media/schools-1619-project-curriculum-historical-errors.

[10] Mairead Elordi, "Nation's Largest Teachers Union Recommends Teachers Read 'Gender Queer,' 'White Fragility' Over The Summer," The Daily Wire, July 5, 2023, https://www.dailywire.com/news/nations-largest-teachers-union-recommends-teachers-read-gender-queer-white-fragility-over-the-summer0.

[11] Tyler O'Neil, "CDC Urges Teachers, Administrators, School Nurses to Adopt LGBT Curriculum, Endorse Transgender Identity," *The Daily Signal,* December 30, 2022, https://www.dailysignal.com/2022/12/30/cdc-urges-teachers-administrators-school-nurses-adopt-lgbt-curriculum-endorse-transgender-identity.

[12] Christopher F. Rufo, "In Portland, the Sexual Revolution Starts in Kindergarten," *City Journal,* July 27, 2022, https://www.city-journal.org/article/in-portland-the-sexual-revolution-starts-in-kindergarten.

[13] Anthony Cash, "Professor Ordered to Complete Free Speech Training After Failing Student for Using 'Biological Woman,'" *The Daily Wire,* July 3, 2023, https://www.dailywire.com/news/professor-ordered-to-complete-free-speech-training-after-failing-student-for-using-biological-woman.

[14] Ingrid Jacques, "Who knows what's best for kids? Hint: Biden and Democrats don't think it's parents," *USA Today,* April 27, 2023, https://www.usatoday.com/story/opinion/columnist/2023/04/27/biden-government-dictate-kids-education-schools-not-parents/11743676002/.

[15] Paul E. Peterson and Samuel Barrows, "Teachers More Likely to Use Private Schools for their Own Kids," *Education Next,* January 11, 2016, https://www.educationnext.org/teachers-more-likely-to-use-private-schools-for-their-own-kids/. .

[16] Mark J. Perry, "Why Do Public School Teachers Send Their Own Children to Private Schools at a Rate 2X the National Average?," AEI, October 9, 2013, https://www.aei.org/carpe-diem/why-do-public-school-teachers-send-their-own-children-to-private-schools-at-a-rate-2x-the-national-average/#:~:text=Public%20School%20Teachers%3A%20Nationally%2C%20more,four%20times%20the%20national%20average.

[17] Andrew Walker, "NYT Op-Ed: Parents Who Don't Send Their Kids To Public Schools Are Racist Theocrats," *The Federalist,* July 31, 2017, https://thefederalist.com/2017/07/31/nyt-op-ed-parents-dont-send-kids-public-schools-racist-theocrats/.

[18] Aaron Garth Smith and Jordan Campbell, "Homeschooling is on the rise, even as the pandemic recedes," The Reason Foundation, May 31, 2023, https://reason.org/commentary/homeschooling-is-on-the-rise-even-as-the-pandemic-recedes/#:~:text=Pre%2Dpandemic%20data%20published%20by,desire%20to%20provide%20moral%20instruction.

[19] Martin-Chang & Gould, *The Impact of Schooling on Academic Achievement,* 2011.

[20] Algar, Selim. "Harvard professor wants to ban homeschooling because it's 'authoritarian.'" *New York Post,* April 23, 2020. https://nypost.com/2020/04/23/harvard-professor-wants-to-ban-authoritarian-homeschooling/.

Chapter 10:

[1] Adam Kredo, "PRIDE MONTH: Here's How the Navy Is Training Sailors on Proper Gender Pronouns," *The Washington Free Beacon,* June 20, 2022, https://freebeacon.com/national-security/pride-month-heres-how-the-navy-is-training-sailors-on-proper-gender-pronouns/.

[2] "Army recruitment video features lesbian wedding" Fox News, May 13, 2021, https://www.foxnews.com/us/army-recruiting-lesbian-wedding-video-cia-woke.

[3] Craig Huey, *The Deep State: 15 Surprising Dangers You Should Know,* Election Forum 2021, 193-194.

[4] Jessica Gresko, "The Supreme Court rules for a designer who doesn't want to make wedding websites for gay couples," Associated Press, June 30, 2023, https://apnews.com/article/supreme-court-gay-rights-website-designer-aa529361bc939c837ec2ece216b296d5.

[5] Louis Casiano, "Sen. Tom Cotton on 'woke' CEOs who run to GOP to escape Dem regulation: 'Best of luck,'" Fox Business, December 6, 2022, https://www.foxbusiness.com/politics/sen-tom-cotton-woke-ceos-run-gop-escape-dem-regulation-best-luck.

[6] Ibid.

[7] Rahm Emanuel, "Rahm Emanuel on the Opportunities of Crisis," *Wall Street Journal,* 2008 CEO Council video clip posted to YouTube, November 19, 2008, 0:14, https://www.youtube.com/watch?v=_mzcbXi1Tkk.

[8] Steve Warren, "No More Church Bans: CA Gov. Newsom Ordered to Pay $1.35M in Legal Fees for Shutting Down Churches" Christian Broadcast Network, May 21, 2021, https://www2.cbn.com/news/us/no-more-church-bans-ca-gov-newsom-ordered-pay-135m-legal-fees-shutting-down-churches.

[9] "About Us – Freedom Starts Here," First Liberty Institute, https://firstliberty.org/about-us/.

[10] "Supreme Court Sides with "Praying Coach" Kennedy, Upholding Right to Public Prayer," National Religious Broadcasters (NRB), June 30, 2022, https://nrb.org/supreme-court-sides-with-praying-coach-kennedy-upholding-right-to-public-prayer/.

[11] "KENNEDY v. BREMERTON SCHOOL DISTRICT," Supreme Court of the United States, Decided June 27, 2022, pages 5, 11, https://www.supremecourt.gov/opinions/21pdf/21-418_i425.pdf.

[12] "The Bill of Rights: A Transcription," National Archives, https://www.archives.gov/founding-docs/bill-of-rights-transcript#:~:text=Bill%20of%20Rights.%22-,Amendment%20I,for%20a%20redress%20of%20grievances.

[13] Leif Le Mahieu, "Coach Who Won Landmark SCOTUS Prayer Ruling Steps Away From Football To Advocate For Religious Liberty," *Daily Wire,* September 6, 2023, https://www.dailywire.com/news/coach-who-won-landmark-scotus-prayer-ruling-steps-away-from-football-to-advocate-for-religious-liberty.

[14] Amy Howe, "Court strikes down Maine's ban on using public funds at religious schools," June 21, 2022, https://www.scotusblog.com/2022/06/court-strikes-down-maines-ban-on-using-public-funds-at-religious-schools/#:~:text=Court%20strikes%20down%20Maine's%20ban%20on%20using%20public%20funds%20at%20religious%20schools,-By%20Amy%20Howe&text=The%20Supreme%20Court%20on%20Tuesday,schools%20that%20provide%20religious%20instruction.

Chapter 11:

[1] "Woke," Merriam-Webster Dictionary Online, Accessed September 13, 2023, https://www.merriam-webster.com/dictionary/woke.

[2] "White Supremacist," Merriam-Webster Dictionary Online, Accessed September 13, 2023, https://www.merriam-webster.com/dictionary/white%20supremacist.

[3] Kamal Sultan, "As Walmart shuts down four stores in crime-ridden Dem-led Chicago, DailyMail.com lists all the big box shops - from Macy's to Target - which have closed due to millions in losses from rampant theft," *Daily Mail,* April 16, 2023, https://www.dailymail.co.uk/news/article-11965589/The-stores-closed-doors-rampant-theft.html.

[4] Ailan Evans, "Dem-linked dark money network quietly funds the 'misinformation' research industry," Alpha News, January 2, 2023, https://alphanews.org/dem-linked-dark-money-network-quietly-funds-the-misinformation-research-industry/.

[5] Ailan Evans, "A Dem-Linked Dark Money Network Is Quietly Funding The 'Misinformation' Research Industry," *Daily Caller,* December 26, 2022, https://dailycaller.com/2022/12/26/arabella-network-dark-money-misinformation-research/.

[6] "Remarks by President Biden on the Continued Battle for the Soul of the Nation," The White House, September 1, 2022, https://www.whitehouse.gov/briefing-room/speeches-remarks/2022/09/01/remarks-by-president-bidenon-the-continued-battle-for-the-soul-of-the-nation/#:~:text=There%20is%20nothing%20more%20important,must%20%E2%80%94%20we%20must%20always%20be.

[7] Jake Tapper, "VP Biden Says Republicans Are 'Going to Put Y'all Back in Chains'," ABC News, August 14, 2012, https://abcnews.go.com/blogs/politics/2012/08/vp-biden-says-republicans-are-going-to-put-yall-back-in-chains.

[8] "Entitlement Spending: Federal Spending In Fiscal Years 2019 through 2022, In Billions," Federal Safety Net, https://federalsafetynet.com/entitlement-programs/entitlement-spending/.

[9] Jordan Peterson, "The Power Of Writing And The Path To Critical Thinking," *Daily Wire,* https://www.dailywire.com/news/the-power-of-writing-and-the-path-to-critical-thinking?fbclid=IwAR0z2-PTUo3xDbHM1KpqB3zMtJcqTZgMvMvfHffgfw-TqihglYk41-Tcd2o.

Chapter 12:

[1] Michael A. Memoli, "In California race, a test run for the Obama campaign," *Los Angeles Times,* July 13, 2011, https://www.latimes.com/politics/la-xpm-2011-jul-13-la-pn-obama-hahn-20110713-story.html.

[2] Ibid.

[3] "Organize Your Community: Sharebank," Democratic National Committee, https://events.democrats.org/event/583773/.

STAY UPDATED ON NEW DEVELOPMENTS AND TRENDS!

Receive a free weekly newsletter in your email inbox filled with concise, need-to-know information, little-known trends and insider insights.

Sign up for Craig's FREE weekly newsletters.

✓ *Reality Alert*

(Christian worldview on key events and trends)

Sign up today at:	**electionforum.org**
Follow us on Facebook	**@realityalert**
and on Twitter	**@Reality_Alert**

✓ *The Huey Report*

(powerful insights on politics and economics)

Sign up today at:	**craighuey.com**
Follow us on Facebook	**@CraigAHuey**
and on Twitter	**@CraigHuey**

✓ *Direct Marketing Update*

(advanced direct response and digital advertising and marketing strategies and tactics)

Sign up today at:	**cdmginc.com**
Follow us on Facebook	**@cdmginc**
and on Twitter	**@CDMGINC**

Order Your Copy of

The Great Deception:

10 Shocking Dangers and the
Blueprint for Rescuing The American Dream

Order 10+ Books or More and Receive
20% Off ... and a Free Election Special Report

3 WAYS TO ORDER

Order on now at
TheGreatDeceptionBook.com

Order by phone at
(615) 814-6633

Send this form to:
Media Specialists, ATTN: Craig A. Huey
1313 4th Ave N. Nashville, TN 37208

☐ YES! Please send me my discounted copy of ***The Great Deception: 10 Shocking Dangers and the Blueprint for Rescuing The American Dream*** — plus my Free Election Special Report.

TWO PURCHASING OPTIONS (CHECK ONE):

☐ Save 10%! Send me 1 copy of ***The Great Deception: 10 Shocking Dangers and the Blueprint for Rescuing The American Dream*** — valued at $16.99 for only: ***$14.99,*** along with my Free Election Special Report.

☐ Save up to 20%! Send me ________ copies of ***The Great Deception: 10 Shocking Dangers and the Blueprint for Rescuing The American Dream*** — valued at $16.99 for only: ******$12.99,*** along with my Free Election Special Report. *minimum 10 books

METHOD OF PAYMENT:

____ Check or money order made out to Media Specialists

Charge my: ______ VISA ______ MasterCard ______ American Express _____

Name (as it appears on card) ________________________________

Card Number ________________________________

Exp Date ____________________ 3- 4- Digit Security Code ______________

Signature ________________________________

Street Address ________________________________

City ____________ State __________ ZIP ________________

Email ____________________________ Phone # ______________

☐ Please sign me up for *The Huey Report* and *Reality Alert* — Craig's weekly newsletters on need-to-know news, shocking discoveries and insider insights for politics and economics *(The Huey Report)* and Evangelical Christians (*Reality Alert*).

Mail this form to:

Media Specialists
Attn: Craig A. Huey
1313 4th Ave N., Nashville, TN 37208

Or, visit: TheGreatDeceptionBook.com to purchase a copy online today.

CRAIG A. HUEY

Craig Huey is a speaker and the author of 5 books and the publisher of one of the largest political/economic newsletters *Huey Report* and The Huey Alert podcast, which he and his wife co-host.

He is a frequent commentator on TV broadcasts, radio, and podcasts including Fox News, CBN, Newsmax, and CSPAN.

Over a million voters follow his non-partisan recommendations every election with his voter guides, including judgevoterguide.com.

Craig also owns the 111-time award-winning ad agency CDMG, which has turned dozens of companies into multimillion dollar corporations. He is one of the top digital and direct response marketers in the United States and teaches how the Republicans, Conservatives, and Libertarians are 10 years behind in their marketing.

Craig has authored five books including *The Great Deception: 10 Shocking Dangers and the Blueprint for Rescuing the American Dream, The Christian Voter: How To Vote For, Not Against Your Values To Transform Culture And Politics, The Deep State: 15 Surprising Dangers You Should Know, The New Multichannel, Integrated Marketing: 29 Trends for Creating a Multichannel, Integrated Campaign to Boost Your Profits Now* and *23 Equity Crowdfunding Secrets to Raising Capital.*

Craig speaks at conferences and seminars internationally on economics, politics, Christianity, and marketing and advertising.

Made in the USA
Las Vegas, NV
23 April 2026